SUPERSUB:

THE STORY OF FOOTBALL'S MOST FAMOUS NUMBER 12

SUPERSUB:

THE STORY OF FOOTBALL'S MOST FAMOUS NUMBER 12

DAVID FAIRCLOUGH
WITH **MARK PLATT**

First published as a hardback by deCoubertin Books Ltd in 2015.

deCoubertin Books, Studio N, Baltic Creative Campus, Liverpool, L1 OAH

www.decoubertin.co.uk
First Hardback Edition.

ISBN: 978-1-909245-28-0
Special Edition ISBN: 978-1-909245-32-7

A CIP catalogue record for this book is available from the British Library.
Cover design by Leslie Priestley.
Special Edition Design by Steve Welsh.
Typset design by Allen Mohr.
Layout by Sabahat Muhammad.

Printed and bound by Standart.

To my Mum and Dad, who have given me so
much love and support.
And for Janet the love of my life and soulmate,
who once asked, when I first discussed writing my
autobiography,
'Who's interested anyway?'

CONTENTS

FOREWORD
BY GÉRARD
HOULLIER

ON THE NIGHT OF WEDNESDAY 16 MARCH 1977, I HEARD DAVID FAIR-
clough's name for the first time. Liverpool defeated St Etienne in the quarter-final of
the European Cup and he famously scored the winning goal.

As a proud Frenchman, I should loathe him for burying the hopes of my nation.
Yet he is someone who I have nothing but the utmost respect and admiration for. To
be invited to write this foreword to his autobiography is a huge honour.

When this local discovery was suddenly propelled into the European spotlight
I was starting out on the road to becoming a coach. Yet I was there at Anfield as
a spectator on that legendary night, travelling up from France in a car with three
friends. I remember there was lot of excitement surrounding the tie. St Etienne
was the outstanding team in France at that time and almost the entire country was
willing them to become the first French team to lift the coveted trophy.

My friends were all passionately rooting for 'Les Verts' and I guess my loyalty
should also have been with the team from my homeland. However, I had a strong
affinity with Liverpool too, having previously spent time working as a teacher in
the city. So it was with mixed feelings that I went through the turnstiles at Anfield.
In a way, I couldn't really lose. Secretly though, if I'm being honest, deep down I
favoured Liverpool slightly more.

As anyone who was lucky enough to also be present at the game will testify, the
atmosphere was incredible and the match is one I'll never forget. We drove straight
back to France afterwards and the sense of disappointment among the St Etienne
fans was overwhelming. They couldn't believe that their team had been knocked out

of the competition by this previously unheard of player called David Fairclough.

For me, it was a privilege to be there; to experience one of Anfield's most special nights and to witness the rise of the legend that is Supersub. There have been many memorable moments in the history of European football and that was one of them.

It's a goal that has haunted St Etienne ever since and it remains one of the most infamous moments in French sport. The name David Fairclough is perhaps as well-known in France as it is in England. He may not have been the biggest star in the Liverpool side but, for his antics when coming off the bench that night, it is he who is remembered most.

It is because of his exploits back then, the term Supersub quickly became part of footballing parlance and he set the standards for the rest to follow. Not that many have managed to replicate it on the scale he did. I remember during my time as Liverpool manager that Manchester United's Ole Gunnar Solskjaer emerged as a prolific goalscoring substitute but there'll only ever be one Supersub in my eyes and that is David Fairclough.

It wasn't until I took charge at Anfield that I was lucky enough to meet him for the first time. I then got to know him more and found him to be very amicable and generous, someone who was always supportive of me and my staff. It was clear to see that this club is in his blood. He wanted what was best for the team and, having played abroad, he understood the motives behind some of the ideas we were trying to implement.

It's good to know that David is still involved at Liverpool as regular face on LFCTV. He's a legend at the club, one of the many who have played a key role in establishing it as the world famous institution it is today.

His story is a fascinating one and I'm sure that football fans everywhere will enjoy reading it, even those in France who can still remember the pain he inflicted on them all those years ago.

Gérard Houllier
August 2015

1

TWELFTH MAN

A typical match day at Anfield – circa late 70s/early 80s . . .

THE FINAL SHRILL OF THE REFEREE'S WHISTLE BRINGS ANOTHER ROU-tine Liverpool victory to a close. As the Kop roar their appreciation, Tannoy announcer George Sephton tries his best to be heard when reading out that afternoon's final scores. A few local youths break free from the terraces to congratulate their heroes as they leave the pitch, while those in the stands politely applaud. In the dugout members of the coaching staff rise to exchange pleasantries with the opposition, content in the knowledge of yet another 'job well done'. In the home camp it's smiles all round. Or so it seems.

There is one glum face. It's mine. Having been sat helplessly on the bench for the past ninety minutes I struggle to share the collective joy that is resonating around the ground. Ronnie Moran wrings out the 'magic sponge' that he would use to treat injured players and chucks the cold water out of his white bucket. He hands the bucket to me and I place the spare ball inside before trudging disconsolately down the tunnel. It is my only worthwhile contribution on the afternoon.

*

TO ME, THAT WHITE BUCKET SYMBOLISES MY FRUSTRATION AT being Liverpool's twelfth man. For some reason it became an unwritten rule that if I hadn't been sent on as substitute it was my job to carry the bucket. How it started

I don't know. I assume Ronnie must have barked at me to do it one day and it then just became an accepted ritual. Now, whenever I see a white bucket it takes me back to the disappointment I felt at that time; a sense of uselessness as my team-mates cantered to victory without me. It would be the same if a win had been secured narrowly, or if the game had ended in a draw. Or even on the rare occasions they lost. If I had played no part, it meant nothing to me.

During the course of my eight years as a first-team player at Liverpool I made a total of 154 competitive appearances. Sixty-two of those came as substitute – a club record for the pre-Premier League era and bettered, at the time of writing, by only Danny Murphy, Vladimir Smicer and Ryan Babel. It's not a record I'm proud of. With the exception of my first few months as a first-team member I honestly hated being substitute. Worse than that was being an unused substitute, and there were a further 76 occasions when I was forced to keep the bench warm for the entire 90 minutes.

That would leave me feeling totally hollow and in a state of limbo. If we'd won everyone would be congratulating each other but amid the handshakes and back-slapping I was left feeling like a phoney. I'd contributed nothing meaningful to the day. I was like an outsider at a party. Someone who'd been invited but for what reason nobody knew. To be on the outside looking in as the lads basked in the glory of what they'd just achieved, or even as they dwelt on the disappointment of defeat, left me in a desperately awkward and uneasy situation. Even getting a shower brought with it a sense of guilt. I wasn't dirty. I hadn't sweated. In my eyes I hadn't earned the right to a shower. It was ridiculous when I think back, but that's how I felt. What do you do? Obviously, I had to get a shower because we'd have had oil rubbed into our legs pre-match. But it didn't feel right.

'What are you moaning for? You got your win bonus and didn't even have to work for it!' That's what some people would say but to me it was never about the money. I was living comfortably enough so financial gain was never a motivating factor. For a young lad like I was at the time I welcomed the money. Of course I did, who wouldn't? And given Liverpool's record at the time there were plenty of win bonuses coming my way. But, hand on heart, I just wanted to play football. Pure and simple. I was a footballer. That was my job. What I got paid for. So to not play and still get paid didn't seem right. Don't get me wrong, I wasn't about to give up my weekly wage every time I was an unused substitute – and just as well, because I'd have been skint if I had – but to me, spending money always felt better when I knew I'd earned it.

Down the years it's often been said that to accept the situation showed a lack of ambition on my part. But that was never the case. In fact, I'd say it was very much the opposite.

*

LIKE ALL THE LADS, I WOULD PUT IN A LOT OF HARD WORK ON THE training ground during the week but for me there had to be an end product. The match of a Saturday, the grand climax to the week, was what we all worked towards and to not be involved when that day came was always a huge disappointment.

Come Friday, I'd be raring to go. I would be as pumped up and mentally prepared as anyone. But whereas most of the lads could rest assured that their place in the starting eleven was safe, for me this would be the most anxious of times. In those early days, no matter how well I'd done in the game before or in training during the week, I'd always be on edge come Friday. Would I or wouldn't I be involved the following day?

Had we worked on team shape in training during the week then we'd have possibly had a better idea of what side the manager had in mind. But our training back then would mostly consist of six, seven or eight-a-side games and therefore there was never any hint of what Bob Paisley was thinking with regard to team selection for the next game.

Team news was all that mattered to me as the week drew to a close. I'd be on high alert listening out for any possible clues that could maybe help me second-guess what the boss was thinking selection-wise. Whenever I was in earshot of the coaching staff I'd strain myself to try and overhear any whispers that would possibly give something away.

Invariably though we'd be kept waiting until the last minute. Even after training on a Friday it was very rare for Paisley to put us out of our misery and tell us the team face to face. The likes of Jimmy Case, David Johnson and Terry McDermott are three other players that spring to mind whose place in the team, at one stage or another, could never be taken for granted. We'd all be in the frame for one of the cherished places in the starting eleven, but I'm sure it was myself more than others who this affected most because, like I say, my involvement always seemed to be in the balance.

The only possible hint you would get of what the team would be was on the back page of Friday's *Liverpool Echo*. Michael Charters, who covered the club for many years, was very close to Bob and whatever he wrote you could be sure had come straight from the horse's mouth. Reading his articles was just like listening to the boss. He even used the same terminology so it was obvious where he'd got his information from. Bob must have had had his reasons for operating this way but to me it was a cowardly method of delivering bad news to the players who wouldn't be involved.

If I was substitute then I have to confess that mentally I wouldn't switch on until given the nod to warm up. I wasn't the type of player who kicked every ball while sat watching from sidelines. I never enjoyed a game from the bench. It might have been a ten-goal thriller but I could take no enjoyment from it if not involved.

I remember the first time I was sub for the reserves. Afterwards, Ronnie Moran asked if I'd enjoyed the experience. As a young kid, hoping to forge a career at the club I love, I suppose I should have been grateful just to be given this chance and I know there would have been a queue of thousands just to be in my shoes. But I genuinely didn't enjoy it. And I wasn't being an arrogant teenager when I told him, in no uncertain terms, that it was rubbish.

There were times in later years when, as a substitute, I probably appeared a little distant. My mind would be elsewhere and I'm not ashamed to admit that I'd be thinking about myself and nothing else. This may sound selfish, the ramblings of a spoiled brat who sulked because he hadn't got his way and wasn't in the team. But was it wrong for me to feel this way? I don't think so. Let me explain. This was my club, the one I'd supported all my life. As long as we were winning, nothing else should have mattered. But you become a different type of supporter once you become a professional footballer. When the game is your livelihood you view it through a different perspective. It's a ruthless profession and to succeed you have to look after number one. To me, every game Liverpool won, or even played, without me was a slight on my ability and a setback for my career.

Football, of course, is a team game. The romantic notion is that everyone in the squad is in it together. Yet that couldn't be further from the truth back in my day. The team spirit at Liverpool was second to none. Like most clubs there'd be certain cliques within the dressing room, but by and large the lads got on. But as I've explained, not everyone could say they had played their part and there was even a real stigma about being substituted back then. Even if the team was winning by three or four a player would still be angry about being brought off for the last ten minutes or so; they saw it as a slur on their reputation rather than about them being rested in order to give the sub a run-out.

I once coined a phrase that used to have my mates roaring with laughter. When someone went down injured I'd say, 'I hope it's nothing trivial.' It was a tongue-in-cheek comment but one barbed with a semi-serious undertone. Harsh, I know.

But that's just how it was. Of course, I wouldn't have wished a serious injury on any of the lads, but there was certainly no sentiment. It was very rare for one of your team-mates to sympathise with you if you were suffering with an injury. At Liverpool everyone was out for themselves. They really were. One player's misery could be your joy. And vice versa.

We all wanted what was best for the club but every player genuinely believed Liverpool Football Club would be better off with them in the team, me included. It was a dog-eat-dog environment and you had to be tough to survive.

It was on the occasions when I was an unused substitute that I really questioned what I was doing there. In those days, not to use your substitute was common practice but I think it showed a lack of foresight. It was a waste, really. I'm certain that games involving Liverpool during this time could have been changed if the manager had been more willing to embrace the role of the number twelve.

It doesn't happen now. The rules have changed and there's a totally different attitude. Managers can choose any three from seven subs and it's very rare they don't use them. The players in the starting eleven accept that they are going to be taken off more often. It's an accepted way of playing in the modern game, meaning the situation I too often found myself in would be a lot easier to cope with nowadays.

But back then no one gave the substitute a second thought. Until something untoward happened, you were just incidental to it all; slumped in the old brick dugout that Bob Paisley had helped build back in the mid-50s, shortly after he'd hung up his boots as a player.

FOR A SATURDAY GAME AT ANFIELD THERE'D BE RONNIE MORAN, Joe Fagan and, more often than not, myself. For a midweek match it'd be the same, plus maybe Reuben Bennett and in later years, if the reserves didn't have a game, Roy Evans. Obviously, this small space would become even more cramped on a European night when we'd have five substitutes to choose from.

I became an expert at reading the situation regarding any possible changes and I'd get to know when a substitution was going to be made. Bob would come down from his seat in the directors' box. My ears would instantly prick up and once I heard those magic words, 'I'm throwing Davey on', I'd be up for it. 'Go and have a little run up and down,' he'd say, and off I'd go. A lot of the time it would be John Toshack or Jimmy Case who I'd come on for. But if he then went back upstairs my heart would sink. That meant he wasn't too sure and was leaving the final decision to Joe Fagan and Ronnie Moran. When this happened, I'd say more often than not I'd not go on.

I'd normally just do a few sprints up and down the touchline then some light exercises to stretch the muscles. That's all my warm-up would consist of. I wouldn't overdo it.

Footballers have certain habits on a match day and one of the things I always have a memory of is the young lad who used to walk around the cinder track at Anfield selling sweets. This one day he threw me a packet of Wrigley's chewing gum before I went on and scored. After that, every time I was a sub at Anfield this same lad, without fail, would shout, 'Davey, here you go,' as he walked past and would throw me another packet. It became a routine.

The old grey warm-up jumper I used to occasionally wear was seen as another lucky omen. For the life of me I couldn't tell you how many times I came on and scored after I'd been wearing it, but people would later say, 'I knew you were going to score because you had the jumper on.' It was a load of rubbish really because the weather would dictate if I wore the jumper or not, but it's amazing what people believe.

The Liverpool fans certainly believed in me and I'll be eternally grateful to them for that because apart from my own eagerness to make an impact when sent on I also fed off their belief. It was like plugging in to mains electricity. There'd always be this huge buzz of anticipation whenever I came on. Invariably I was being sent on because things weren't going as expected, so I suppose the sight of me getting ready offered hope. Apart from my home debut against Real Sociedad in the UEFA Cup in November 1975, very rarely can I remember being sent on when we were three or four goals up. It always seemed to be in dramatic circumstances, chasing a lost cause, and there'd be this expectancy every time that I'd just get the ball, run at defenders and have a shot at goal, because this had become my trademark.

If I didn't do this then the talk in the newspapers would be that I'd failed to make an impact and therefore the substitution was branded a failure. And I'd feel the same. There was never any middle ground. I might have gone on, kept things neat and tidy and done a job. But given my early exploits as twelfth man, this was never enough. If I was going on I had to do something. I was never happy to just make up the numbers. What's the point in coming on as a sub if you're not going to try your best to change things?

Of course, I went on plenty of times and never scored, but I always had confidence in my ability to go on and change a game, especially in the early days when it seemed to happen all the time. I never once ran on thinking, it's not going to be my day today. I never suffered from nerves when going on but I'd always be keen to get that first shot in on goal. If I didn't manage to have at least one shot then in my mind it had been a waste of time. My philosophy was that I'd always get at least one chance in a game. I wouldn't know how good an opportunity it was until afterwards so I used to try and take every chance as if it was my last.

To be fair, Bob Paisley was still finding his way in the job when I first broke into the side. The club was on the up and back then when a youngster was pitched into the first team he had to deliver. There was a lot of pressure on us both. If I didn't produce the goods I'd be criticised and so would he. Simple as that. It's just the way it was. No big deal. I knew what to expect and just got on with it.

More often than not a player will need a run of four, five or six games to find their level and produce the form they are capable of. I was expected to produce at the drop of a hat. Other players might have suffered a dip in form but their place in the team was already established and they were therefore given a lot more leeway. The spotlight was more on the young kid who'd been brought in. All eyes would be on me to see what I could do. And when it didn't come off it was tempting to make me a scapegoat. In the very early days, when I started coming on as sub and doing quite well, it wasn't a problem. But after less than a year, probably around the start of the 1976/77 season, I first went in to see Bob Paisley. I just wanted to be playing and it got to a point where I didn't mind whether that was for the first team or the reserves. Just like the first team, the reserves would most weeks play Saturday and midweek, 42 games a season.

Around September that season I was down to be sub one Tuesday night and I remember asking Bob to put me back in the reserves just so I could get a game. He'd made it clear that I'd always be his first-choice number twelve that season so my place in the first-team squad – and the win bonuses that would bring – were guaranteed. But I wasn't happy to just accept that. It was still early in the season but to remain fresh I had to be playing. He did eventually come around to my way of thinking and I was allowed to return to the reserves. Looking back, perhaps I did myself an injustice and talked myself out of more first-team appearances.

If I'd have carried on being sub then more opportunities might have come my way. It only takes an injury to a first-team player for the situation to change but, and it's sad for me to say, even then a distrust of Bob Paisley was festering away inside me. There was a lot of 'what if' in my thinking. What if I got another chance, would I keep my place? Competition for places at the time was fierce. The likes of Tosh, Davey Johnson and Alan Waddle were all in and around the fringes of the first team. There were many different permutations the boss could use and I got the feeling that no matter how well I did I'd never get an extended run in the side.

Hindsight, of course, is a wonderful thing but I was desperate to maintain my match fitness and if I had to drop back into the reserves to achieve this then so be it. At least then, in my mind, when an opportunity to start in the first team came available I'd be better equipped to make a worthwhile contribution. Of course, it could be argued that Bob Paisley only had my best interests at heart. I was just nineteen at that time and by playing first-team football week in, week out I suppose there was a danger that I could become burned out. Not just in a physical sense but mentally as well, because there is a huge pressure attached to it. It's a topic that's still relevant in the game today but I maintain my belief that he was far too overcautious where I was concerned. I've since read that he later admitted he'd have done things differently had he had more experience of dealing with an up-and-coming youngster like I was back then but that is of little comfort to me now.

We can all look back through rose-tinted glasses at the Liverpool team of the late 70s and early 80s. But let's be honest, it wasn't always perfect. There were plenty of times when the team didn't perform to their true capabilities. Sometimes they'd just manage to scrape through games. Occasionally they'd lose, but no big fuss was ever made within the club.

Many a time I'd be sat on the bench watching the team labour to a narrow victory, thinking I could do better than certain players in my position, but continuity played such a big part of the thinking at Liverpool during this time. It stemmed from the days of Bill Shankly. In the title-winning season of 1965/66 he famously called upon just fourteen players and two of them – Bobby Graham and Alf Arrowsmith – played only six games between them. 'What's the team this week, Bill?' journalists would ask. 'Same as last year,' his reply. Tongue-in-cheek it might have been, but this was very much the club's philosophy when it came to team selection. Changes were rarely made. And when they were it was more due to injury than loss of form.

Not that anyone at Liverpool would ever own up to having an injury. We, the players, would know that a certain player was carrying an injury and struggling but they would do their best to disguise it.

On the morning of the St Etienne game, for example, I knew Tosh was badly injured. He'd been suffering with an Achilles problem. My movement was fine, no hint of stiffness. I was as fit as a flea. Tosh's Achilles was crumbling away. There was no way he should have played against St Etienne. As it turned out, it was him who I'd later replace but he shouldn't have started in the first place. That's the way it was at Liverpool back then. No player would ever admit to not being 100 per cent because that would put their starting place in jeopardy. I'll admit I did it myself on many occasions. There was a genuine fear that if you dropped out of the first team at Liverpool you might never get back in.

It was so competitive that some players would resort to taking painkillers, while the sheer adrenalin rush of being involved would sometimes be enough to get players through games. Because the team was so strong, it was good enough to carry a few under-par performers. It's a subject that we've since discussed in-depth when the former players have got together, and the general consensus was that so long as there were eight fully fit players in the eleven we'd be OK.

An accusation that was often levelled at me is that I wasn't fit enough to last ninety minutes; that I was never as effective when starting and only ever effective when coming into a game late on. It's a claim I dispute and I'd like to think that 37 goals in 92 starts dispels that theory.

But at the same time I do harbour a sense of resentment at how my career panned out. Bitter is perhaps too harsh a word to use but – and it's horrible to have regrets in life – there's absolutely no doubt in my mind that I could have made a bigger impact at Liverpool and, in turn, enjoyed a much more fruitful career had I been given more opportunities. In my opinion Bob Paisley didn't fully utilise my potential. He failed to use me in the best possible way. And it's something that still haunts me to this day.

2

AN EVERTON RED

A BORN-AND-BRED, DYED-IN-THE-WOOL LIVERPUDLIAN I WAS, I AM and I always will be. Yet it was in the Everton district of Liverpool that I grew up and in a blue and white kit that I first showed my potential as a young footballer.

The kit belonged to Major Lester, the primary school many a Liverpool fan would have walked past on countless occasions as they made their way up to Anfield. It stood at the Everton Valley end of Walton Breck Road, a Ray Clemence goal kick away from the famous Spion Kop.

I attended that school for four years (1964–68) and started playing competitively when I was just seven years old; first for the under-10s (B-team) and then the under-11s (A-team). Why we played in the colours of the team from Goodison Park I don't know, but despite my allegiances to the red half of the city I wore the Major Lester blue with immense pride.

Our home games took place on Stanley Park, that great divide which separated the city's two major football clubs. If any inspiration was needed during a match you had only to look one way towards the shrine that was Anfield or, if you happened to be the other way inclined, turn your head in the opposite direction towards Goodison, where those of a blue persuasion worshipped.

Football is a religion on Merseyside and with both grounds being in such close proximity to our house I suppose it's no surprise that I was footy mad. We lived in a typical two-up two-down, back-to-back, terrace house: 43 Carmel Street, off St Domingo Road.

I suspect there are very few former Liverpool players who can lay claim to having grown up closer to Anfield than me, the nearest ones to me that I can think of are Steve Peplow who lived on Oakfield Road and Tommy Smith who came from Kirkdale. On a match day I could hear the roar of the crowd from our front step, while the choruses of 'You'll Never Walk Alone' would fill the air.

I can't vouch for other parts of the city at that time but to me football just seemed to dominate the lives of everyone. In our narrow street, which hardly ever had a car parked in it, we had a ready-made pitch and practice area. In the middle of the street was a gap between houses, left to us by the Luftwaffe in World War Two. We called it the 'hollow'. At one end, the wall had Liverpool painted on it; at the other end, it was Everton. It was a rough, uneven surface of rocks and stones but we never complained. In the summer it briefly became our cricket pitch as well. Learning to play football in such cramped spaces meant we devised our own rules for the games, such as keeping the ball below window height or playing one and two touch, which, unwittingly at the time, helped us develop our skills.

Given where we lived, there was just no getting away from the footy. It would have been difficult for anyone not be bitten by the bug and it took hold of me from a very early age.

Every week the streets were alive with people making their way to the match: one Saturday it would be the Reds at home, the next it was the Blues. I just loved the buzz that a match day brought and together with my mates I'd be out early touting to mind the cars of those on their way to the game. It was an extremely competitive business, with most little lads around our way out to do likewise. With both clubs regularly attracting crowds in excess of 50,000 back then, not to mention the lack of 'official' car parks, it was an obvious way to supplement my small amount of pocket money. In return I like to think we offered a valuable service to the motoring match-goers of Merseyside back in the mid to late 60s.

It's often through rose-tinted spectacles and a sense of dewy-eyed nostalgia that people think back to their childhood. It can be all too easy to let emotion fool you into believing it was actually better than it was. But I can honestly say that I couldn't have grown up in a better place. Our neighbourhood was a constant hive of activity. There were local shops or pubs on almost every street corner, lots of people buzzing about and something was always going on. There was also such a strong community spirit and I'm so proud to say I came from there.

Of course, I'm not naive enough to start suggesting everything was a bed of roses, far from it. Everyone in that area had to work hard for a living. Money was tight and I suppose life could be a struggle at times. Within most big cities there were areas like ours. It was also a tough environment in which to live so you certainly had to be street-wise to survive. I remember regularly getting chased around the block by older lads, usually from the local Catholic school, with my escape route usually being the tenement blocks of the nearby Sir Thomas White Gardens, known locally as Tommy Whites, which I knew like the back of my hand.

It's a good job I could run, that's all I'm saying. And I believe it was partly because of where we lived that I had so much pace. St Domingo Road, which ran across the bottom of our street, gradually rose from Walton Road, across Everton Valley and up to one of the highest points in Liverpool. On a clear day it offered terrific views across the Mersey and out to sea. Tackling that steep incline every day worked wonders for my football fitness. Without knowing it, I was in daily training even back then.

It's an age-old cliché, I know, but those long, mainly football-filled, carefree days I spent as a kid on the streets of Everton really were special. I even enjoyed going to school. Academically I was more than competent and Major Lester was a great place to learn. I might have once lost two teeth on the sloping school yard after accidentally butting the concrete floor during a break-time game of football, but I'd still be one of the first in each day, ready to hone my skills once again.

Sadly, the old neighbourhood has changed beyond all recognition now. Carmel Street and Major Lester School no longer exist. Both were bulldozed. Carmel Street, in 1971, shortly after we left, and Major Lester as recently as 2014. But the memories will never fade. I spent the formative years of my life there and wouldn't change a thing. For that I have my mum and dad to thank.

Both my parents, Tommy and Ivy, were from Liverpool, although my grandmother on my mum's side was actually Scottish, a fact I only discovered after my football career was over. Mum was one of nine children and had four older brothers, all of whom were keen Liverpool supporters. My dad was friends with them and that's how he and mum met. Dad was a precision engineer, having previously travelled the world during a short spell in the Merchant Navy. He too was a big Liverpool fan, a passion shared with his brother and two sisters. Strangely, three of my mum's sisters married Everton fans, so that really divided our family on that side, although the banter between us was always good-natured, even when they bought me an Everton strip one Christmas.

When I think back, I only have great memories of growing up in a home where both my parents forever tried their best to see that my sister Lesley and I had a happy home life. They made sure that we spent plenty of time together as a family. Days out would be arranged at every opportunity, mostly to Southport or Harrison Drive in Wallasey, and we enjoyed some great holidays in the likes of North Wales and Devon. In short, we wanted for nothing and they both worked hard to ensure that we were happy kids. We were actively encouraged to do well at school and they certainly supported my love of football, with my dad always happy to enjoy a kickabout with me.

*

COMPARED TO THE OLDER LADS IN THE SCHOOL TEAM I WAS small, but I was always very quick, even back then, and could pack a powerful shot for someone with such a slight build. I lost count of the number of times I smashed windows in Carmel Street through the sheer power of my shooting. It was never done in a malicious way, maybe due to me trying to be too adventurous. On such occasions the other kids would invariably scatter, leaving me to take the blame. Someone had to though because otherwise we'd have never have got our ball back.

There wasn't much else to do other than play football and so the ball would be out at every opportunity. Unless it was World Cup year, the cricket stumps replaced it for a few months, always the day after the FA Cup final, but football was my all-consuming passion and I'd always be there or thereabouts whenever a game was taking place, be it in the street, the park or at school. I steadily earned myself a reputation as a promising player and my friend's dad in particular insisted I would play for Liverpool. Because of my red hair I was often likened to Alan Ball, especially by the Evertonians in the street.

Like most Scousers, my dad had played as a young lad, but apart from the fact that my mum's cousin Alan Banks had been a professional with Liverpool in the late 50s, there was nothing in the family genes to suggest that football would become my livelihood. Alan was an inside-forward who scored six goals in eight games during a three-year stint as a professional at Anfield. His name cropped up in conversation from time to time – he went on to have a successful career, playing for the likes of Exeter City and Plymouth Argyle – but that's all I knew of him until years later when we met at a former players' function and we cleared up how we were related.

He would have been just six months into his apprenticeship with Liverpool when I entered the world on Saturday 5 January 1957. But while my parents might have been celebrating the birth of their first child they'd have also been cursing the fortunes of their favourite football team, because on that same afternoon the Reds were infamously dumped out of the FA Cup by Southend United. Perhaps it was an omen – I too was destined never to have much luck in that competition.

The decade in which I was born was not the best of times to be a Liverpool supporter. The club lost out to Arsenal in the 1950 FA Cup final, their first-ever appearance at Wembley, after which a gradual demise set in that led to relegation in 1954 and an annual failure to regain their top-flight status. Support for the team, however, remained loyal and my dad was among the staunchest of Liverpudlians.

In his younger days he'd have regularly travelled away to watch the team and, although I would only have been about five at the time, I can distinctly remember him going to Leyton Orient during the promotion season of 1961/62. It was only natural that I followed in his footsteps, although in truth he wouldn't have given me a choice. Everton might have been the bigger club on Merseyside at this time but there was never any doubt as to where my allegiances would lie and I am eternally grateful to him for guiding me down the right path when it came to football.

Like most young kids of the time my match-going experience began with the reserves. My dad became a season-ticket holder in the Kemlyn Road Stand when it was rebuilt in 1963 and was therefore entitled to free entry into Anfield whenever the second string played at home. But even before then we were regular supporters of the reserve team and, though I can't remember specific matches from this period, I can still clearly recall how back then you could walk from one end of the ground to the other while the game was in progress. We'd normally go in the Kop and walk along the terracing that used to run alongside the front of the old Kemlyn to the Anfield Road, or vice versa depending on which way the Reds were shooting. Watching the reserves with my dad became a regular thing and I really looked forward to those Saturday afternoons in the early 60s. I was too young to know who was who at this stage but the likes of Tommy Lawrence, Chris Lawler and Tommy Smith, players who would soon establish themselves as Liverpool legends, were then coming through the reserve ranks. Little did I know that one day I would be running out in a red shirt alongside Tommy Smith!

While I might not yet have been too familiar with the names of those in the club's second string my apprenticeship as a Liverpudlian was progressing well and my thirst for knowledge about the club must have driven my dad mad. I was soon scouring the local papers for snippets of information and it wasn't long before I became a regular subscriber to magazines like Charlie Buchan's Football Monthly – if they contained any photographs of the Liverpool team, I would cut them out to put in my LFC scrapbook or pin on my bedroom wall. Kop stars of the time, such as Roger Hunt and Ian St John, used to stare down at me as my dream of one day emulating them developed, but there were so many players in that early 60s team to admire. Bill Shankly's first great side was taking shape and it was difficult not to get swept away by the excitement of it all.

The stories about Shanks are the stuff of legend and he was a messiah in the eyes of all Liverpool fans. Our club hadn't won the league since the first season just after the war in 1946/47 and on the day this long wait was finally ended, in April 1964, I'm proud to say I was there at Anfield. Well, I was for the last quarter of an hour. Something special was occurring almost on my doorstep. My dad was at the game, sat in his usual seat in the Kemlyn Road, and I simply had to be there too, so together with a group of friends we made our way down to the ground just to be closer to the action.

Famous film footage of that day – a 5–0 victory over Arsenal – still exists. It was the afternoon BBC's Panorama visited Anfield and the swaying Kop was in fine voice. A carnival atmosphere engulfed Anfield and there was a party going on outside too, where lots of kids would often hang around waiting for the exit gates to open at what was generally known as three-quarter time. When they did, as the odd fan from the inside made for an early dart, hundreds on the outside would rush past them, eager to catch some of the action. On this occasion curiosity got the better of me and I followed suit.

THE FIRST 'PROPER' GAME I ACTUALLY REMEMBER ATTENDING WAS Anfield's inaugural European fixture against Reykjavik in September 1964. I stood at the front of the Boys Pen and became a regular there throughout that season, although I did watch the odd game from dad's seat in the Kemlyn: row 3, seat 145. It was such a fantastic spec, so close to the action, that I wished I could have sat there every week. Totally smitten with the Reds, it wasn't that long before my dad also started taking me to away games, my first being the following season's visit to Blackburn, which we won 4–1 on the road to being champions again.

Of course, you can't talk about memories of those times without mentioning one of the biggest games ever at Anfield. That occasion was the night world champions Inter Milan came to town for the European Cup semifinal first leg in May 1965. Just days earlier, amid seemingly never-ending celebrations, Liverpool had won the FA Cup for the first time and everyone was on a high. However, taking into account that the ground would be so packed that night and that I had school the next day, I had to make do with following the game back home, via the huge cheers that greeted each goal. In terms of atmosphere that match has gone down in Kop folklore as one of the best and I remember clearly standing out in the street, with a group that included my mum, as the Kop belted out the 'Go back to Italy' chants.

Although I lived in Everton, Anfield was most definitely the closer of the two football grounds. Within three minutes of leaving my house I could be at the top of Robson Street and the Kop was in sight, just a further short walk away, down Vienna or Venice Street. In terms of where we'd knock about as kids it was certainly part of my patch and I'd often wander down to the ground, especially during the school holidays. My mates and I would hang around there almost every day in the hope of spotting the players and collecting more autographs. Another favourite haunt of ours around this time was the garage on Walton Breck Road owned, by Peter Thompson and Gordon Wallace. In the shadow of the Kop we'd regularly sit on the railings around the forecourt in the hope of bumping into Thommo or Gordon. Occasionally other players would call by. Bobby Graham could often be seen there and I actually got to know him quite well as a result of this. He was a very approachable type of guy and as a player he was a hero. He'd burst on to the scene with a hat-trick on his league debut at home to Aston Villa in September 1964 and it was unfortunate that his progress was blighted by injury. Nevertheless, he remained a popular member of the squad and was a big favourite of mine, especially after his goalscoring heroics in the Goodison derby of 1969. That was the match made famous by Sandy Brown's own-goal but I've never forgotten the sublime skill shown by Bobby when he rounded the Everton 'keeper to complete a 3-0 win.

Roger Hunt remained my all-time hero, and I'd never tire of getting his auto-graph, but Bobby was a really down-to-earth fella who was always willing to stop and chat. For a starry-eyed youngster such as myself this was amazing and as an added bonus he'd even occasionally give us programmes from away matches, which we'd show off to the rest of the lads in school.

Among my group of mates there were also a few Evertonians but for three weeks during the summer of 1966 our club rivalries were cast aside. The World Cup had come to England. And of greater importance to us, it was right here on our door-step because Goodison Park was one of the host venues. What made this thrilling spectacle even more special for me was that I was lucky enough to actually attend some of the games after winning a competition in the *Liverpool Echo*. In the weeks leading up to the tournament they ran a series in which you had to pick the eight best players, in various positions, in order of merit. I won in the week they asked readers to choose the world's best strikers.

I was always reading magazines and books on football so considered myself a keen student of the game and picked up a pen and entered. Not for a minute did I think I'd win. I forgot all about it until there was a knock on our door one Saturday morning. It was two men from the *Echo* – a reporter and photographer – who had come to relay the good news. My mum's first thought when she opened the door was that we'd won the 'Spot the Ball', which was a big thing at the time and carried with it a £25 prize. To me, tickets to every World Cup game at Goodison and Old Trafford, plus the final at Wembley, were worth a lot more. Priceless. Once the reporter was informed that it wasn't my dad who had entered but his nine-year old son it quickly became a much bigger story.

The photographer took a photo of me doing keepy-ups in the street and it appeared in the paper the following week. Not surprisingly, I was the envy of all my mates. My dad had said that he was hoping to get tickets for a couple of the games at Goodison but this was beyond my wildest dreams.

It was an unbelievable experience. I remember walking back through Stanley Park from Goodison after one particular game. It was a lovely summer evening and I spotted Helenio Herrera, the famous manager of Inter Milan. I knew all about him from reading my football books. I couldn't believe my luck that he was now stood there in front of us. Although star-struck, I built up some confidence and asked him for his autograph, and he kindly obliged.

It was an amazing month of football and we were so lucky to have so many of the games here in Liverpool. As well as meeting Herrera, I also got to see world-famous stars like Pelé, Eusébio and Garrincha in the flesh, plying their trade at Goodison. Every day during the tournament was like Christmas for a footy-daft kid such as myself. I was also lucky enough to witness some unforgettable games, none more so than the Portugal v North Korea quarterfinal. Hungary beating Brazil was another great memory and how can I forget the final? Unlike in the modern era, our football back then didn't seem so tribal and there were no anti-England sentiments. Everyone was rooting for the Three Lions and I was no different, especially with my favourite player, Roger Hunt, leading the attack.

It's difficult to recall much about the actual game. The whole occasion was so huge that it seemed to pass me by. It was just too much to take in for a nine-year-old. What I can vividly remember is walking up Wembley Way in the sunshine with my dad beforehand. I also have strong memories of West Germany equalising near the end of full-time. Then there was Geoff Hurst's controversial second goal, the one that bounced on the line, which happened almost right in front of where we were sitting. I know there was a lot of controversy surrounding it but if my hero 'Sir' Roger says it crossed the line that's good enough for me. Unfortunately we didn't stay for the presentation because my dad was worried about us getting back to the station on time for the train journey home. Still, it had been such a special time in my life, one I'll never forget. The fact that England are yet to replicate that success makes it even more momentous because there aren't that many people my age who can say 'I was there' when England won the World Cup.

*

OF COURSE, WHEN I WASN'T WATCHING FOOTBALL OR HANGING around Anfield gathering autographs I was out in the narrow cobbled streets of Everton honing my skills. I had a couple of mates in the street where I grew up and was also friendly with the kids I played football with. We only lived within about half a mile of one another so we'd all meet up most days for a kickabout. We'd organise tournaments between teams from the different streets. I remember one day we decided that a trophy should be awarded to the winners. I mentioned it to my dad, who was quite handy at making things, and within minutes he came out with this shield about the size of a toilet seat.

I was always trying to learn new tricks with the ball while out playing in the street. Simple tasks like being sent by Mum to the corner shop for a loaf of bread was turned into a mini training session and I'd never set off without a ball at my feet; dribbling it along the cobbles and doing one-twos with the lamp-posts and walls. You just don't see kids of that age trying these simple type of things nowadays. Even at a young age I was constantly trying to bend the ball with the outside of my left foot and then the right.

What inspired us to try it I don't know because there wasn't much football on the TV back then, although I do remember watching the very first Match of the Day. It was the opening day of the 1964/65 season and in 'glorious' black-and-white I watched Liverpool beat Arsenal 3–2. 'This afternoon we are in Beatleville,' said commentator Kenneth Wolstenhome. I, like countless others, was instantly gripped. Aside from playing, Match of the Day would become the highlight of my week. I'll never forget those Saturday nights as a youngster. It was the one night of the week when my parents would go out to the local pub, the Alexandra (the Alex) on Beacon Lane, which was about 200 yards from our house. They'd often go on a Saturday night with my aunts and uncles for a couple of hours. My gran would babysit but Dad would make sure he came back in time for the football highlights.

Watching Match of the Day no doubt fuelled my ambition to become a foot-baller, as I'm sure it did most boys. Emulating Roger Hunt was my dream but it was an ambition I kept to myself because it was something I never thought was possible. At school, especially in later years, we often had to write down what job we wanted to do when we were older and I was always too embarrassed to put footballer as it really didn't seem achievable.

In local junior football circles though, my stock was gradually rising. I mentioned earlier how I started out playing in the school team at Major Lester as an under-age player. In my first year we won through to the final of the local knockout competition where we played against Springwood from Allerton. Years later I discovered that playing for Springwood that day was Jimmy Case. He was ten and I was seven. The match was played at Everton's training ground, Bellefield, and it was a huge occasion for everyone involved, with kids from both schools making the short journey by coach to support us.

For me to be involved at such a young age made it even more exciting but just before the game the teacher informed me that he was leaving me out. He tried explaining that because I was only seven there would be plenty more opportunities for me to play in games like this, whereas for most of the other lads this was their last chance before leaving primary school. At the time it didn't make me feel any better and the fact they lost compounded the disappointment. But although it hurt watching from the sidelines, it was nothing compared to the pain I would experience in future years when history frustratingly repeated itself. My schoolteacher was proved right, however, but not until my last year at the school when I got the chance to play in another cup final with Major Lester.

That was the year I scored in every game en route to the semifinal of the major Liverpool schools' competition, only for us to lose against the mighty St Teresa's, for whom my future Liverpool reserve team-mate Alex Cribley starred. It was tough for Major Lester coming up against these more powerful school sides and although we managed to reach the final of our second target, which was a creditable enough achievement, we again came up against one of the powerhouses of local schools' football back then and lost 4–1 to Toxteth.

Despite the disappointment of that defeat I thoroughly enjoyed the experience of those cup runs with Major Lester and I always look back on 1967 as a fantastic year for me personally, because I was also selected to play for the Liverpool Primary Schools team. I was the only player from Major Lester to be invited for trials and it was a proud achievement to be chosen, not just for myself but for Mr Corrin my head teacher and all the other teachers who had been a constant source of encouragement in terms of my football. Although my school work had to come first, they knew I was addicted to the game and I will be forever thankful to them for all their support.

I was only the second boy from Major Lester to represent the city at this level and the first to play regularly. To play for the Liverpool schools team was a great experience and another invaluable learning curve. Our manager was Mr Ernie Carr and also in the squad were Max Thompson and Colin Irwin, two more players I would later play alongside at Anfield. I was one of three ever-presents that season and top-scored with what was then a primary schools' record eighteen goals in twelve games.

One of the highlights was a four-game tour of London over the Easter holiday. It was a great trip, the first time most of us had been away from home for any length of time. People who knew me back then may beg to differ, but I think of myself as being a very shy kid. I was always talkative with people I knew, a bit of a chatterbox at school, but take me out of my comfort zone and I'd clam up. Trips such as this certainly helped me to come out of my shell a bit more.

Seventeen boys travelled and we came through unbeaten, winning three and drawing one. On Good Friday we were treated to a day out at White Hart Lane, where we saw Tottenham defeat Leeds 2–1. My abiding memory is of the goals I scored, two against South London the following morning and then five in our final match on Easter Monday; an emphatic 5–1 win over Islington, after which we returned home on the train to Lime Street. A write-up on the tour appeared in the *Liverpool Echo* a few days later and, referring to my scoring exploits, it commented, 'David is certainly the modern striker.'

Playing for Liverpool under-11s and getting a mention in the paper was certainly a big thing in those days. I'd be lying if I said it wasn't nice to read such praise and it no doubt contributed to my name becoming more familiar around the school football scene. But while it might have been obvious to others that I had some talent there was never much of a fuss made at home. My mum and dad would have been the last people to get carried away. They remained very much in the background when it came to my football and, in turn, it seemed no big deal to me.

Down the years it has always been widely assumed that I was right-footed. And while it was on the right that I first played for the Liverpool Primary Schools team, I was actually naturally left-footed and left-wing was the position I started out playing at school before drifting more into the centre as an inside-forward. With the help of my cousin and my dad, I worked tirelessly to build up my strength in the right foot. By the time I was nine or ten you'd have been hard pushed to spot which was my better foot. In later years, being two-footed became a disadvantage to a certain extent because it meant I would often get played in different positions, but as an aspiring young footballer it undoubtedly aided my progress and would continue to do so after leaving primary school.

Although football took up a lot of my time I was also quite good academically.

Major Lester was a good school and I passed the old eleven-plus exam comfortably before moving on to Evered Avenue Grammar School in September 1968. Because of the reputation I had forged as a junior footballer I always felt the teachers there were a bit tougher on me, making sure that I remained focused on schooling and constantly stressing that there was more to life than football.

It was not a very sporty school and therefore didn't have the best facilities. We had the use of a church hall to play volleyball, while the only other option was cross-country running. The playing of football was confined solely to the school teams of a Saturday morning. I needed to be playing more regularly than that so I also started to play in a Sunday league for the first time. Previously my parents had felt I should rest from football on Sundays. It used to kill me knowing other lads would be out there playing, and after some persuasion they finally gave in and allowed me to join some of my new schoolmates who played for Fazakerley Colts in the very competitive Bootle & Litherland League.

The standard of junior football back then was extremely high. I'm sure it was similar elsewhere in the country but on Merseyside there seemed to be so many flourishing youth leagues, with the Bootle & Litherland definitely among the strongest. At the end of one season the Colts reached the final of a competition called the Cookson Cup. We eventually lost 5–4 to Royal Oak Juniors but it was dubbed the 'match of the season' and watched by a crowd of over 300, one of whom was quoted in the local newspaper as saying, 'Why go to see senior football when there are matches like this on your doorstep?'

It was a terrific environment for youngsters to learn the game and I've no doubt that all these experiences helped shape me into the player I was to become.

3

ANFIELD CALLING

AS THE 1960s CRASHED INTO THE 70s EVERTON USURPED LIVERPOOL as the city's top club. Thankfully, as the saying goes, 'form is temporary, class is permanent', and it was only a temporary blip on the Reds' part. Bill Shankly was about to begin the process of assembling his second great team at Anfield and, while he did, Harry Catterick stole a march on him by leading the Blues to the First Division title in 1970.

Casting my red bias aside for a moment, it was a great team they had across the park, the so-called 'School of Science'. Big Joe Royle up front, the much-lauded trio of Kendall, Ball and Harvey in midfield, Brian Labone at the back and Gordon West in goal. England international West was a larger-than-life character, a firm favourite among my Evertonian mates and a player who enjoyed a great rapport with the Kop. He was an outstanding keeper too. During that championship-winning season he conceded just 34 goals, the best record in the division, and managed to shut out Liverpool's strike-force in the Anfield derby of March 1970.

Just two months earlier, though, I succeeded where Ian St John, Bobby Graham and Alun Evans would fail. I had just turned thirteen and had been nominated by my uncle to take part in a national penalty prize competition that featured on ITV's Saturday lunchtime football show On the Ball. The top four in the country went through to a final which was held at Wembley on the day of that year's League Cup final between Manchester City and West Brom, and there was a lot of publicity surrounding the competition. The Merseyside heat took place at Goodison, with the late great Gordon West in goal. I was one of two local lads chosen to battle it out for a place in the final, the other being Alex Cribley, and the *Liverpool Echo* even sent a photographer along to cover the occasion.

I might have been a rabid Red but the prospect of running out at the home of our great rivals Everton was still a massive thrill. To take part the school gave me the afternoon off and I'd been so excited during the morning lessons that I struggled to concentrate in class. Goodison, while not the most modern of playing arenas nowadays, has always been a grand old stadium. It was the first time I'd played on a football league ground and even though it was eerily empty it lived up to my expectations.

Unfortunately, in front of the Park End terrace where Liverpool fans used to stand on derby day, my hopes of stepping out at Wembley evaporated. I'd scored 35 goals in just 13 games for my school that season so wasn't short on confidence as I stepped up in the blue-and-white stripes of Fazakerley Colts to take my first kick. Gordon was a big imposing figure between the sticks so I kept aiming for the bottom left or right corners in the hope that he'd struggle to get down for them. Unfortunately, in doing so I ended up knocking a few wide. Out of ten kicks, I converted just three, while Alex scored six to claim the victory. Afterwards West, along with his Everton and England colleague Brian Labone, who had been watching from the side, both explained that they thought I was trying to vary my kicks too much whereas Alex kept putting his in pretty much the same place. I was disappointed but appreciated the feedback and took their advice on board. Still, what an experience it had been! And one that only served to whet my appetite to play at these big grounds on a regular basis in the future.

My Wembley dream would have to wait, but that disappointment was to be tempered by some significant developments later that same year. While my penalty-taking experience hadn't gone as I'd have liked, back with the ball at my feet in open play everything still seemed to come naturally and, as I was soon to discover, this hadn't gone unnoticed.

NOT LONG AFTER PITTING MY WITS AGAINST GORDON WEST I WAS playing in a local tournament on the old gravel pitches at Stanley Park, where football fans now park their cars before games at Anfield or Goodison. As I came off at the end, a guy I'd never met before approached. He introduced himself as a scout from Liverpool FC and asked me my name. I told him, he noted it down and I walked off home with my mates.

It didn't cross my mind at the time but he hadn't asked where I lived so how he would have ever contacted me again I don't know? Just because he'd asked my name I wasn't automatically thinking it would lead to anything but in my excitement I hadn't given such minor details a thought.

I never did find out who that scout was and in the end it wouldn't have mattered if I had have given him my address because within about six months we had moved to Cantril Farm, a new development on the outskirts of the city, just beyond the boundary of West Derby, where Liverpool's Melwood training ground was situated.

Like a lot of inner-city properties around this time, our house in Carmel Street was due to be knocked down as part of the regeneration process and families were moving out in their masses to these new sprawling estates in the nearby suburbs.

Others moved to places like Speke, Halewood, Huyton, Kirkby and Skelmersdale, but my parents opted for Cantril Farm, probably due to the fact that my mum's sisters had already relocated there. That certainly made settling in a whole lot easier and, in addition to my cousins, I also knew a lot of other kids who had moved from the Everton area.

Although our new home was only about five or six miles from Carmel Street it seemed like a totally new world. Where we had been used to row upon row of cramped terraced houses and cobbled streets, here we were greeted by wide open spaces and plenty of grass to play football on. It was like being out in the countryside. Although sad to leave the place I had called home for thirteen years, the move to Cantril Farm opened up an exciting new adventure for us all. It later got a bad name due to a lot of theft and vandalism, and locally it was cruelly rechristened 'Cannibal Farm' in the early 80s, but for us it was a great place to live.

Being a melting pot of small communities from all over Liverpool it, not surprisingly, could also be quite rough at times. There were a lot of gangs about and it became a very territorial area. Football saved me (not from ending up in a gang but certainly from a couple of beatings). These gangs would often roam about of a night and if your face wasn't familiar or you had ventured into the wrong parts of Cantril Farm you'd run the risk of being chased and beaten up. Thanks to my exploits on the local football pitches I quickly became quite a well-known face around 'the Farm' – not hard I suppose when racing about with a distinctive mop of bright orange hair – and so they used to leave me alone.

Football-wise it was an area rich in talent. A lot of the kids attended school in nearby Huyton and Huyton Boys won the English Schools Trophy in 1970. Among the players of note from Cantril Farm who went on to play professionally are striker Mick Quinn of Newcastle, Portsmouth and Coventry fame, and midfielder Ian

Bishop, who became a firm favourite at Manchester City and West Ham. Both were a bit younger than me. The big names in my age group were Kenny Ward, who later joined Huddersfield, and a lad called Tony Jones, who went on to become an apprentice with me at Liverpool. He was a very good centre-half with great energy, especially at under-16 level. Unfortunately for Tony, he probably didn't grow as much as he needed to for that position and didn't progress much further.

The move from Everton curtailed my participation in the Bootle & Litherland League because it was too far for me to travel. My dad often had to work on a Sunday and the bus services between Bootle and Cantril Farm were difficult on a weekday, never mind a weekend. Luckily, my new neighbourhood had its own thriving youth league made up of teams from all the different areas in Cantril Farm. Most kids played for the team that represented the area they lived. Our new house was in a place called Cremorne Hey, and because there was still a lot of development going on around there I was deemed a free agent and so could play for who I liked.

Fazakerley Colts then were quickly swapped for a team called Little Moss. There were quite a few teams who wanted to sign me but a couple of kids I knew from Everton played for Little Moss so I had no hesitation in joining them. They weren't considered the biggest or best team in Cantril Farm but we had some decent players, with a spine that included the best goalkeeper in the league, a great centre-half and me up front.

Like the Colts, Little Moss also enjoyed a fair degree of success and it wasn't long before I started making a name for myself in my new colours. In my first season with them we were Intermediate League champions and I got to meet former Prime Minister Harold Wilson, who presented us with our medals after we also triumphed in the inaugural New York Police Cup (The trophy was donated by the New York Police force, a member of which was a relative of a Cantril Farm resident). Wilson was the MP for nearby Huyton and had travelled up from London especially for the occasion. We would have completed a glorious treble had it not been for a 3–2 defeat to our big rivals Barons Hey in the final of the Ploughman Cup.

Of much greater significance to me personally, Liverpool had followed up their initial interest in me. Apparently my name had been cropping up more and more in conversations between various Football League scouts who had seen me play in Everton, Bootle and now Cantril Farm.

One Saturday morning I returned home for lunch after playing for the school at Yew Tree Comprehensive, which was only a short walk from where we lived. 'There's a man been here for you, from Liverpool,' said my mum. 'He wanted to watch you play today but just missed you. He's coming back tomorrow,' she added. The next day I was playing for Little Moss, who at this point I hadn't long joined. Again, we were up against Barons Hey and, believing it was going to be a tough game, I was a bit worried about the scout coming to see me play this day, even though I had scored four for my school the previous morning.

During the warm-up kickabout I remember seeing my dad in the distance walking towards the pitch with these two men, one of whom was obviously the scout from Liverpool. I was unaware of them once the game started. We won 6–1: I scored two and had a really good game. Afterwards my dad explained that they wanted me to go to Melwood on the Tuesday night. I was thirteen at the time and at this point I honestly didn't know where it was leading. I didn't know what to expect but I was very excited. So I went along, watched a bit of training and had a look around the dressing rooms before being asked to sign on as an associate schoolboy.

Everything was explained to my dad but the only sticking point was that my school also had to authorise this and it was not something they were in favour of. To them it was a distraction to my education. Fortunately they eventually relented. Thirteen was the youngest age a boy could sign for a professional club and I've still got a copy of those first forms I signed, dated 1 October 1970.

As can often happen to boys of that age, it would have been easy for me to have then sat back and been content in the belief that the path was now clear for me to go on and fulfil my dream of becoming a professional footballer. In reality though, I had not yet achieved anything and fortunately I was always aware of this. Yes, I was proud of the progress I had made. To be one of the youngest associate schoolboys on the club's books was a real achievement but the words 'made it' never entered my head. I knew there was a lot of hard work ahead and although I always had confidence in my ability, a future career in professional football was never something I took for granted. If I ever did show signs of falling into the trap of resting on my laurels there were plenty of good people around to ensure I was promptly brought back down to earth, including my family, friends, those on the coaching staff at Liverpool and at school. My teachers did their best to make sure I remained academically focused and because of the amount of homework that came my way I never had too much time to dream about becoming the next Roger Hunt.

This was also the year that I was selected to represent the city schools once again. Unlike nowadays when young players are forbidden from playing any schools football by their respective academies, it was to the club's credit that they actively encouraged my participation with Liverpool Boys. That was down to the recently appointed Youth Development Officer Tom Saunders. A former manager of the England Schoolboys team, Tom was a legend in schoolboy football and what an acquisition he turned out to be for Liverpool Football Club. His role at Anfield was a revolutionary one and he was to become a hugely influential figure within the club for many years to come, his words of wisdom lapped up by anyone lucky enough to come into contact with him. I also had good reason to be thankful to the head teacher at Evered Avenue who kindly let me play for the city boys' team, because at the time this went against school policy. Pursuing a sporting interest was not actively encouraged as Evered saw itself as more of an academic school, but the fact I had played for the city under-11s went in my favour. At that age it was a tremendous honour to be picked out as one of the best dozen or so players in the city. To have played for Liverpool Schools at under-11 was great, but this was the point that football started to get serious. Although it meant I couldn't attend those Tuesday and Thursday evening training sessions at Melwood, Tom reassured me that representing the city schools was in the best interests of my development.

Liverpool were more than happy to keep me on their books while closely monitoring my progress from afar. The only time I returned to Melwood during that first year was to make up the numbers for the annual Easter trials that the club used to hold, which saw lads from all over the UK try out in front of the manager and his coaching staff.

The following year was much the same and I hardly trained at Melwood at all. Under-15 level is a big year in the schools' football calendar and Liverpool Boys were challenging for honours on numerous fronts. We lifted the Merseyside Cup after defeating Kirkby in a two-legged final but narrowly missed out on the Lancashire Cup when losing to Manchester in a replayed final at Old Trafford. Then, in the more prestigious English Schools Trophy – the yardstick by which every Liverpool Boys team is measured – we embarked on a thrilling run that saw us battle our way through to the semifinal before losing to eventual winners Chelmsford. That was a crushing blow. Nevertheless those two years with Liverpool Boys was an invaluable experience.

Give or take the odd player, the squad remained much the same during the course of those two years. We came from schools all over the city but we were a really close-knit squad. Several of us ended up on the staff at Anfield, including Max Thompson, who I've already mentioned, Jeff Ainsworth and Mick Branch, whose son Michael later went on to play first-team football for Everton in the late 90s.

With Liverpool Boys I also got to travel the country and play on a lot of the major Football League grounds, something I would never have got to do at that age under the present Academy system. Our home games were played on a pitch in Penny Lane, an area in the south end of city made famous by the Beatles. When it came to the big matches though, Anfield and Goodison, much to our delight, were regularly used. My first experience of running out in front of the Kop, albeit a deserted one, came in October 1971 against a London Boys team that included Ray Wilkins and Ray Lewington. We lost 2–0 in front of over 5,000 but it was still a thrilling experience.

This annual match was often seen as one of the highlights of schoolboy football. Given the size of the two cities, London always had the advantage as they could pick players from every borough in the capital. In comparison our selection area was tiny but that never dented our pride or confidence in thinking we could match them and the games were always close. On this occasion, though, Wilkins stole the show. He was brilliant and everyone knew he was set for stardom. Nevertheless, from a personal perspective, to play on the hallowed turf of Anfield for the first time was a magical moment for me. I played outside-right and was happy with my performance, the only disappointment being that I didn't score.

Of course, it's during these early to mid-teenage years that boys begin to fill out in terms of size and strength. It's fair to say that some of us grew up a bit quicker than others and I was still very much on the slight side. There is a picture of me in that Liverpool schoolboy team of 1970/71, taken a just few months before my 14th birthday. We are lined up in order of height and I am at the front, the smallest. I was only about five foot seven. The likes of Max Thompson, for instance, would tower over me. It wasn't until I was sixteen that I started to shoot up in size but being too small never really entered my head. Nowadays, I think too much is sometimes made of a player's strength and size. 'Is a player big enough? Is he strong enough?' It's too early at schoolboy age to write off a player's prospects just because he might not have filled out yet.

Thankfully it was never an issue in my day. You only have to look at Sammy Lee. He was a couple of years behind me at schoolboy level and smaller still. It didn't hamper his development and nor did it hamper mine. I always remember Liverpool youth coach John Bennison constantly banging on about the reasons why the club had signed me. 'It's because of your blistering pace and skill with the ball,' he would say. 'Concentrate on your strengths and the rest will come.'

One lad who certainly had no problems in terms of stature was Jimmy Case. He was a few years older than me but trained at Melwood on Tuesdays and Thursdays as an amateur. He was actually working as an apprentice electrician during the day and would turn up, bag over his shoulder, in his jeans and denim bomber jacket. I can remember him distinctly and with his long hair he certainly stood out from the crowd and looked hard even then.

Among the other lads I recall from those twice-weekly sessions were Joe Joyce, John Higham and Bob Johnston, lads I would become friendly with and later play alongside in the youth team. With his mop of blond hair, high-school background and all-round clean-cut image, Bob was a bit of a golden boy back then and a more than decent player too. He captained the youth team but failed to progress much further after breaking into the reserves. Trevor Birch (later to become a very influential football executive), Colin Irwin and Tommy Tynan were three more of my contemporaries who all had high hopes of breaking through at Anfield.

For me, Jimmy was always the player most likely to make it. He was a tough lad and had this image of being a handful. I wasn't spending enough time at Melwood to come in regular contact with him during these early years. It was only later on when we played in the reserves together that I really got to know Jimmy, but he was a player I always admired.

Those training sessions were as tough as anything I've experienced. They were run by Tom Saunders, John Bennison and George Paterson, an old Scottish guy who had played a few first-team games for Liverpool shortly before the war. Tom was the one who oversaw everything.

Reuben Bennett would be there on the occasional Thursday and, on those nights, training would be even harder. At the time it was the hardest training I'd ever done and some of Reuben's drills left me seriously doubting if I had what it takes to be a Liverpool player. When people talk of Liverpool legends this man, made of Scottish granite, has to be up there with the best of them. The part he played in Liverpool's success during the 60s and 70s was incredible.

Despite thinking at times that it was too hard for me, I really did love training at Melwood. It was all about being taught how to do the basic things right. There was never any room for fancy tricks or back-heels. 'Just pass the ball from A to B, keep it simple and the rest will follow.' This was the mantra that was constantly drummed into us. Anything else and you could be sure that Ronnie Moran would be scowling at you. The other coaches would often be quite hard on us too, but over time I learned that they only moaned or shouted because they cared so much and they knew you were capable of doing better.

Apart from the times when I was studying, football dominated my life, even more than it had done before. I was also still playing for my school and turning out in the Cantril Farm junior league. It was hectic at times and I had to make sacrifices but I was living the dream and would have wanted it no other way. Just getting the chance to train at Melwood made it all worthwhile because to me that really was something special. I appreciated that all my mates would have swapped places with me in an instant so I made sure that I enjoyed every moment. To walk through those gates as a Liverpool player, albeit a schoolboy player, was an enormous thrill; one I can still remember to this day.

It was a magical time: nervous and exciting in equal measure. Just making my way through the car park used to give me such a buzz. Then to enter the changing rooms in the old pavilion, where the first-team players would sit before training each day, just like my footballing heroes of the past had done, was awe-inspiring. After so many years as a fan on the outside, knowing that I was now one of the select few who were actually allowed inside the inner sanctum of the club was a great feeling.

There was now no doubt in my mind that I wanted to be doing this for a living. I'd had a taste and wanted more. Yet in 1972 I turned down the club's offer of a full-time apprenticeship in order to continue with my studies. If I'm honest, I'd have signed there and then, but to leave a grammar school at fifteen was unheard of and my teachers made their feelings perfectly clear. In fairness, they were completely right. There was no guarantee that I was going to make a living out of football so I had to consider the fallback options. Sports journalism was the other occupation that really interested me and unless I managed to get some qualifications behind me that would be a definite non-starter.

The club were understanding about the decision, Tom Saunders had been a headmaster himself so he agreed with my school's thoughts and confirmed to my dad that there would be another offer on the table in twelve months. In the meantime my contract as an associate schoolboy was simply extended for a further year. I'd be lying if I said I had no concerns about it. A lot of the other lads did take up the offer of an apprenticeship and my big worry was that I'd fall behind as a result of not training with them every day. Thankfully, I needn't have worried.

Despite studying for my O levels I continued to train at Melwood twice a week and would play for one of the junior teams of a weekend. I also got to represent the club in the FA Youth Cup for the first time, which, for a fifteen-year-old, was a big deal. There's always a lot of prestige attached to this competition and, having lost in the previous season's final to Aston Villa, Liverpool were still waiting to get their hands on the trophy for the first time. Hopes were high that we could go one better and I was really excited to be selected in the starting eleven for our second-round tie at home to Coventry. Unfortunately, it ended in a disappointing 2–0 defeat.

Off the pitch I managed to pass just three of my O levels and, in truth, I know I should have done much better. The football became too much of a distraction and I could sense the school's disappointment in me. All the end-of-term reports throughout my time at Evered Avenue had constantly spelled out that I was bright enough to go on to higher education. They had high hopes for me academically and there was even talk of university. I could have still pushed on with my studies but in summer 1973 my mind was set.

Anfield was calling and my boyhood dream was edging ever closer to reality.

4

LEARNING THE LIVERPOOL WAY

CHRISTMAS 1973 WAS ONE I'LL NEVER FORGET. MUSICALLY, IT WAS the era of glam rock and Slade topped the charts with 'Merry Xmas Everybody'. Bell-bottoms and silk scarves were the height of fashion on the football terraces, while space hoppers were the must-have toy for the kids. My seventeenth birthday was looming so the days of waking up to a stocking full of presents had long gone. But, without knowing it at the time, the best gift anyone could have ever given me was lying in wait.

I'd been a full-time apprentice at Liverpool for six months. I signed on the same day as four others: Ronnie Madine, who I'd played with for Liverpool Boys; Tony Dilworth, an ex-England Schoolboy who came from Preston; Tony Jones, my mate from Cantril Farm; and Jimmy Fitzsimmons from Bootle. We all arrived with blossoming reputations but that now counted for nothing and it was here that the real hard work began.

The other four signed in the morning but I had to sit an O level exam in school before completing the leaving process so had to wait until the afternoon. After the exam I handed all my school books back and went around the various teachers to get the relevant forms signed. Most seemed aware that I was leaving. Mr Stebbings, who taught us British Constitution, had always been one of my favourite teachers and he asked, 'Where are you off, Fairy?' I told him I was signing for Liverpool as an apprentice. 'You must be mad, giving up school,' was his reply. His reaction took me by surprise. We had always shared a mutual love of football and Liverpool FC so I thought he would be pleased for me, but nothing was going to change my mind about what I wanted to do. The next time our paths crossed would be in Rome 1977, him a travelling Reds fan, me a part of the European Cup winning squad. It was good to see him again and we laughed about this moment when he tried to put me off football.

After school I rushed up to Anfield and met my dad. Together we made our way inside to where Bill Shankly and Tom Saunders were waiting in the manager's windowless office. It was a great moment for me, obviously, but also for my dad who as well as seeing his son sign for Liverpool also got to meet Shanks for the one and only time. As they went through the finer details about what signing as an apprentice now meant I could barely listen – 'Just give me the forms to sign', was the only thought running through my head.

When the formalities were finally completed we left with Tom to go to his office, just a few yards down the corridor. As we walked through the door Tom made a prophetic statement that lodged in the back of my mind. 'We signed four other lads here this morning,' he said. 'We told them they might as well go off and be binmen because they will not be footballers, but you've got a chance though, it's all up to you.' I was stunned – it seemed so cruel, but I never forgot it.

It's such a crucial time in the career of any prospective professional footballer, a make-or-break period that sees so many fall by the wayside. Naively we never discussed the prospect of failing, but it is a subject that should never be taken lightly. For one reason or another, it sadly didn't work out at Liverpool for the others and they progressed no further than the B team before drifting out of the game for good. Apart from Jimmy, who went on to forge a very successful career in the police, I don't know what happened to them. But on that summer day in 1973, when together we put pen to paper on our apprenticeship forms, we shared the same dream.

I remember my life as an apprentice fondly. It could be tough at times but it was generally fun. Just walking into Anfield and down the players' tunnel every day was a dream come true. I would gladly run errands for the first-team players and to sit on the coach alongside the likes of Keegan, Hughes and Smith on the way to training every day, then play alongside them at Melwood, was paradise.

Of course, there were also plenty of jobs to complete each day before and after training. Putting the kit out for training then collecting it in afterwards was an eye-opener. Growing up, I'd always been fussy about my kit and was a stickler for it being clean and well turned out, whoever I'd played for. At Liverpool, the kit you wore on a Monday was the kit you wore on Friday, unwashed and by Friday not exactly smelling of roses – your socks stood up on their own by the end of the week. The jumpers we wore over our shirts were washed just once a year! The giant drying room was a health hazard but we survived.

Aside from looking after kit we cleaned boots, pumped up and prepared the footballs for training, mopped and brushed up the dressing rooms and cleaned the big communal baths. The jobs were allocated on a weekly rota, so it was never monotonous. When I look back I realise that it gave me a terrific grounding in life and I'm thankful for some of the tips I learned away from the football pitch.

As an extra duty each first-team player had what we called a 'bootboy', a paid servant really who looked after their particular training boots, and for that you hoped you receive a little bit of extra pay on a Friday. I was given John Toshack and Peter Cormack to look after, which was lucky really because they just happened to be my favourites in the first team at the time. Peter was great and very fair. He would pay me a pound every week. Tosh paid a little less frequently and I think that was the reason no one was doing his boots at the time, but it didn't matter, I loved Tosh and he once gave me a pair of brand-new Puma King boots so that made up for everything.

I knuckled down and got on with the jobs but couldn't wait to get my own boots on and be out on that training pitch showing the coaches what I could do. The chance to occasionally train with the first team was incredible. For apprentices to share the same pitches as the big stars was probably common throughout the country in those days and was a key factor in player development. Sometimes we would have a small-sided competition morning where the teams would consist of two first-team players, two reserves and two apprentices. How good was that? The opportunity to play with some of Liverpool's biggest stars formed a massive part of your education. To be bawled at by Smithy or Emlyn at sixteen or seventeen years of age was a real test of your character. I had loads of stories to report back to my mates back in Cantril Farm, and they were fascinated.

Training was mostly football-based but, as you'd expect, with a reasonable amount of fitness thrown in. The old-style shuttle runs could be a killer. I think the ideas were based on the notion of increase and demand, which developed your speed of recovery. Added to that, you received a real grounding in the likes of how to pass and receive a ball, with the old shooting boards at Melwood central to an awful lot of that training. With the football knowledge, experience and personalities there at the training ground it's no surprise we picked up invaluable lessons that moulded our thinking for life.

Just like the first team, everything was geared towards the game of a weekend. Whatever team you were in, Saturday was match day. That's the way it should be, unlike today where games are continually moved around and there is no pattern to the schedule. It's no wonder that young players these days get so frustrated by the infrequency of fixtures. Because we regularly played on a Saturday our chances of watching the first team were very few and far between, but at this point in our lives playing was the only thing we wanted to do.

On the pitch I also continued to make decent progress. I was mainly in the B team under John Bennison, playing on the left side. I'll never forget how delighted I was the day I scored my first hat-trick for 'Benno' at Burnley. I can't recall the actual goals that clearly but as a reward he gave me 50p, which supplemented my £8 a week very nicely. I felt that my game had come on leaps and bounds, and as the halfway point of the 1973/74 season approached I was more than happy with how life as an apprentice was treating me. I soon earned a promotion to the A team, but our coach George Paterson was much more frugal and there were to be no more 50p rewards for scoring hat-tricks.

At the same time I was also in the team that competed in the FA Youth Cup again. As a full-time apprentice I now felt much more prepared for what was the major competition at this level and we were determined to make up for the disappointment of being knocked out in the first round a year earlier. This time around we were drawn at home against Nottingham Forest. The match took place at Anfield on a Wednesday afternoon and with both Shankly and Paisley watching from the stand it was quite daunting. We'd never played Forest before at that level so were unaware of any of their players or reputations, which I suppose was a good thing because we went out with no preconceived ideas and just played our natural game.

As it was, we ran out comfortable 3–0 winners and it was only a couple of years later, looking at the match programme, that I noticed it was the first time I played against Viv Anderson, who had marked me that afternoon, and Tony Woodcock, who played up front. In truth neither of them had stood out that day but I was to come up against them a few more times in later years when the stakes were much higher and they certainly got their own back in some of those encounters.

In the next round we faced Manchester City, which was a chance to play against a couple of lads I'd known from schoolboy football, including winger Peter Barnes. Frustratingly, it took two games to get past City but at least I got the chance to play at Maine Road for the first time, which would later become one of my favourite away grounds.

Hopes were now high that we could go on a really good run in the competition, but Middlesbrough stood in our way at the next stage. On a rainy Wednesday afternoon in the north-east we got off to a slow start and were 3–0 down before we woke up. At half-time we must have received a real ear-bashing because we managed to pull two goals back before really throwing the kitchen sink at Boro for the remainder of the game. Unfortunately, the home side held out and our Youth Cup aspirations were over for another season. It was undoubtedly the biggest blow yet of my fledgling career but I'd soon return to Ayresome Park for an occasion that would more than make up for this loss.

*

WITH ONLY THE FIRST TEAM DUE IN FOR TRAINING ON CHRISTMAS Day I was looking forward to a rare day off and planned on doing nothing more than relaxing at home with the family. That was until myself and Max Thompson were called in to put their kit out. It was nothing out of the ordinary, there were always two apprentices in to help out, but I don't know if our names had randomly been pulled out the hat or whether there was another reason. Either way, we felt a little hard done by.

Sensibly we kept these thoughts to ourselves and after doing what was expected of us we hung around in the dressing room, eavesdropping on the conversations that were taking place between the players. The majority of it was general chit-chat: what time their kids had been up that morning or the condition of the roads on their way into training, that type of thing. But the thing I remember most was hearing Peter Cormack say he had bought his missus a car for Christmas. I was staggered and so, it seemed, were the other players. 'A car? For Christmas?' It was unheard of. To my knowledge not many players even had two cars in those days so to buy one for your wife seemed a massive extravagance.

It was a 1000cc Datsun Cherry, worth about £850. It doesn't seem like much now but to put it into comparison, as an apprentice I was earning £16 a week. We used to get it in two brown envelopes, £8 cash in each. One envelope was for me individually, the other was for lodgings. Luckily I was living at home and my mum only took £4 and put the rest in a bank account for me, something only a mum would do. Obviously I knew that the first-team players were paid a lot more than I was but I was never fully aware of just how wealthy they were until then. Maybe I was naive but it really opened my eyes.

As soon as training was finished my dad came to pick me up to enjoy what was left of the day. I was still a little peeved that, along with Max, I'd been singled out to come in but, as I was soon to discover, there was a method in what I perceived to be their madness. A couple of weeks later, after one of our Saturday morning games, Tom Saunders pulled me to one side at Melwood and asked if I could report to Anfield the next morning, on what should have been another scheduled day off. It struck me as odd but I didn't ask any questions and thought nothing else of it.

The next day, as my dad was in work, I got the bus up to Anfield and Max Thompson was there. Obviously he'd been told the same and as we stood waiting in the corridor we became more and more intrigued as to what we were there for. Max joked that we might have been signing professionals forms, as both of us had just celebrated our birthdays, but that hadn't even crossed my mind.

Saunders eventually arrived with another man I'd not met before. He introduced himself as Martin Day, a researcher from the popular children's television programme of the time, Magpie. As Martin talked to us in a dimly lit players' lounge it was him who let the cat out of the bag, telling us that we were going to be signing on as professionals and that we would be getting filmed for a feature on his show. To say that Max and myself were a bit taken aback by this news was an understatement. I found it amazing that no one from the club had thought of telling us but that was typical of Liverpool at that time, to make no big fuss of the fact we were about to turn professional. What was surprising was that the club were now going to allow Magpie's cameras in and that they would build a programme around our life-changing experience. I made my way home and told my mum the incredible news.

We remained apprentices for another couple of weeks until the big day arrived; it was nerve-racking enough to be signing professional but to do it on television was even more daunting. We received our instructions and then had to play to the cameras. Both of us ran out of the tunnel with one of the show's presenters, Mick Robinson, who looked more like a rock star than a footballer with his long curly hair and wiry frame. The three of us had a kickabout at the Anfield Road end of the pitch and were asked a few questions for the show. All we really wanted to do though was sign the forms.

After what seemed an eternity, we were eventually summoned into the Anfield boardroom where, at the far end of the long table, Bill Shankly was sat with two contracts and a pen. It was rare for players to be invited into this inner sanctum of the club and adding to the sense of occasion was the presence of two glittering pieces of silverware; the League Championship and UEFA Cup that had been won the previous season and freshly polished for the cameras. With our training gear on we must have looked a bit out of place but despite the importance of what we were about to do and the presence of the television cameras, the boss immediately put us at ease.

Max had been an apprentice for a year longer than me but being only six months into my apprenticeship, I wasn't expecting it at all. I naturally assumed I'd do at least another year before there'd be any hint of signing professional. It was beyond my wildest dreams, to be honest. To have Shanks there, with his arm on my shoulder, as I put pen to paper was just fantastic. Although there was still a long way to go in terms of reaching my ultimate goal, it was a significant moment on my career path. Financially, my wages were instantly doubled to £32 which, for a seventeen-year-old still living at home with his parents, was a small fortune – although still not enough to buy a Datsun Cherry!

THE ONLY DOWNSIDE TO TURNING PROFESSIONAL AT SUCH AN early age, if there was one, was that I trained less with the mates I'd been an apprentice with. They now had to make sure my kit was ready each morning and then pick it up off the floor to be washed after training, like they did with the other professionals and just like I'd been doing. I must admit this created a bit of an awkward situation because these were the lads I'd come through the ranks with and who I'd still go out socialising with. My attitude towards them never changed but there might have been a bit of resentment on their part and when I think back now I can't blame them if there was. I wouldn't call it jealousy but at the same time none of them were exactly queuing up to pat me on the back and offer their congratulations. I think in the back of their minds some of them would have been muttering under their breath, 'He's one of us, what are we doing put the kit out for him?' If I'd have been in their shoes then maybe I'd have been the same because, as I was soon about to learn, that's the way it was in football. The only person anyone really cares about is themselves. A football club is an unusual place – success is achieved as a team but everyone in there is looking for personal glory and to build a career.

For a short while this attitude used to really bother me and I would worry about what other people thought. I'd read too much into certain situations and at times would let it get to me. Luckily I had the support of my friends outside of football, and of course my family, to fall back on, and this was crucial when making such a big step. Knowing how proud they were of me was a massive boost and, not wanting to let them down, it soon dawned on me that I couldn't afford to be affected by the actions of others because on the pitch there was now a lot more pressure on me to perform.

All of a sudden I was getting changed alongside players who I'd previously cheered from the terraces. Obviously, the majority were a lot older than me and it was difficult not to feel a bit overawed around them. It certainly took time to feel comfortable in their company but that was to be expected. Happily, my good fortune continued. Everything seemed to be happening at once and a couple of weeks later I made my debut for the reserves.

The reserve set-up back then was a lot different than it is today. Just like the first team, we'd usually play almost every Saturday and in midweek, playing in the Central League, the competition for reserve teams of clubs in the North and Midlands. If the first team were playing at home to a Central League club the reserves would invariably play the same opposition away, and vice versa. Home games would be played at Anfield, albeit in front of just a few hundred spectators.

Players wouldn't pick and choose when to play in the reserves. If they were required to play they'd be told and that was it. You'd occasionally get the odd unhappy first-teamer who had been dropped from the senior side but by and large the second string was made up of promising youngsters eager to make an impression, seasoned professionals who had been injured and were attempting to fight their way back into the first-team fold, or new recruits who were in there to learn the 'Liverpool Way' before hopefully making the step up. Either way, almost everyone in the team had something to play for and a point to prove. No wonder we did so well. The players were hungry. And no one more so than me. I might have only been seventeen but was determined to make the most of this chance.

Ronnie Moran was the coach and he had a very good squad of players at his disposal. The team had been Central League champions in four of the previous five seasons and was once again riding high in the table, sometimes attracting crowds of up to 1,000. To get anywhere near this team at such a tender age was a real honour and away to Bolton on 26 January 1974 I was bursting with pride when named in the starting eleven for the first of countless appearances for the Reds' second string. The fact that Ian McDonald, a recent signing from Workington, was also making his debut this day perhaps eased the pressure on me slightly. Most eyes were on him and, although he might have stolen the headlines with our third goal in a 3–2 win, I was pleased with how I played and felt I more than justified my inclusion.

The reserves went on to clinch another title that season and although I played out the remainder of the campaign back in the A team I continued to make good progress. The ultimate dream for all us young lads was to play in the first team and to see Max Thompson called up for his senior debut that May was a massive boost. At 17 years and 129 days old he was the then youngest player ever to play for Liverpool. I was really pleased for him and it gave us all hope that we could one day follow in his footsteps. Max's big moment came away to Tottenham, four days after Liverpool had crushed Newcastle 3–0 to win the FA Cup at Wembley.

The final had been a wonderful occasion. I travelled down with the rest of the youth and reserve team players and to top it off we stayed at the famous Waldorf Hotel. It was a perfect way to end an eventful season and as thoughts turned to that summer's World Cup I found myself on a plane for the very first time, also bound for West Germany, with the Liverpool under-21 squad for the prestigious Dusseldorf youth tournament.

The fifteen-man squad was made up mainly of players from the title-winning reserve team so to be included was a huge vote of confidence in me. It was an enjoyable trip, the first time I'd been on a plane and my first experience of playing in continental competition, something I always found more enthralling than a run-of-the-mill league or domestic cup fixture. There was just something extra special about travelling abroad to play in unfamiliar surroundings against teams with unpronounceable names and players you knew nothing about.

Being away with the lads was new and exciting and it certainly whetted my appetite for more of the same in the future. My only disappointment was that I didn't play more. Of the four games we played en route to winning the trophy I played just once, in a 3–1 victory over Ujpest Dozsa of Hungary in the final group game. By this stage our place in the final had already been secured and a Tommy Tynan goal eight minutes from time against Denmark's Vejle ensured we became only the second English team after Burnley to prevail in this tournament.

Coming just a few weeks after the first team's FA Cup triumph, our victory in Germany added to the feel-good factor at the club as the close-season dawned. I too had plenty to feel good about. My first six months as a professional had gone as well as I could have hoped and I headed into the summer break on cloud nine following a chance meeting with Shanks.

I'd previously never had that much contact with him. He was obviously the main man about the place and I had only just turned professional. As apprentices, we generally tried to keep out of his way. We were continuously under the microscope. Who brushed the floors well? Who was keenest in training? Every little detail would be noted by the coaches and all this information would ultimately form a mental dossier that, obviously along with your ability on the pitch, would go some way to determining which players would eventually be elevated to the next level or not. Now, as professionals, we were always hoping to catch his attention for the right reasons.

I had been brought up to respect my peers and behave in an acceptable way at all times so there was never much danger of me incurring the wrath of Shanks or the coaches. I was never a troublemaker or malicious in any way. From a very young age my mum instilled into me that because of my distinctive mop of red hair if there was ever any trouble I'd always be the first one to get the blame, so I was forever conscious of keeping a low profile.

I'd also come through the ranks of the Liverpool schoolboys team and this had given me a good grounding in how to conduct myself on and around the football pitch. There were key rules associated with the schoolboys and it would be constantly drummed into us that we were representing ourselves, our families and our city at all times, and we had to behave in the right manner. I took this with me to Liverpool. I was proud to be in the position I found myself in and would never have jeopardised that by stepping out line.

Of course, as with any group of young lads, there'd be a lot high jinks and a fair share of pranks. I remember a couple of the apprentices getting behind the wheel of the coach that took us to training one day and taking it for a spin around the Main Stand car park. It was funny at the time and we all laughed but you would never have found me doing that sort of thing. I was definitely more than conscious that if I was going to attract the attention of Bill Shankly it had to be for my football ability.

On the last day before we 'broke up' for the summer I remember standing directly outside the bootroom as Shanks walked by. 'Next season is going to be a big one for you, son, you're going to be left-winger for the reserves.' Well, you can imagine how this made me feel. I just stood there transfixed. It was a massive boost to my confidence. I walked out of Anfield that day feeling ten foot tall and couldn't get home quickly enough, eager to tell everyone that the messiah had spoken to me.

It was also a big incentive for me to make sure I kept in shape that summer, ready to return fitter than ever for the start of pre-season training. My first full campaign as a professional beckoned and life at Liverpool Football Club would never be the same again.

5

THE BIG
TIME
BECKONS

NOT FOR THE FIRST TIME WHEN IT CAME TO FOOTBALLING MAT-
ters, Bill Shankly was right. I would soon be a regular on the left-wing for Liverpool
reserves and pushing for a place in the first team. Unfortunately, I would never get
the chance to play under the great man. On 12 July 1974, one of the most sensa-
tional footballing stories of all time broke: Shankly had resigned. It was Liverpool's
very own JFK moment. Everyone knows where they were on that afternoon.

It was just after midday and I was enjoying my last day off before reporting back
to Anfield for pre-season training. Only a matter of weeks had passed since Shanks
had spoken to me in the corridor at Anfield and when the news came through that
he had stepped down I just couldn't believe it. It was such a shock. Nobody saw
it coming. The FA Cup final victory over Newcastle was still fresh in the mind
and further glory seemingly lay on the horizon. Liverpool without Bill Shankly was
unthinkable and, like everyone, I was devastated.

The appointment of Bob Paisley as his successor was less of a surprise. I recall that a few potential names were bandied about in the press, including future
Republic of Ireland boss Jack Charlton, who at the time was doing a good job at
Middlesbrough, but the board opted for 'continuity' and announced they would be
keeping things in-house. It was a decision that was well received within the club.
Paisley, who had been Shankly's right-hand man, was a highly respected member of
the backroom staff but apparently he took some persuading before finally accepting
the job. I remember being in the dressing room the day he walked in and addressed
everyone as manager for the first time. He made it clear that he hadn't wanted the

job but also that it was the start of a new era and we all just had to get on with it.

I always worked as hard as I could during pre-season and the summer of 1974 was no different. In a football sense, the transition between Shankly and Paisley would be a smooth one.

With very little changing in terms of playing personnel there was that extra incentive there for everyone to try and impress the new manager. There's always a feeling in situations such as this that the slate has been wiped clean and that everyone is starting off again from scratch so it was important that I got off to a good start, which fortunately I did.

Although in later years we would have our differences, Paisley took a real shine to me during his first days in the manager's job. A lot of the lads who had worked under him previously believed him to be something of a tough character and generally tried to stay out of his way for fear of getting on the wrong side of him. The stories went that if he picked on you then you really were in trouble. I saw none of that and found him personally very supportive. He'd occasionally pull me to one side after training and give me a few pointers on where I might have been going wrong or could have done a bit better. He'd gladly pass on his advice and there came a stage when some of the lads even used to joke that he had a soft spot for me. I think he just saw my potential and was keen to nurture it. So in that respect, while I idolised Shanks, I saw it as no bad thing that Paisley had taken over from him.

Shankly, of course, would still occasionally turn up at Melwood. It must have been extremely difficult for him to forget he'd retired and his presence around Melwood made the atmosphere strained for a while until he was told how awkward it was for the new manager and the players, who were now calling both men 'Boss'.

He'd often just wander across the training pitch and have a word with us, ask how we were doing and offer words of encouragement. Although I'd not had much direct contact with him myself, the few times that our paths had crossed had been memorable for me and I have no doubt that he'd have had some say in me being offered a professional contract and my eventual promotion to the reserve team, so I'd always be grateful to him for that. On a personal level, it was great for me to see Shanks about the place every day. He was still such a huge icon in my eyes, although I could see why others viewed his continued presence at Melwood as an inconvenience. Eventually we saw less and less of him and his successor Paisley was allowed to get on with the unenviable job of following in his legendary footsteps.

*

IT'S OFTEN SAID THAT IT'S MUCH TOUGHER FOR A LOCAL LAD TO break through into the first team at Liverpool. And while many had done it before me, there was also a much longer list of those who had tried and failed. With a professional contract now under my belt this was obviously my number one ambition and I took inspiration from the likes of Max Thompson and his namesake Phil, another local lad who was well on his way to establishing himself as a first-team regular, having broken through a couple of seasons earlier.

For the time being, a more immediate target of mine was to become a regular starter in the reserves, and although I began the 1974/75 season in the A team it wasn't long before I was turning out for the second string on a much more frequent basis.

My good early-season form had attracted the attention of the England youth selectors and I was invited to Lilleshall for trials. Although I didn't make it into the team – Peter Barnes getting the nod ahead of me – I was put on standby a couple of times. It was still heartening to know that I was making an impression. My chances of breaking into the reserve team on a more regular basis were boosted when fellow wingers Hughie McAuley and then Peter Spiring were sold to Plymouth and Luton respectively.

After warming the bench as an unused substitute at home to Blackpool, I started a fortnight later against Blackburn and made my mark on the left wing, setting up the first goal, scoring the other two in a comfortable 3–0 victory and going close to completing a hat-trick. The papers were fulsome in their praise with descriptions ranging from 'striking discovery' to 'a very useful future prospect'.

It wasn't until late in the season that I began to command a regular place, and a further three goals – including the winner at Goodison in a 3–2 mini-derby triumph – helped secure yet another Central League Championship. I now considered myself a regular in the reserve team set-up.

Our defence of the Dusseldorf International Tournament, however, was not so successful; even though we were the only unbeaten side in the competition. The crucial game was the opener against VFL Bochum, which ended goalless. I hit the post in that match and although we didn't realise at the time it was to prove costly. We won our remaining two group games, with yours truly netting the winner against FC Turu, but it was Bochum who progressed to the final on goal difference. The only consolation was that I scored another in our 2–1 victory over Partizan Belgrade in the third/fourth place playoff tie.

I managed to carry this good form into the following season. I was still operating as an out-and-out left-winger, an old-fashioned number eleven if you like, and was starting to perform more consistently. My dad and I regularly discussed the progress I was making and during the summer we'd agreed that a realistic goal for the year ahead was to fully cement my place as a starter in the reserves. Until then, there was no point even thinking any further forward, such was the phenomenal strength in depth at the club during this time.

Bob Paisley had a wealth of attacking options at his disposal. The almost telepathic partnership of Keegan and Toshack was a seemingly immovable force up front, while Steve Heighway's electrifying pace and scintillating skill would have graced any of the top teams in Europe.

Even beyond Paisley's regular starting eleven there was fierce competition for places. Ray Kennedy, Terry McDermott and Jimmy Case, a trio of future European Cup winners, were yet to fully establish themselves in the first team, so were often hovering around the fringes and occasionally dropping down to the reserves, while experienced professionals like Brian Hall and Phil Boersma, both of whom had played a key role in the success of the early 70s, were nearing the end of their Anfield careers but still had plenty to offer.

Also joining the long queue of players waiting to seize their chance should an opportunity come their way were a number of seasoned reserve team regulars. These included players like Alan Waddle, a tall striker in the Toshack mould who'd been signed from Halifax. He scored a derby winner in his first season at Liverpool but not even that could guarantee him a regular place in the senior side. Another was Tommy Tynan, a prolific goalscorer who had won an apprenticeship at the club through a competition in the *Liverpool Echo*. Despite topping the reserve team goalscoring charts for the past two seasons he was still waiting to make his debut. As was Kevin Kewley, a highly promising attacking midfielder from Kirkby, who captained the reserves.

They were chomping at the bit to step up and prove their worth but it was a difficult situation and I could sense their growing frustration. Being two years younger, I had more time on my side and was of the mindset that there was still a long way to go before I was even considered to be in the reckoning. I was under no illusions about the size of the task that lay ahead of me. Not that I was complaining. Bob Paisley was only a year into the job and had reassured me that I had a bright future at the club, while in Roy Evans I was playing under a reserve team coach for whom I had nothing but the utmost respect.

'Evo' had been a Reds player himself and I actually played alongside him a few times in the reserves, with both of us operating down the left side – him as full-back, me on the wing. The backroom reshuffle in the aftermath of Bill Shankly's resignation saw him promoted to the coaching staff. It may have come as a surprise at the time but it was an inspired appointment. He was only 26, the youngest coach in English professional football at the time.

With him in charge of the reserves the atmosphere changed and things seemed more relaxed. Compared with Ronnie Moran, Roy's approach was a lot calmer. 'Bugsy' could be scary and sometimes had you on edge but now I felt more at ease and playing for Roy used to give me great confidence.

I started in each of the opening sixteen Central League games of 1975/76, with the stand-out fixture for me being the mini-derby at Anfield in early September. I was on fire that night and scored one of my best ever goals in a 2–0 win. I'd been in reasonable form, scoring five goals in the previous four games, but this was something special. Both clubs named very strong sides – in our starting eleven only myself, Kevin Kewley and goalkeeper Peter McDonnell had no first-team experience – and there was a relatively big crowd of just over 3,000 there to see it. The goal was similar to a famous one I would later score in a 1977 FA Cup tie at home to Middlesbrough, though on this occasion I cut in from the left and hit the ball with my right foot as opposed to coming in from the other side.

I was aware that I had played well and delighted with how things were going but I couldn't believe it when I was featured on the front page of the following evening's *Liverpool Echo*. Because of the goal people were suddenly starting to go overboard about me. Fortunately, my strong form continued and, along with all this positive press I was attracting, a momentum began to steadily build.

In addition to scoring goals, a big feature of my game back then was dribbling past the full-back and during this spell I was managing it almost every time. I read the odd reference that I should be called up to the first team but I wasn't thinking about that. By late October I had nine Central League goals to my name and was the leading scorer at the club. Against Manchester United at Old Trafford I scored another memorable solo goal, although what I remember most about that game is the running argument I had throughout with Tommy Smith.

Tommy, a former Liverpool captain who had lifted the League Championship and UEFA Cup just two years before, was a much-revered figure at the club. I was one of his biggest fans and he was a player who commanded the utmost respect. He'd recently lost his place in the first team and had dropped into the reserves to maintain his fitness. Whether it was his frustration about this situation boiling over I don't know, but for some reason that day he just wouldn't let up in giving me stick.

I overheard him after the game talking to Evo about this 'little bastard with the red hair' and how the 'deserved kick up the backside' he had given me had helped me go on and score what proved to be the winning goal. I didn't agree with him at the time but to be fair to Smithy he was probably right.

The following midweek we played at home to Sheffield Wednesday. Again, I played reasonably well, bagged another goal and was afterwards told, along with Kevin Kewley, to report to Anfield in the morning, on what should have been our day off. Unbeknown to us, a couple of first-teamers were struggling with injury, so we were brought in as a precautionary measure. We trained on our own, away from the main squad, but Kevin somehow got wind of a rumour that was going around Melwood that one of us might be involved in the senior side at Middlesbrough that weekend.

Kevin was a couple of years older than me and captain of the reserves so the likelihood was that it would be him who'd get called up first. Even so, I was absolutely staggered just to be in contention. After training we went for a bite to eat in a local café, where the prospect of travelling up to the north-east with the first team dominated our thoughts. Come Friday, Kevin trained with the reserves as normal but for the first time I joined the 'big heads'. All the talk after training was that Steve Heighway wouldn't be fit enough to play against Boro and that I would be taking his place. I couldn't believe what I was hearing. A million thoughts were rushing through my mind and all I remember was being told to report back to Anfield for the coach journey to Middlesbrough later that afternoon.

There were no mobile phones in those days so I couldn't get home quickly enough to share this fantastic news with everyone. For some reason, the bus journey back to Cantril Farm that day seemed to take forever but when I finally got home everyone was overjoyed and plans were hastily made for my mum, dad, sister, auntie and uncle to travel up to Teesside the following day.

On the coach journey north I barely said a word. The only two players I really knew were Phil Thompson and Joey Jones so I just kept myself to myself. I was a bit in awe of everything but one thing that put my mind at ease a little was the fact that Steve Heighway wasn't on the coach after failing to prove his fitness. That didn't necessarily guarantee my involvement because we had a thirteen-man travelling squad, but the papers were reporting that I was set to make my debut and more often than not in those days the journalists were very well informed.

I was gobsmacked by the amount of money that was being gambled by the players in the card schools during the coach journey. Three-card brag was normally the game of choice among the Liverpool players. I'd never seen so much money sitting in one pot before. My wages might have recently risen to £32 a week but the lads were gambling a lot more than that. Obviously they were earning much more but to me it seemed unbelievable.

Tommy Smith was back in the first-team picture and, again, he was doing his best to wind me up. 'Eh lads, you won't get near the bogs tomorrow, young Davey's going to be parked in there,' he was saying. Everyone laughed, myself included. It was just good banter and, even though it was at my expense, just being involved in the jokes and wisecracks that were being bandied about made me feel more part of the team. But Tommy was wrong in assuming I'd be a bag of nerves. I didn't suffer from this at all. I was really at ease with myself, taking everything in and just looking forward to the game.

I was more nervous about who I would room with than the football. Luckily I roomed with Joey, which was good because we were mates, and from memory managed to sleep OK – I certainly don't recall having any nightmares. The next morning couldn't come soon enough and I was like a kid at Christmas.

In much the same way that birthdays and significant anniversaries are recalled, 1 November 1975 is a date that will forever be ingrained in my memory. In some respects it now seems a lifetime away but my recollections are vivid. In his team-talk at the hotel the manager spoke about how I fully deserved my place in the team and how I wasn't going to let anyone down. It was a strange feeling, one mixed with excitement and disbelief that this was really happening to me.

I remember a press photographer calling by the hotel at lunchtime to take my picture and everyone wishing me well before we left for the short drive to Ayresome Park. I think I just sat quietly on the way to the ground. Once in the old away dressing room I'd visited a year earlier with the youth team it all felt familiar, so I found my place before going out with the others to have a look at the pitch.

When I got back inside I was handed a pile of good-luck telegrams, mainly from family and friends back in Cantril Farm, including one from the junior football league I used to play in. It was great to know they were all rooting for me – but no surprise because that's the type of community it was, one in which they took great pride in seeing one of their own doing well. It was very humbling.

As the clock ticked towards kick-off I was impatient to get my kit on. I know it's a well-worn cliché but as I sat getting changed I really did have to pinch myself that I was about to make my Liverpool debut. It was a moment I had dreamed of all my life, one I had worked so hard to aspire to, one that every young Liverpudlian who had ever kicked a ball around the city's streets would have given their right arm for. I looked around at the faces beside me. Including myself, this was the team chosen by Bob Paisley as Liverpool looked to win only their second away league game of the season against a Middlesbrough side that had yet to taste defeat at home. Ray Clemence, Phil Neal, Joey Jones, Phil Thompson, Tommy Smith, Ray Kennedy, Kevin Keegan, Brian Hall, John Toshack, Ian Callaghan and substitute Terry McDermott. Household names, the lot of them. And I could now class them as my team-mates.

As I pulled on that classic white Liverpool away shirt I thought about my dad, a Liverpool supporter all his life, who was up in the stands waiting to watch his only son make his first senior appearance for the club. An immense feeling of pride surged through me. This moment was as much for him and all my family and friends as it was for me. It had come much earlier than I'd anticipated but I was ready and in no mood to let them or anyone else down, including Bob Paisley, the manager who had put his neck on the line by placing his faith in me.

The referee's buzzer went to summon us to leave the dressing room and I took my place in the line-up to go down the tunnel, I don't know where I was in the line to start with but by the time we got to pitch my mum said I was almost ahead of captain Kevin Keegan, – such was my excitement.

In front of a partisan full house on a horrible wet day I played well and was really happy with how it went. Apart from scoring a goal I couldn't have asked for a better debut. When I think back now a few stand-out moments remain. One was an incident early on when Tommy Smith sent a long ball over the top of the Middlesbrough defence, one that was way too long for me to latch on to. I went chasing after it anyway but it was to no avail and Smithy didn't seem best pleased. Here we go, I thought, it's going to be like last week in the reserves all over again, but straight away Kevin Keegan jumped to my defence as I jogged back towards the centre circle, yelling back at him, 'Fucking hell, Smithy, give the kid a chance.'

As it transpired, chances were very few and far between in the game. I didn't get a sniff of a chance in the first half but I made more headway in the second and I almost scored with one – it wasn't to be my day in front of goal, but that didn't worry me too much. Middlesbrough had a good side at the time, one of the best in their recent history, and it was a tough match that could have gone either way until the 71st minute. In what was maybe an ominous sign for things to come later in my career, the only goal of the game was scored by a substitute, our number twelve Terry Mac who had come on to replace the injured Brian Hall early in the first half.

The other stand-out moment in the game was the sending off of Joey Jones six minutes from full-time. It came following an incident with John Hickton, which resulted in the Boro striker losing five teeth, for which Joey later served a one-match ban, but we hung on. The two points were vitally important as they kept us in hot pursuit of the top four that included, in reverse order, Derby County, Queens Park Rangers, West Ham United and Manchester United. It was to also kick-start an impressive run of results that would see those above us soon pegged back, but more of that later.

On our way back from the north-east I remember we stopped off at a hotel in Ripon for a meal. The exertions of the day, combined with the nervous tension that went with making my senior Liverpool debut, had combined to leave me absolutely shattered but it was a great feeling.

When I eventually got home my parents had been out to buy that night's *Football Echo*, which in those days carried what was almost a minute-by-minute report of the match, so the first thing I did was scan that for any mention of my name. It featured quite heavily, which to me was a good sign, and I spent the remainder of that night reading it over and over again as it all slowly sank in.

The following morning I got up and went across to the local playing fields in Cantril Farm to watch some of my friends play their Sunday League games, just as I normally did. I still felt shattered, with every muscle in my body seemingly aching. It was normal to feel tired after a game but this was different to what I felt after playing for the reserves. Not that I was complaining. For the first time in my life I felt like something of a local celebrity. I was quite well known within the local community anyway but the reaction on this occasion was different. All of a sudden, people who I didn't know were looking and pointing over at me, while others were queuing up to say well done. It was a fantastic experience.

This was it, the big time had arrived and it was something I quickly had to get used to.

6

A LEGEND IS BORN

THE OFFICIAL LIVERPOOL TEAM PHOTOGRAPH THAT HAD BEEN taken in readiness for the 1975/76 campaign offered no hint that my life was about to change beyond all recognition.

Just three months prior to my first-team debut, the lads had lined up at Anfield for the annual photoshoot. Eighteen red shirts posing alongside the boss as the invited photographers snapped away, capturing for posterity the Liverpool squad Bob Paisley was pinning his hopes on for the season ahead.

I say squad in the loosest of terms because there wasn't a 'squad system' as such back then. Only on European nights when you could name five substitutes. Otherwise, it was just the starting eleven plus one on the bench. And, given that on a week-to-week basis team changes at Liverpool were usually nonexistent or, at the least, kept to a minimum, the first team was looked upon as something of a closed shop – especially to those who hadn't even been included on the pre-season photograph.

Not surprisingly at the time, I didn't think I was near it. After all, I was still just an eighteen-year-old with one year of reserve team experience. The caption for the image taken on that August afternoon in 1975 read like a who's who of Liverpool greats: Lawler, Heighway, Keegan, Lindsay, Kennedy, Clemence, Thompson, Toshack, McDermott, Jones, Case, Boersma, Callaghan, Smith, Hughes, Hall, Cormack and Neal.

Fifteen of those pictured were (or were soon to be) internationals and the remaining three, Case, Boersma and Hall, can justifiably lay claim to be among the

51

best players never to be capped by their respective countries. It's another example of the phenomenal strength in depth at the club and it meant that if anyone was to drop out of the normal match-day 'squad' there was a queue of quality players waiting in the wings.

At the outset of 1975/76 my primary aim was to continue doing my best for Roy Evans' second string. Things can move quickly in football though and, just like I hadn't expected to make my senior bow so early, I didn't anticipate what the remainder of the campaign had in store for me.

*

MY DEBUT PERFORMANCE AT MIDDLESBROUGH HAD SUDDENLY pushed me firmly into the first-team picture. Ten days earlier I'd been sitting on the front step of a friend's house, two doors down from where I lived, listening to the radio commentary of Liverpool's UEFA Cup tie away to Real Sociedad. Never once did it cross my mind that I could have been in with a chance of taking part in the second leg. Bob Paisley later revealed that it had always been his plan to blood me against Sociedad and only injuries had forced his hand into pitching me in earlier than anticipated at Boro. But that was news to me and was typical of the 'Liverpool Way'.

There's a long list of players who'd come through the ranks to make their first-team debut, only to never be seen again. I was desperate not to be another name on that list of 'one-game wonders'. At the same time, I was equally aware of the need to remain patient and bide my time for another opportunity.

Once you have experienced the big time though, no one wants to go backwards and, even if it was a little bit ahead of schedule in terms of my expected career development, I was eager to sample life in the first team again. I may have started the season way down the pecking order when it came to challenging for a place but now that I'd made the initial breakthrough things moved faster than I could ever have anticipated; my career was about to take off in a way I could never have imagined.

Some newspapers were reporting that I'd be involved in the return tie with Sociedad but I was taking nothing for granted. As it happened, Steve Heighway was fit again so I dropped down to the bench, one of five substitutes. It was the game in which my reserve teammate Brian Kettle made his first-team debut and although I'd have loved to have been out there alongside him from the start it was a great feeling just to be included in the match-day squad for the first time at Anfield.

As a contest the tie was quickly put to bed. We led 3–1 from the first leg and by half-time another two goals had been added to that tally. Our progress to the next round was assured. Kevin Keegan even missed a penalty during a one-sided first half. Not that I remember much else of it. I was too busy savouring the occasion to concentrate on what was happening out on the pitch. In fact, my head must have still be in the clouds during the half-time break because although we were cruising to victory it didn't cross my mind that I was about to be thrown on for my home debut. It was only towards the end of Bob Paisley's team-talk that he casually mentioned I would be taking the place of Ian Callaghan for the second half. Apparently, Cally wasn't feeling too well. Ronnie Moran then came over with a few simple instructions.

Given that I'd enjoyed a decent debut on the Saturday I sensed that the majority of supporters were eager to catch a glimpse of me. Those who hadn't made the trip to Middlesbrough had obviously read the reports and they no doubt wanted to see what all the fuss was about. I was aware that there would be a lot more focus on me now and, playing down the right-hand side, I was determined to impress. It had rained all day and in those days Anfield was hardly the bowling-green surface it was to become. I remember the pitch being a touch on the heavy side which, for someone as light on their feet as myself, wasn't the best but after a few early touches I soon got into my stride as we attacked the Anfield Road end.

There were no further goals until the 72nd minute when a misplaced pass came my way inside the box. Without thinking, I just turned and knocked it into the net from about twelve yards out. It was a bit of a gift but one I gratefully accepted. The finish was a touch nonchalant and I probably made it look easier than it actually was. The angle was quite tight and it would have been much more difficult if I'd taken my time and really thought about it. As it was, within a split second of receiving the ball I'd turned and hit it. It wasn't the best goal I ever scored and with the ground being less than half full it was not greeted with the deafening roar we'd become accustomed to on a European night at Anfield. But to score my first senior Liverpool goal meant so much. That it had come as a substitute was a sign of things to come.

The main thing was that I was off the mark; scoring had always been a big part of my game and we can all remember strikers who had a tough time netting their first goals. My only slight disappointment was that it hadn't come at the Kop end. That would have to wait.

Within seven minutes our advantage was doubled as Ray Kennedy, with his second of the night, Steve Heighway and Phil Neal quickly added to my strike. It was an emphatic victory and to cap it all, two minutes from time, my old mate from Liverpool Schoolboys Max Thompson also came on, meaning a trio of Liverpool teenagers had featured in the same game, a rare occurrence in the days before squad rotation. For reserve team boss Roy Evans and the club's youth development system it was seen as a real success. Later that week, underneath the headline 'Liverpool's Likely Lads', myself, Max and Brian were photographed side-by-side on an empty Kop terrace, each raising a triumphant arm in the air to suggest we had 'arrived'.

What made our success even more special was the fact that we had all stood on the Kop as kids. Three young Liverpudlians living out their boyhood dreams. It was a terrific local-lads-make-good story. Unfortunately, our careers were to follow different paths. Max didn't play for the first team again, while Brian made only three more appearances. Both later played in America before seeing out their careers on the local non-league circuit. In an ideal world we would have progressed together but this was the harsh reality of life at the top level.

Of course, there was no guarantee back then that I would do any better, so I relished every moment of this new-found fame. It had been an amazing four days, comic book stuff, really. I had made my senior Liverpool debut and scored my first goal but I knew there was still a lot of hard work ahead if I was to push on and firmly establish myself in the team. The following Saturday I was back in the reserves away to Newcastle, although the feel-good factor was still in place and I enjoyed another decent game, scoring with a memorable 25-yard strike.

In the next round of the UEFA Cup Liverpool faced Slask Wroclaw of Poland and I would have played a part in the home leg of that tie had I not been sent off while playing for the reserves the previous weekend. It was away to Blackburn Rovers and I received my marching orders for retaliation. Back at Anfield on the Monday, Bob Paisley informed me that I was now suspended and therefore he couldn't pick me to play in the European tie as he'd planned to do. I was absolutely gutted and I cursed my stupidity even more as I watched Jimmy Case memorably score his first senior hat-trick to book Liverpool's place in the quarterfinal. It certainly taught me a lesson.

Over the next few months my role in the first team was restricted to a series of minor substitute appearances, one of which was a dour goalless draw at Bramall Lane; memorable only for the fact that on a personal note I roomed with Kevin Keegan. I must admit, sharing with the only team-mate I was ever in awe of was a nerve-racking experience. Only months earlier I'd been telling my mates in Cantril Farm that KK had talked to me. Now he was making my tea and running me a bath, a story that had the rest of the team roaring with laughter when he relayed it to them the next morning.

I later roomed with Kevin on a number of other occasions and always found it fascinating listening to him. Like a duckling follows a mother duck, I one day followed him through Harrods. He had such an aura about him that passers-by would stop and stare. He later told me, 'When people recognise you in places like London you know you are making a name for yourself.' It was a moment that would flash back to me in very different circumstances a season later.

Though Kevin was only to stay with Liverpool until the summer of 1977, playing alongside him was also fantastic. He set very high standards and seeing him enjoy his success probably inspired me and a number of others to aspire to greater things. I was living on a council estate and going to training on the bus but I dreamed of one day driving a sports car and living out in the country like him. Despite his fame and all the trappings that brought, he remained a very genuine person, a great role model and the best footballer I have ever seen with fans. Never once did I see him refuse an autograph. He was the perfect example of a working-class lad achieving great success and retaining humility.

More often than not when I was substitute I'd get at least a good ten-minute run-out to show what I could do, although on one occasion at home to Newcastle in February 1976 I came on during a very, very late break in play. I replaced Tommy Smith and was on the pitch for less than three seconds before the final whistle blew. I didn't even touch the ball. It must have made me a contender for a place in the Guinness Book of Records for the shortest ever involvement in a match, yet I still collected my bonus following the 2-0 win.

It was all part of my learning curve and gradually I began to make a more meaningful impression in and around the first-team squad. So much so that when a thigh injury ruled John Toshack out of what was a big top of the table clash away to Derby County a few weeks later the boss had no hesitation in handing me my next senior start.

The Baseball Ground was a venue that had not been particularly kind to Liverpool in previous seasons and its pitch was notorious as the worst in the league. Since the Rams had come back up to Division One in 1969 we had failed to register a single win there. They were viewed as our bogey team and there was a big rivalry between the sides at the time.

Just a month earlier a Roger Davies goal had knocked us out of the FA Cup. Liverpool might have been league leaders but Derby were the reigning champions and sat just two points adrift in fourth place. Not surprisingly then, it was billed as a massive match – one which we were delighted to come away from with a 1–1 draw, with me setting up the equalising goal for Ray Kennedy just three minutes from the end. If I couldn't score myself then an assist was the next best thing and I was more than pleased with my overall level of performance, which again drew widespread praise in the press.

It was enough for me to retain my place in the starting eleven for the first time when European competition resumed following its winter break. It was to be my first taste of continental travel with the senior squad, and the midweek trip behind the Iron Curtain, where Liverpool had been drawn to play against East Germany's Dynamo Dresden in the first leg of the UEFA Cup quarterfinal, was an amazing experience. The attention to detail throughout the entire trip was a real eye-opener. It was nothing compared to the luxury players experience nowadays but for me it was the first time I felt special as a footballer and where I'd normally have been sat at home listening to a game like this on the radio, there I was walking out behind the referee for match of massive importance.

Dresden were extremely strong opponents on their own patch and we were glad to return with a share of the spoils following a tough goalless draw, best remembered for Ray Clemence pulling off a crucial penalty save. I received a kick on the sole of my right foot in the opening minute that eventually led to me being subbed just after the hour mark, but up until then I'd been happy with how I'd played.

It was initially feared that the injury would force me to miss the next match at home to Middlesbrough, thus denying me the chance of a first start at Anfield. I was desperate to recover in time and delighted when the swelling eventually subsided. My full home debut, however, was a huge anticlimax.

A very poor game saw us lose 2–0 and surrender top spot in the table. It was the first real setback I had encountered since being part of the first-team scene. Boro got off to a strong start and we struggled to get back on terms. I remember there being a strange atmosphere there that day. The crowd were stunned and it was rare to play with such an air of desperation hanging over Anfield. No one played well; it was an off-day for us all. In typical Liverpool fashion no big fuss was made but it certainly acted as a wake-up call.

There was no blame culture at Anfield when results didn't go our way. No one ever pointed the finger. Defeats were rare, home defeats even rarer. This loss to Middlesbrough was one of only eleven suffered on home soil in the league by Liverpool throughout the entire 1970s. As always, the message from the coaching staff was simple: 'Just go out there next time and ensure it doesn't happen again.'

I can never remember there being a knee-jerk reaction to any defeat during my time at the club. I know that Shanks ripped up his first great team following an infamous FA Cup defeat at Watford in 1970 but Liverpool was a club that didn't enter into change for the sake of it. They embraced a tried and trusted method of playing the game. And it was one that had proved very successful. A lot of it was based around two-touch football, which we'd work on a lot in training, but that's not to say the club was stuck in its ways and not open to an alternative approach from time to time. The sages in the bootroom were certainly always looking for ways to improve the team; a prime example being how a tactical switch in the aftermath of a European Cup exit to Red Star Belgrade in 1973 had prompted a new 'European' style of playing from the back.

Though people often remember these times for fast-flowing football, this Liverpool team also knew how to get results and often we went away with the intention of almost strangling teams in the early part. Our greater expertise would see us grow in strength as the game wore on and, more often than not, we'd come through to win late on. Hard-working grafters complemented the odd flair player and in certain games there would also be this element of having one free man; a player who had licence to roam and run at defences when in possession. It was a common-sense, grown-up outlook; one that worked because of the trust the manager had in his players.

During my early years in the team the free man would, more often than not, be me. My greatest asset was dribbling with the ball at speed, taking on defenders and going for goal. It was a more cavalier approach in terms of how Liverpool normally played but Bob Paisley and his coaches realised just how effective this could be, especially back in the days when I was looked upon as a novice and still something of an unknown quantity in the eyes of the opposition.

For sure, they would work on trying to polish my rough edges, but the creativity and flair side of my game was actively encouraged. Some coaches would try to knock this out of a young player and instruct them to conform to how the rest of the team played. At Liverpool I was given the freedom to express myself because I offered an alternative (some would say refreshing) option. I didn't have the same restraints placed on me as most of the other players did and therefore when I received the ball I didn't have to automatically release it. Generally, I was told not to dribble anywhere near our own goal, but thirty yards away from the opposite end and the message was: 'Don't be scared to take defenders on.'

I played off-the-cuff and would try to take the opposition by surprise. Bob Paisley would often comment, 'How do the opposition know what he's going to do? He doesn't even know himself.' The press often referred to me as the secret weapon in Liverpool's attacking armoury and I don't ever remember going into a game back then thinking about who I'd be up against. I had enough belief in my ability to think, 'Let the opposition worry about me'. Not the other way around. There was no one quicker than me in the First Division at the time and I feared no one. I was unaware of reputations, of whether a defender was weaker on a certain foot or the like.

In that game away to Derby, for example, which was only my third appearance in the first team, the player marking me was David Nish, an England international. Alongside him were Colin Todd and Roy McFarland. But I went out there with no preconceived ideas of how I was going to play against them; whether I was going to try and beat them on the inside or the outside, whether it would be best to go at them using pace or skill. My mind was completely open and I think that worked in my favour because if I'd have given them too much thought I might well have been overcome with fear. It was only when I was about to go on that Ronnie Moran or Bob Paisley would say, 'If you get the chance, have a go at this full-back.' Apart from that I had no idea of the situation I was being pitched into and therefore just played my normal carefree game.

It was the way I had always played, ever since I was a kid. And if I were instructing young players now I'd tell them not to get too bogged down with thoughts about the opposition. Some people may argue that this approach smacks of arrogance, but innocent, youthful exuberance should never be knocked out of a player if they are talented enough to get away with it. As the 1975/76 season entered its thrilling final straight it certainly did me no harm.

WITH THE TEAM CHASING GLORY IN BOTH THE LEAGUE CHAMPI-onship and UEFA Cup excitement was steadily building and towards the end of March I scored my second goal for the first team. It was the match-winner in a crucial 1–0 win away to Norwich, a result that kept us on the coat-tails of surprise table-toppers Queens Park Rangers. Reigning champions Derby and recently promoted Manchester United were the other teams locked in this intriguing four-horse race for the title. Just two points separated first and fourth so there was little margin for error.

I played all ninety minutes at Carrow Road, again in place of Tosh, but found myself back on the bench seven days later for Burnley's visit to Anfield. I wasn't best pleased but didn't make a fuss. Obviously I'd have liked to start every game but time was on my side. Bob Paisley had gone on record admitting that I was one of the best young prospects in the country and I didn't doubt that he valued me. This was his first experience as manager of dealing with a young aspiring player and he was very mindful that my talent had to be nurtured carefully. So while I was constantly wanting to play, at this stage I understood his reasoning, especially as I'd been receiving treatment throughout the week on a bruised right instep that I'd suffered at Norwich.

Against Burnley the boss was forced to send me on much earlier than he had planned after Steve Heighway suffered a nasty-looking eye injury shortly after the half-hour mark. From the bench I'd watched how fellow nineteen-year-old Gerry Peyton in the visitors' goal had pulled off a string of heroic saves under the shadow of the Kop, and you got the sense that it could be one of those days. The Clarets were struggling near the foot of the table and seemed content to sit back and hopefully soak up what we had to throw at them.

I had different ideas. I don't remember it as one of my better games, partly due to the slight injury I was carrying, but I'd been on the pitch for just four minutes when I managed to break the deadlock. Keegan flung over a corner which I met with my head at the far post. True to form, Peyton was there to parry it away but only on to the post and from the rebound I bundled the ball over the line with my thigh. It wasn't pretty but I didn't care. It was my first senior goal at the Kop end and the thrill was something else, one I'd never experienced before. I'd stood on that terrace and celebrated hundreds of goals like that in the past. The roles were now reversed and I was re-enacting my boyhood dreams. For that moment I was King of the Kop.

My foot was still bothering me and I had it strapped up during the half-time break. As a result I came out with much more of a spring in my step and sealed the two points by doubling the advantage in the 61st minute, this time with a more straightforward close-range finish. Neither goal was what you would call a classic, though the second featured in the BBC's Goal of the Month selection, but for both I was in the right place at the right time – a priceless knack for any striker and one acknowledged by Kevin Keegan in his post-match interview. Praise from a superstar like Kevin was hugely satisfying and very reassuring. As was seeing my name plastered across the back-page headlines yet again. With each passing week the games were gaining in importance, so this was another vital victory and the role I had played in it was not underplayed.

Of course, I'd come off the bench to score before but this was the moment that gave birth to the 'Supersub' legend. I honestly had never heard it before and it was only in the wake of the Burnley game that I first came across it. I don't know which journalist or newspaper first coined the phrase but over that last weekend in March 1976 it appeared in a number of places. It was a double-barrelled word back then and one that had never previously been used. Substitutes had only been introduced in the Football League in 1965 and at first they were only permitted if a player was injured. Charlton Athletic's Keith Peacock was the first ever substitute used in English football, while on the same day Bobby Knox of Barrow was the first sub to score a goal, so I suppose he can lay claim to being the first ever Supersub.

The following month Geoff Strong was the first ever substitute used by Liverpool and he scored thirty minutes after entering the fray in a 1–1 draw at home to West Ham. Substitutes were rarely called upon back then though, and it wasn't until 1967, when a change in the rules allowed substitutions to be made for tactical reasons as well as injuries, that they became more commonplace.

Phil Boersma had since become the club's most prolific scoring sub with four goals to his name as twelfth man, but no big fuss had ever been made about it. Apart from maybe Roger Davies of Derby, I can't recall there ever being any other comparable goalscoring substitutes about back then.

Of course, my reputation as a 'Supersub' was still very much in its infancy and although it was a nickname that I would soon live up to, at this stage it was all just press hyperbole. Still, it quickly caught on and soon everyone was using it. Although it would eventually become annoying, back then as I began to make a name for myself I must admit it made me feel about ten foot tall whenever I heard it because it gave me a unique identity.

*

A LOT IS MADE THESE DAYS ABOUT TEAMS BEING TIRED THE weekend after a big European game but you would never hear a Liverpool player admitting to this back in the 1970s. You gave up a place in the first team at your peril. In these times of 'rotation' can you imagine Bob Paisley telling Tommy Smith, Emlyn Hughes or Kevin Keegan that he thought they were tired and would miss out on a Mersey derby?

Cup finals aside, weeks don't get much bigger than a UEFA Cup semifinal away to Barcelona followed by a home clash with Everton. At times like that the sheer adrenalin gets you through it and that's what we were running on as the season's climax drew ever closer.

Having scored in the previous two games against Norwich and Burnley, I was disappointed to miss out on playing in the Nou Camp against a Barca team that included the legendary Dutch duo Johan Cruyff and Johan Neeskens. This tie between two clubs of such immense stature was something very special and one that caught the imagination of everyone. According to Michael Charters in the *Echo*, the manager's plan had been to play me from the start but he was worried about my bruised instep and opted for the experience of Tosh instead. Nevertheless, just being part of the squad for such a massive occasion, in one of the world's great stadiums, was an unbelievable experience and the fact Tosh scored the only goal in a notable victory maybe went some way to justifying Bob Paisley's decision.

The night was also memorable for the post-match actions of my fellow substitute Joey Jones. As the Barca fans showed their displeasure in defeat by throwing seat cushions on the pitch, Joey returned them Frisbee-style as quick as he could – it was hilarious, particularly when Bob Paisley almost threw him down the players' tunnel in disgust!

With the big games coming thick and fast, Liverpool's starting eleven virtually picked itself and I was content in the fact that, at the very least, despite Brian Hall being the only substitute used in the Nou Camp, when it came to the league games I was now almost assured of the number twelve shirt.

The lads were high on confidence upon our return from Spain. No one was complaining of tiredness. The fact that next up were local rivals Everton obviously heightened the excitement within the city and no matter how hard you tried it was impossible not to be affected by it. I was no stranger to the unique atmosphere of the fixture, having grown up attending them, but to be in with a chance of playing in one was a whole new ball-game for me and this was to be something else.

It was a morning kick-off – the first in the history of the fixture – due to the Grand National taking place in the afternoon at nearby Aintree – and the night before we stayed at a hotel in the Liverpool suburb of Gateacre. It was very rare for the first team to kick-off so early back then and most of the lads would have found it strange, so the management tried their best to ensure it didn't throw anyone out of their normal routine too much. For someone as young as myself it wasn't that unusual because I'd obviously been used to playing on Saturday mornings for my school and also in the A and B teams when coming through the youth ranks.

From my vantage point on the bench, I must admit the game passed me by and I don't remember much of the first 64 minutes. There hadn't been a goal scored in the derby for two and a half years, since Alan Waddle netted the winner at Goodison in December 1973, and this was drifting towards another goalless stalemate.

Tosh then suffered a bang to his head and the next thing I knew I was being told to go on. It was a huge moment for me but thankfully I didn't have much time to comprehend the scale of it. This was the game every young football-loving Scouse lad dreams of playing in. There were almost 55,000 inside Anfield that day, by far the biggest crowd I had ever played in front of. I've since seen brief video clips of the game and, although I didn't look to be wracked with any sense of trepidation when entering the field, I must admit I could sense the magnitude of the occasion and just what was at stake. I couldn't wait to get on. My warm-up consisted of just a few quick sprints along the touchline. My tracksuit was then quickly ripped off before I tucked my shirt into my shorts and was pushed into the action by Ronnie Moran.

The game was petering out, both sides looked to have settled for the draw and I think all thoughts were turning to that afternoon's big race at Aintree. Everton had a throw-in near the halfway line on the Kemlyn Road side and I remember drifting over, lurking with intent and then winning the ball by intercepting Roger Kenyon's return pass to Martin Dobson, who had taken the throw.

From my earliest days my natural instinct was to dribble with the ball and at that moment my first thought was to take on the man in my way. I was tight to the line so had little option. The following twenty seconds were probably the most exhilarating of my career. In desperation, a flurry of blue shirts ran at me, so I just made sure they couldn't get near me or the ball. Aware there was very little time left, once I was in the penalty area I never had time to consider that Kevin Keegan was waiting, unmarked, in the six-yard box.

My job was to score goals. It's what I had been sent on for and that's what I intended doing. So without hesitation I shaped my body to shoot and pulled the trigger, aiming low and hard in the direction of the near post. Luckily, Dai Davies failed to stop it. The ball hit the back of the net and all hell broke loose. It was like being back in the schoolyard, football how I like to play and watch it.

The longest goal drought in Merseyside derby history – 469 minutes in total – was finally over and, more importantly, a vital two points were heading Liverpool's way. I turned towards the Kemlyn Road, the stand traditionally occupied by the more discerning, older generation of Liverpool supporters. Normally they would be only too keen to give you a piece of their mind if they thought you weren't pulling your weight. It was a running joke among the Anfield faithful that they'd always be among the first to leave the ground, even when we were winning. Not on this day though. My goal sparked an unprecedented commotion, the likes of which had probably not been experienced in the Kemlyn since the tea bar ran out of Eccles cakes!

If any proof were needed of just how big a moment this was, a mini pitch invasion ensued. Not the type that required the intervention of mounted police, which was sadly an increasingly common occurrence at some grounds during this time. No, this was nothing more than an overspill of unbridled joy. It took something special to get the regulars in the Kemlyn off their feet, never mind on to the pitch, so I think that said it all.

What had been a nondescript derby had suddenly exploded into one of the most memorable. There was still a couple of minutes left as I got back to the halfway line and as I prepared for the game to resume my mind started drifting to what the headlines were going to be in the following morning's papers. Unprofessional, I know, but for me to be on the verge of scoring the winner in my first ever senior derby game was scarcely believable, especially given the circumstances: on as a sub and netting in the dying minutes, or to be more precise one minute and twenty-two seconds from the end, as one newspaper reported it the following day.

My head must have been in the clouds because I don't remember having another kick, no recollection whatsoever, although in my scrapbook there's a press cutting in which I'm interviewed post-match and I tell the reporter that, 'I should have scored again after that but my concentration had gone.'

The reaction of the other players was one of shock at what I'd done. No one had expected it and given the recent derby stalemates such drama was not the norm. It had come completely out of the blue and maybe that had an effect on what happened next. I had been thrust into the role of local hero and all I wanted now was for the ref to blow the final whistle. You can imagine how I must have felt then when we immediately attacked again and got a penalty. I couldn't believe it and, to my shame, I couldn't help but think that this was going to ruin my moment of glory.

Up stepped Phil Neal, who had taken over from Kevin Keegan as Liverpool's regular penalty-taker just a few months earlier. As he strode forward to try and put the result beyond all doubt I must have been the only Liverpudlian in the ground praying that he'd miss. His previous track record was faultless – four successful conversions out of four – so I didn't hold out much hope. Ensuring we claimed maximum points was obviously more important, but this was a once-in-a-lifetime opportunity for a local lad like myself – the kind of scenario you lay in bed dreaming about as a youngster. But lo and behold, Nealy only goes and puts his effort wide of the post. Amazing. As a huge collective sigh rolled over the majority of the ground I did my best to conceal my delight, but on the inside I was screaming, 'Yerrrrrrrs!'

And that was it. Time was up. Clive Thomas blew his whistle to signal that the last ball had been kicked, meaning I had scored the winner on my derby debut and etched my name into local folklore. Elation and relief were my overriding emotions as I struggled to comprehend what had just happened. I felt like a character from the Roy of the Rovers comic . It was a moment I'll never forget as long as I live.

While the game itself was hardly a classic, it is still fondly recalled as one of the most memorable derbies of all time. Whether it would be if that penalty had gone in, I'm not too sure. Most people have long since forgotten about Nealy's penalty miss, which I'm sure he won't be too bothered about. He didn't miss many during the course of his career but I'll always be grateful to him for that one.

There had been plenty of late winners in the fixture before and many more since but I firmly believe that few, if any, have been more significant than the one struck at around a quarter to one on Saturday 3 April 1976. Its importance really cannot be underestimated and it was to have serious repercussions in terms of Liverpool's history because it spurred us on to the glory that followed and, in turn, what was to come after that.

The quality, timing and importance combined to make it a goal that's never been forgotten but as the sporting focus switched to events down the road – where Rag Trade beat the people's favourite Red Rum to win the Grand National – I was genuinely nervous about what the reaction to it would be. Obviously I knew all the Liverpudlians would be queuing up to congratulate me but at the same time I'd upset the other half of the city and I didn't know what quite to expect. There were a couple of notorious hard-core Evertonians living in Cantril Farm back then and it was with some trepidation that I walked over to the local shops to pick up a 'Pink' *Echo* later that evening. I needn't have worried: I didn't come across any Blues and even in the days that followed the comments were only good ones.

Though a special goal for me, the game wasn't covered by the BBC so it didn't feature in their 'Goal of the Season' competition – that award in 1975/76 going to Gerry Francis for his effort against Liverpool back on the opening day. I'm more remembered for another famous strike, one that I'll cover in a later chapter, but I think this derby winner is the best I ever scored.

Highlights of the game were shown on Granada TV's The Big Match the next day. Manchester City manager Tony Book was the studio guest and he gave me man-of-the-match. To commemorate the occasion I was awarded a special mirror, inscribed with the 'Big Match' motif and details of the game. I gave it to my mum and she still has it hung up on a wall at home.

I don't need anything to remind of that day. It is right up there among the greatest moments of my career – a kid born in Everton scoring a derby winner at Anfield. It was the stuff dreams are made of and it was to thrust me into the spotlight more than ever before.

7

TIME OF MY LIFE

HAVING SCORED FOUR CONSECUTIVE LEAGUE GOALS, AND BEEN elevated to the role of local hero, the whole mood around me changed and would continue to do so for the remainder of the 1975/76 season. I was suddenly the centre of attention wherever I went. Everyone was talking about this 'young red-headed striking sensation' and the press were queuing up to write features about me.

Seeing my name and face in the papers was nothing new, especially where the local press was concerned. They had been tracking my progress since I started making a name for myself in the reserves but now that I had scored a few goals in the First Division I became the subject of widespread interest from the national media.

One story in the Daily Express pictured me sat on the 12C bus that I used to catch every morning from Cantril Farm to Anfield on the way to training. I'd actually passed my driving test just three weeks before the Everton game and had since bought my first car, a three-year-old orange Ford Escort, but the article was emphasising how, in such a short space of time, my life was rapidly changing.

It's funny when I think back to it now. Can you imagine today's rising stars ever travelling to Melwood on the bus? Never mind being photographed on one. This type of thing just doesn't happen any more. Nowadays, young players are wrapped in cotton wool from a very early age with some even chauffeured to and from training every day. Down the years I've heard plenty of stories about players from previous generations travelling to home games with the fans on a bus and although I never did that, my weekday journey to training helped keep my feet on the ground.

In one interview I admitted that all the publicity made me feel 'a bit daft' but at the same time I didn't know what the future held so if I had never kicked a ball again this was would have been my five minutes of fame. I therefore tried my best to just take it all in my stride and enjoy it. In truth, it was a bit overwhelming. I was a just a shy and quiet 19-year-old lad who was coming to terms with being in the spotlight.

It certainly increased the pressure on me to maintain the good form I had shown but if you wanted to play for Liverpool then that was to be expected. It's par for the course for any young footballer who has just broken through into the first team and, as the expectancy levels around me rose, supporters almost began to believe that me coming on as a substitute brought with it a guarantee of goals.

That's quite a responsibility to be placed on the shoulders of a player so young. At the same time, once I'd made the breakthrough I had a strong self-belief that I now deserved to be in the team. If you are going to play for Liverpool then you have to believe you are equal to everyone else and that when you take to the pitch you can be the one who will make the difference. I wasn't there to make up the numbers. I thrived on the pressure and knowing that the supporters believed in me was a big help.

I was level-headed enough to deal with it. My feet were planted firmly on the ground. The family and friends I had around me made certain of that. And, of course, the number one rule at Liverpool Football Club was that you never let success go to your head. I'm sure that had I shown even the slightest sign of cockiness the coaching staff and my team-mates would have come down on me like a ton of bricks.

I said it at the time and it was true; it was great to have a bit of glory but the most important thing was making sure I did it again the next time. I didn't change off the pitch and I didn't change on it. I just tried to do what I did best. That's what had got me into this position so why change it now? When you're in a good vein of form things just come naturally to you and you do certain things without having to think.

It no doubt also helped that I was part of a team competing for the title and chasing glory in Europe. It was an incredible time. Since scoring at Norwich, no other Liverpool player had managed to get their name on the score-sheet in the league and as we closed in on the title I was seen as the lucky charm, even though I still wasn't a regular starter. Three nights after my much-lauded derby goal I found myself back on the bench against Leicester. We eventually won 1–0 but at one stage were really struggling and when I was warming up along the touchline I could hear nothing but the crowd appealing for me to come on.

After we were held to a goalless draw at Aston Villa, Queens Park Rangers moved a point above us at the top and, with each passing week, the pressure was mounting.

There was a growing clamour for Bob Paisley to start me in the team more regularly. As the title race entered the final straight I was raring to go but he continued to stress the need to use me carefully and explained that he would only put me into situations where he thought I could have an impact. With just three games remaining the boss was playing it carefully and biding his time with me.

The first of those games was at home to Stoke on 17 April 1976, Easter Saturday. It was a great match, played amid a fantastic atmosphere. They took the lead and, for a while, gave us a real fright. By the time I came on midway through the second half the lads had managed to turn it around and led 3–2. Within six minutes the result was safe. Emlyn Hughes scored our fourth before I rediscovered my scoring touch to add a fifth. Stoke netted a late consolation and a lot of people still remember that game, purely because of there being so many goals scored. It was rare for Liverpool to be involved in a goal-fest such as this. Scoring five at home was nothing out of the ordinary but to concede three was really unusual. Nevertheless, Anfield really was bouncing that day.

Our defence was not yet the formidable rearguard that would leak just four league goals at home in 1978/79, but it had recently kept six successive clean sheets and would end the season with the meanest goals-against record in the division. The Stoke game would have no doubt concerned the backroom staff, but at this stage of the season it was points rather than performance that were the priority. Saying that, as we walked off that afternoon I don't think any of us were aware of just how important a win it was. Only when we got back inside and heard the news that Queens Park Rangers had lost at Norwich did the significance hit home. We were back on top, just two games remained and the destiny of the title was now in our hands.

With a place in the UEFA Cup final having also been secured the previous midweek, this season was suddenly shaping up to be one of the most momentous in the club's history. Shanks had guided the Reds to a League Championship/UEFA Cup double three years before and Bob Paisley, having not yet even completed two years in the job, was on course to repeat the feat.

Not that any of us were allowed to think that far ahead. It's a well-worn cliché, I know, but the mantra at Liverpool was always to take one game at a time – next up, just two days later, was the vital Bank Holiday Monday trip to Maine Road.

Manchester City were a strong and attractive team, by no means a side you'd take lightly. They'd won the League Cup earlier in the season and would be our main title challengers the following campaign. I started in place of Jimmy Case and, for me personally, it was to be a near-perfect afternoon. It's funny how some people remember my career though, because in his autobiography, penned years later, Bob Paisley recalled things a little differently, writing that when he needed to change things late on he brought me on as substitute to 'save the day'. It must have been force of habit.

By the time we kicked off, QPR had already beaten Arsenal and therefore regained top spot. The pressure had been cranked up but we would run out 3–0 winners. For the kick-off I was positioned out on the right wing and as the ball was first played to me it bobbled over my foot and went out for a throw-in. It was an embarrassing start but things got better. I laid on the first goal for Steve Heighway and then scored the other two.

To go there and win by such an emphatic score-line was absolutely massive. As far as performances go it was not just our best during that season's run-in but also one of the finest I was ever involved in as a Liverpool player. Defensively we were back to our resolute best, limiting City to just the odd chance, while offensively there was no stopping us once the deadlock had been broken.

Until then it looked like we would have to settle for just a single point in what was an extremely tight encounter. But this team was going for the championship and, backed by an enormous army of travelling fans, we couldn't give up. We kept probing and eventually got our reward. My memories of the goals are a bit sketchy. For some reason there were no TV cameras in Moss Side that afternoon and to this day I've never seen them back. What I can recall is that there were about sixteen minutes left when we opened the scoring. I jinked past Peter Barnes and Alan Oakes before crossing from the byline to Heighway, who made no mistake in steering the ball home at the far post from six yards out. Conscious of the need for more goals to improve our goal average (it was the last season goal average rather than goal difference was used), we continued to push forward and in the 86th minute I doubled the advantage, beating Mike Doyle twice before striking a left-footed shot past Joe Corrigan. It might have taken a slight deflection on the way but it was always going in and had the keeper well beaten. The third came in the final minute, from a Keegan pass. I had the easy job of finishing it and with just Corrigan to beat, made no mistake with a subtle little dink as he raced off his line to narrow the angle.

The newspapers were unanimous in their declaration that I was man of the match . . . 'a new star is born', was how one journalist (Horace Yates of the *Daily Post*) ended his report and, although previous match-winning performances had yielded similar glowing testimonies, what pleased me more about this showing was that I had proved I was more than just an impact player. I'd completed the full ninety minutes and given a more than decent account of what I was all about as a footballer.

The following morning I was approached by a photographer on my way over to the local shop. By the time I returned home our modest council house had been besieged by a posse of pressmen. This little corner of Cantril Farm had never seen anything like it and they soon had me posing for pictures once again, first with a gang of kids out in the street and then inside with my mum and sister Lesley. My Dad missed out on all the excitement through being at work but he was such a private man that I doubt he'd have been complaining. He was happy just to sit back and observe my progress from a distance. To have this much attention on our doorstep was all a bit surreal. I'd slowly been getting used to being the subject of interest from the press but this day took it to another level.

It also prompted talk of an international call-up, which I found flattering given the fact that I had been disappointingly overlooked by my country at junior level. I harboured genuine ambitions to represent England but having only been in Liverpool's first team for less than a full year I didn't expect all this. It was remarkable and a further sign of just how far I had come since the summer.

In this day and age I probably would have been called straight up into the squad. I was arguably the country's most in-form player. England had failed to qualify for that summer's European Championship finals but had been invited to take part in the Bicentennial tournament in America. Having just half a season behind me wasn't enough. You had to be an established first-team regular to earn a full cap back then. They weren't just dished out to the latest youngster in the headlines.

While such talk was good for my ego it was club not country that remained uppermost in my thoughts. More importantly, from a team perspective, victory over City made us firm title favourites. We had one game left to play, away at relegation-threatened Wolves. If we won that, the likelihood was that we'd be champions. QPR were still viewed as our main challengers but Manchester United could have mathematically still pipped us if they won their three remaining games. Given our better goal average that was always an unlikely scenario and two nights later they ruled themselves out of the equation altogether by slumping to a shock home defeat against Stoke. This left just us and QPR but the outcome would not be resolved for another fortnight. Due to John Toshack and Joey Jones being called up to play for Wales in a vital European Championship qualifier against Yugoslavia on the final Saturday of the Football League season, the club requested that our scheduled game at Molineux be rearranged.

It meant that the title decider would now be sandwiched in between the two-legged UEFA Cup final with Bruges. Obviously, it would have been nice to have had the championship wrapped up before such another important fixture but there were two ways of looking at it and the postponement allowed us more time to prepare for our first leg with the recently crowned champions of Belgium.

It had been a long hard season – an unforgettable one for me no matter how it unfolded from here – but one that, overall, would be defined by what happened in the next three games. In situations like this it's usually the team which can hold its nerve that comes out on top.

For the likes of myself, Jimmy and Nealy it was all new, but a lot of the other lads had been involved in the double success of 1973 so their experience was invaluable. In contrast, the two teams standing in our way were far less experienced when it came to dealing with the high-octane pressure that we faced. Maintaining our focus was key. The prospect of finishing the season empty-handed, while still a reality, was not one we contemplated. We'd come this far. It was not in the club's mindset to pass up a chance to win silverware. Now was the time to finish the job.

It had been nine days since the City match but my performance had not been forgotten. I retained my place in the eleven and it was a real boost to my confidence that Paisley placed his faith in me for such an important game. I had been an unused substitute for the semifinal against Barcelona so this was my first real taste of playing at Anfield on a big European night. And what an occasion it turned out to be. It was a lovely sunny spring evening and I remember the usual big-match atmosphere having a slightly surreal feel to it due to a Belgian brass band playing in the paddock area.

Our opponents were by no means household names in Europe at the time but under the guidance of legendary Austrian coach Ernst Happel, Bruges were entering what is now considered their 'golden era'. Earlier in the competition they had over-turned a 3–0 first-leg deficit to eliminate Ipswich and beaten Roma, AC Milan and Hamburg en route to the final. Still, we were the clear favourites going into the tie and, although never one to underestimate opponents, the boss, with perhaps one eye on the Wolves game, was no doubt thinking it would ease the pressure if we could get at them from the first whistle, score a few goals and give ourselves a comfortable cushion ahead of the return leg.

I was given the number eight shirt and asked to play out on the right side, with Tosh and Kevin as usual through the middle. This was the plan. But it was Bruges, attacking the Kop end, who were first into their stride with a stunning start that had them two goals up after just fifteen minutes. Anfield, normally such a cauldron of noise on nights like this, was temporarily silenced. Shocked into near submission.

Our 'double' dream was fading fast before our very eyes and there seemed nothing we could do about it. The Belgians were threatening to run away with it and half-time couldn't come quickly enough. The interval allowed us to regroup and take stock. We weren't playing too badly but this final was in danger of running away from us before we could even start thinking about a second leg, so something had to be done. It required the intervention of a 'Supersub'. It was the type of situation I'd have revelled in but with me already on the boss had to look elsewhere. He opted for Jimmy Case. Tosh was replaced and it was an inspired choice. Attacking the Kop, the scene was set for a memorable second half.

The change meant Jimbo returned to his usual wide-right position while I moved into the middle and within twenty minutes of the restart the whole complexion of the tie had changed. The switch worked to perfection. The crowd rediscovered its voice and they roared themselves hoarse as we completed a miraculous comeback. In a frenzied seven-minute spell, goals from Ray Kennedy, 'Supersub' Jimmy and a Kevin Keegan penalty saw us snatch a breathtaking 3–2 victory.

It was an amazing game. European finals are often dull, cagey affairs. Not this one. For me, apart from a goal by myself, it had everything. And when I think back to it now I'm proud to say I was part of it. It's a pity it often gets forgotten about when people talk of Anfield's great European occasions. At most other clubs it would be hailed to high heaven and forever spoken about in revered terms. At Liverpool it's just recalled as another memorable match among a cast of thousands. For it not to be ranked that high just goes to show how great a continental pedigree this club has. We've become Euro snobs, almost spoiled by our incredible success on the continent.

Despite our second-half heroics, the slender margin of victory and the fact we had conceded two 'away' goals meant this tie was far from over and our hopes of lifting the trophy hung in the balance. With the return leg to come three weeks later the feeling afterwards was more of relief than celebration and, given our situation in the league, the pursuit of UEFA Cup success had to be quickly put to the back of our minds.

The immediate priority now was to wrap up a record-breaking ninth League Championship. QPR had completed their campaign with victory over Leeds – a result that saw them again leapfrog us into first place. I've no doubt that the neutrals would have loved Dave Sexton's side to have stayed there. They had been the surprise package of the season, that's for sure, and with a team that included players like Stan Bowles, Don Givens and the England captain Gerry Francis they certainly didn't lack quality. In many ways their style reminded me of Liverpool in 2013/14, a team playing with no fear against the odds.

Having to wait and see if we slipped up at Wolves must have been agonising for them but there's no such thing as sympathy in football and they were certainly getting none from us. We knew what was required at Molineux on 4 May. A win or low-scoring draw would be enough to see us crowned champions and our mood was one of determination. So while the QPR players sat in a specially set-up television studio to watch the deciding game, the red army invaded Wolverhampton.

If any extra incentive was needed it arrived with the news that seemingly half the male population of Merseyside was converging on the Black Country in the hope of witnessing our coronation. I remember being woken up by Ronnie Moran at the team hotel in the afternoon, and the normal practice then would be for us to have some tea and toast. On this occasion though, we were told we had to get straight to the ground because it was already heaving with supporters and the congestion was only going to get worse. This was at four o'clock in the afternoon, three-and-a-half hours before kick-off. It was obvious then that this was going to be a special night.

When we got to the ground it was absolute chaos. There were huge crowds everywhere and just getting the coach to the players' entrance was a struggle. Fans were climbing up the floodlight pylons and everyone was desperate to get inside. Some were even allowed in through our dressing room, which was hilarious. Molineux was an old-fashioned stadium then and the big sash windows in the away dressing room opened out on to the street. We watched the scenes outside standing on the wooden benches and a number of us spotted lads we all knew. There were thousands out there but I managed to spot a couple of my mates, as did the likes of Thommo and a few of the others.

Bob Paisley agreed to let a few in and they were asked to line up outside in an orderly fashion. To the ticketless Scouse hordes this was a chance they were never going to pass up so as the boss opened the big wooden doors, what seemed like an entire army stormed through. We were partly changed as this almost never-ending sea of supporters made their way past us. They were all wishing us luck as a now panic-stricken Paisley single-handedly struggled to shut the door, much to our amusement. I couldn't imagine it happening nowadays but it was great of the boss to allow it and I think it played a part in helping everyone relax.

It was great to know that we had such support with us that night. Liverpudlians always travelled in large numbers so we expected a more than decent following but this was just off the scale. The sheer size of our support really became apparent when we went out on to the pitch for our pre-match walkabout. Red and white filled all sides of the ground. The turnstiles had been locked hours before and we could have been forgiven for thinking we were back at Anfield.

SUPERSUB

I always enjoyed playing at Molineux. Before it was redeveloped it had been a traditional old ground that had a real sense of history about it, perhaps most famous for the series of pioneering floodlit friendlies against some of the best teams in Europe during the early to mid-50s. Those games have gone down in folklore as being the forerunner to what we all know now as the Champions League but I doubt it had ever witnessed anything quite like the scenes on this night.

It's easy to forget that, while it was a vitally important game for us, there was just as much at stake for Wolves. They needed a win to have any hope of avoiding relegation so for the home fans to be so outnumbered was remarkable. A lot is spoken about the impact supporters can have on a match and the Liverpool crowd has often been referred to as 'the twelfth man'. This was one of those nights on which that particular legend was cultivated.

The front cover of the match programme called it right with its old theatre-style front cover billing it as 'The Great First Division Drama'. It was certainly the most important match I had been involved in to date but after starting the last two I found myself back on the bench. If I'm honest, it did come as something of a surprise, but I tried to understand the reasoning behind it. As Roy Evans suggested to me some time ago, 'just because you was number 12, how do you know you weren't the first name on the team sheet and that it was always his plan to use you in the latter stages of a game?' It's an interesting theory and this could well have been one of those times. Also, having sparked the transformation against Bruges, Jimmy's claims couldn't be ignored and in a team full of experience I suppose leaving me out was the obvious option.

I was disappointed but mindful of just how far I had come these past few months. I took my seat on the bench and, like everyone else, was gripped by the unshakeable tension that filled the ground. We again started slowly, a touch nervously even, and were punished when Steve Kindon raced past Emlyn to open the scoring after just thirteen minutes. Fortunately, no one in a red shirt panicked. As the game wore on I was becoming more eager to get into the action. It was always the same whenever I was a substitute, but even more so on this occasion and the reason was twofold: firstly because I felt I could help change the game; and secondly because I needed to get one more appearance under my belt in order to qualify for a championship medal, should we turn it around.

As the clock ticked towards the hour mark I was given the nod to get ready. I came on for Jimmy but there was to be no instant impact this time. The title was edging its way towards London. Just fifteen minutes now remained and despite enjoying all the possession we still had nothing to show for it. Lesser teams might have panicked but this Liverpool side was made of sterner stuff. We continued to knock the ball about and a minute later the vital breakthrough finally came.

Fittingly it was KK, the Footballer of the Year elect, who got the goal. Momentum had swung back in our favour and the travelling Kopites, who had backed us relentlessly throughout, spilled on the pitch in celebration. When Tosh and 'Razor' Ray Kennedy then put the outcome beyond any doubt with a goal apiece in the last five minutes the scenes were unbelievable. The fans had been encroaching closer and closer towards the touchline since the opening goal and it's a wonder we were able to finish the game given the thousands that ran on to greet the second and third goals. As they did, you could almost hear the groans of despair back in Shepherd's Bush.

At the final whistle the title-winning party began in earnest and again the supporters came pouring down from the terraces to congratulate us. The greasy Molineux playing surface became a sea of ecstatic dancing Scousers. I remember being mobbed and for a split second it was quite frightening because I went down under a deluge of bodies. It was all good-natured though. I was just as excited as them. After all, I would have been on those terraces myself had I not been part of the team. Such actions may be frowned upon in this day and age but there was no malice involved and it was great that we could celebrate in unison.

There's always been a terrific bond between the players and supporters but it was never better illustrated than on this night. When we finally made it back to the dressing room everyone was going berserk. The champagne was flowing and there were all sorts of people in there, including a load of fans who must have remembered how they came in this way and were now performing a triumphant conga as they headed towards the exits.

Going back on the coach took forever. Not that we minded. Everyone was in celebratory mood and the champagne continued to flow. For long stretches of the journey, traffic was at a complete standstill and supporters were partying on the hard shoulder of the motorway while we handed out bottles of bubbly. In terms of the celebrations that greeted other Liverpool title triumphs I could remember, the scenes of jubilation were unprecedented. It was like Liverpool had never won the league before.

When we eventually got back to Liverpool most of the lads went on to Ugly's nightclub on Duke Street. It was where the players always used to go after a midweek match and on this occasion they took 61-year old Reuben Bennett with them and got him dangerously drunk. Luckily he just about survived the experience.. I'd won my first championship medal and just wanted to go and see my Mum and Dad so I headed home to reflect on the drama that had unfolded at Molineux and let it all sink in. To win the league in such circumstances, at the end of my first season in the team, made it without question one of the best nights of my career.

In his post-match interview Bob Paisley had explained how it had made him 'proud to be a Liverpudlian' and I couldn't agree more. It was moments like this that we all strived for and to experience it at such a young age made it even more special. I could still vividly remember how I'd sneaked into Anfield at three-quarter time to hail the Liverpool championship winning side of 1963/64. This was an equally historic occasion and I too could now call myself a champion. It felt fantastic.

But while the curtain had come down on a thrilling domestic campaign the small matter of the UEFA Cup final second leg meant we couldn't afford to switch off just yet and a long fifteen-day wait lay ahead.

While the traditional end-of-season Home Internationals were being contested, during which time Bayern Munich collected their third successive European Cup by beating the highly rated French team St Etienne at Hampden Park, we prepared for our own final test. There was more silverware to be won and, although Bruges might have been confident of overturning the 3–2 first-leg deficit on home soil, we were hell-bent on going out in a blaze of glory.

It came as no surprise to me that the boss named an unchanged team, meaning I was one of the five substitutes. Of course I'd have loved to have started. But, as with the Wolves game, I placed my disappointment into perspective. When the UEFA Cup run began back in September I was nowhere near the first-team reckoning, I was the youngest member of the squad that travelled to Belgium and, despite the fierce competition for places, there was a fair chance I would come on at some point during the night.

In the 65th minute I did exactly that. Sent on to replace Tosh, I became the first teenager to represent Liverpool in a European final. Another proud milestone, but one I admittedly wasn't too aware of at the time. With the score on the night tied at 1–1, the tie was finely balanced, so there were more pressing matters for me to contend with. We'd fallen behind to an early penalty by Lambert but KK had promptly restored our aggregate advantage with a sweetly struck free-kick. We came under a lot of pressure in the second half and spent a lot of time with our backs against the wall. My instruction was to try and get Bruges running the other way and perhaps snatch a goal to put the outcome beyond reach of the hosts.

That was easier said than done. Bruges knew just one goal would see them re-claim the advantage and they laid siege to Clem's goal. We found ourselves pinned back in our own half for long periods of the time that remained and it was difficult for me to get on the ball, never mind carve out a scoring opportunity. Despite the best efforts of our travelling fans the atmosphere was so tense. The destiny of the trophy was so tightly balanced, but thankfully we hung on. The feeling at the final whistle was sheer relief, quickly followed by a joyous burst of adrenalin as the scale of our achievement sank in.

League champions, now UEFA Cup winners. Paisley had emulated the feat of Shanks three seasons before and issued an ominous warning to the rest of Europe that this Liverpool team was a force to be reckoned with. As the celebrations commenced we swapped shirts with our beaten opponents and Emlyn famously dropped the cup, leaving it without a base for our triumphant homecoming the following day.

My first season as a senior player was over and it had all played out beyond my highest expectations. Others played more and scored more during our march to glory in 1975/76 but I couldn't have been happier with the contribution I made. Seven vital goals in fourteen vital games, two trophies (three if you include the Central League) and a growing reputation as one of the most promising young players in Europe; not bad for a teenager who hadn't even figured on the official team photograph at the start of the season.

8

SUPERSUB STRIKES AGAIN

REAMS OF TOILET ROLL STREWN ACROSS THE PENALTY BOX IN front of a baying Kop. Gerald Sindstadt commentating for ITV and opponents sporting a futuristic-looking green strip that could well have been dipped in Kryptonite. It can only mean one thing. St Etienne. Two words that would come to define my entire career.

No matter what else I achieved, even if I'd have gone on to score hundreds of goals, won countless more trophies and become one of the leading players in the world, nothing could have left a more indelible mark than that unforgettable night of Wednesday, 16 March 1977.

It was the European Cup quarterfinal second leg and Liverpool looked to be heading out of the competition at the expense of the French champions until my 84th-minute intervention. What happened next would cement me a place in Anfield folklore. It was to change the course of the club's history and is what I'll forever be most remembered for. Hardly a day goes by without the words 'St Etienne' somehow being mentioned and I'd have it no other way.

*

ST ETIENNE WAS THE FAIRY-TALE SEQUEL TO WHAT HAD BEEN A scarcely believable debut campaign. Yet rewind a few months, to when the draw for the last eight of the European Cup first paired Liverpool with the champions of France, and the likelihood of me playing a starring role in such an important game seemed a long-shot. In fact, it couldn't have been further from my thoughts. For all I'd achieved during the previous season, my first-team career had seemingly stalled. I was yet to make a senior start and was to see in the New Year playing in front of just a few hundred spectators in the less than salubrious surroundings of Gigg Lane.

To say it was something of a comedown would be a massive understatement. From the UEFA Cup final in Bruges to a Central League fixture away at Bury; all in the space of just over six months. It had been a rapid descent in my eyes. As fast as I'd appeared on the first-team scene, I was now in danger of drifting out of it. Hardly how I'd envisaged it during the long hot summer of 1976, when I basked in the glory of breaking into the senior side and helping them to a League Championship/ UEFA Cup double.

Despite my new-found fame it had been a pretty low-key close-season for me. Amid a three-month heatwave and endless hours of sunshine, I did what any recently crowned League Champion and UEFA Cup winner would do – I holidayed at Butlins in Skegness with my parents.

The summer of 1976 was a scorcher, but it wasn't the sole reason for us having an English holiday; it had been booked well before my dream ending to that season had begun. After enjoying such an amazing end to the previous campaign I suppose I should have been somewhere like the Côte d'Azur rather than on the English east coast.

It was a memorable holiday nevertheless. We did ordinary things and it was great to spend time with my Mum, Dad, sister and my then girlfriend. Many people will have fond memories of their activity-packed holidays at a Butlins camp. They were great places to spend a week or two in the summer and I loved them as a young lad. This time around I was a little more reluctant to wholeheartedly join in with the activities than I had been in the past.

One afternoon, as we stood watching the weekly sports day, my dad wickedly dared me to go in for the 100-yard sprint. Among those lining up to take part I spotted fellow footballer Brian Talbot, then of Ipswich Town. Dad suggested Talbot would win. I disagreed, saying he wouldn't if I entered. 'Go on then,' urged my dad. I rose to the bait and won the last of the heats to qualify for the final alongside Talbot and about ten others, who I then beat to claim the overall prize.

My dad's smile as I returned told me he knew I'd win all along, while the fact not one other person on the camp knew who I was is a measure of how the game has changed and how lucky we were back then to be able to live our lives without the kind of intrusion a modern footballer has to cope with.

Despite winning the race, all I really wanted to do was get back to Melwood and pick up where I'd left off the previous season. I'd had a taste of success and wanted to sample it again. I was desperate to get back to training that summer and kick on. My aim was to build on what I'd achieved already, become an accepted member of the first team and not someone looked upon as just being on the periphery.

We went to Holland on our pre-season tour and I figured in all three games, completing the full ninety minutes of the first two. But in the build-up to the Charity Shield against FA Cup winners Southampton Bob Paisley came to me and casually explained his team plans for that game. The way he put it to me was that the team which played in the season's annual curtain-raiser was a 'pat on the back' to those who had won the league. I could accept that. Yes, I had played my part in the title win but only during the run-in, whereas those in the team picked to play Southampton had been regulars throughout the season. Despite the impact I had made I was not yet a fully established member of the first team. Keegan, Toshack and Heighway were the established front three and I could have no arguments about that.

It would have been nice for my contribution to have been recognised too, with at least a run-out as substitute. To play at Wembley for the first time would have been a fitting end to an unbelievable few months but, disappointingly, I never got on. Where was my 'pat on the back' for the vital role I had played the previous season? It might have only been the Charity Shield, a glorified friendly if you like, and I didn't read too much into it at the time, but it was another sign of things to come, even if I did return home with another medal in my pocket.

When the spoils of the previous season were proudly displayed at Anfield the following week, prior to the season-opener against Norwich, I was at the Hawthorns playing for the reserves and scoring our first in a 2–1 win. Back at Anfield a new face was making his debut. Just days after the Charity Shield Liverpool had splashed out £200,000 to sign Ipswich and England striker David Johnson. Naturally, it meant increased competition for places and you'd expect my reaction to be one of concern. However, it was a signing that didn't necessarily worry me. Nor did it surprise me. It was not uncommon for Liverpool to freshen things up with a new signing from time to time. It never did any harm introducing a new body into the dressing room. It kept everyone on their toes. Johnno offered something different to me, more of a central striker than a wide player. In my eyes, it was an indication that I was maybe viewed as more of an option for the wide areas, rather than a direct replacement for Kevin or Tosh.

It was a move that made sense and one that I saw only as a positive; another part of the evolution of Paisley's team. There were growing doubts over Tosh's long-term fitness, as he'd been struggling with an Achilles complaint for a while, and Kevin was on the verge of announcing that he was to join Hamburg at the end of the 76/77 season.

Since breaking into the first team I'd got to know Kevin a bit more. He might have been the superstar in this Liverpool team and really popular in the dressing room but no one seemed to have a hint of the news he would soon deliver. He was a very private person who enjoyed living in North Wales well away from Liverpool and I certainly wasn't one who he'd have confided in. Like all Reds fans I'd only heard myself through the newspapers that he would be leaving Anfield at the end of the season. Kevin was ambitious and wanted to test himself abroad. It was as simple as that and although the news of his impending departure wasn't too well received among the fans, and a few did voice their disapproval, it was not an issue among the players.

There was always a good camaraderie in the dressing room at Anfield. Tommy Smith and Emlyn Hughes had their much-publicised differences but by and large everyone got on, even if we didn't always socialise as one big group. There were never any real cliques as such but the likes of the Formby gang – Tosh, Emlyn, Clem, Nealy and Steve Heighway – would generally stick more together, while as a local I stuck to those who lived in the city.

Although I was friendly with Joey Jones, and more than comfortable in the company of Thommo and Terry Mac, my big mates were still those from the reserves – the likes of Jeff Ainsworth, Colin Irwin and Sammy Lee – lads who I'd grown up with through Liverpool schoolboy teams.

I never ever felt I was big time. Despite what I'd achieved the previous season I didn't find it hard to keep my feet on the ground. I was still living with my mum and dad in Cantril Farm. My dad, in particular, was determined to ensure that I never got above my station. He was always prepared to hand out little messages about my attitude if I ever threatened to step out of line. I was in my late teens now, almost twenty, don't forget, but I remember coming in after midnight once and he read me the riot act. I remember it vividly as he confronted me at the top of the stairs. I got the message and he didn't have to do it again.

Life was a lot different back then though. Pubs closed no later than eleven o'clock and nightclubs finished at two so there was not as much temptation to stay out all night as there is nowadays. I never classed myself as a big drinker. In an era when there was a big drinking culture in football this could have been problematic. There was a tendency at times to bow to peer pressure and try to keep up with the bigger drinkers within the squad but it quickly became apparent if you were out of your depth.

Don't get me wrong, I didn't mind the odd drink and I never lived like a monk, but heavy drinking and nightclubs were just never really my thing. It's no secret that there were a few at Liverpool who could have a skinful and still be able to train better than anyone else the next day, notably Terry McDermott. I just wouldn't have been able to do that. Some people might have looked upon it as being boring but that didn't bother me. I was happy enough and knew my limits.

I mentioned that the signing of David Johnson didn't duly concern me but with him going straight into the first-team group, chances to play became even thinner on the ground. It's why I suggested to the manager that it might be best if I started the season back in the reserves. I felt it would do me more good than sitting on the bench most weeks. It wasn't an ideal situation and something of a risk to drop out of the first-team picture altogether, but I just wanted to be playing football and scoring goals. Even though I was missing out on win bonuses I was much happier at that point of the season getting some games under my belt. If I couldn't do that in Liverpool's first team then playing alongside my mates in the reserves was the next best thing.

I was well grounded so there was never any danger of me thinking that Central League football was beneath me and I was able to prove that I'd lost none of my sharpness. In particular, I hit a rich vein of scoring form in October, netting four against Southport in the final of the Liverpool Senior Cup, which had been held over from the previous season, and grabbing hat-tricks away to Manchester United and at home to Blackburn.

It still wasn't enough to earn me a starting place back in the first team. Up until the end of October I'd made just six substitute appearances and, although I was yet to score, I felt my form for the reserves warranted another chance. After being honest with the manager at the outset of the season I now wanted him to be fair with me. I was fast becoming frustrated and during the half-time interval of our game at Sunderland in early November he spotted my mood. Whereas José Mourinho readily admits that he doesn't like to be surrounded by unhappy players, this didn't bother Bob Paisley. He had no time for going round and making sure all his fringe players were happy. He was concerned only with the players he had selected in his starting eleven and so long as they were doing the business out on the pitch that's all that mattered to him.

Although he'd ignored my moodiness many times before, this time he decided to speak to me. I was the twelfth man again and following an uninspiring goalless first half I was in the toilet as he came and stood next to me. 'Take that look off your face, and pick your chin up, we are going to need you here and you will be going on soon,' he said.

I didn't reply and nor did I believe what he was saying because if we'd have scored a few minutes after the break the likelihood was that I'd have remained on the bench. Fortunately for me, there was still no score when midway through the half Paisley emerged from his seat in the stands to join us on the bench. I was told to warm up while he had a discussion with Joe and Ronnie, then I was thrown into the fray at a packed Roker Park.

I'd been on for only a minute when, with just my second touch of the ball, I broke the deadlock. It will be remembered as an easy tap-in from two yards out but it could have been more memorable had my initial diving header not been saved by Barry Siddall – instead, as KK retrieved the loose ball I scored my simplest goal ever. Not the greatest of goals, but it proved to be the decisive moment in the game, enough to clinch two vital First Division points that kept us out in front at the top of the table.

It was a reminder of what I had to offer. That I was no one-season wonder. Bob Paisley was deservedly praised for the timing of his substitution and lauded for how he was carefully nurturing my development. I wasn't exactly seeing it that way any more and just wanted him to have a bit more faith in me.

It was in a newspaper interview shortly afterwards that I first expressed my displeasure at the Supersub tag. I told the reporter that I was 'sick of it' and had 'come to hate it'. I was speaking in the heat of the moment so my feelings were no doubt running high. On reflection I probably shouldn't have spoken out so strongly about it in public but that's how the situation was starting to affect me. It would really get me down at times.

I was hopeful that my winning goal at Roker Park would be the catalyst for a change in the manager's thinking but again, much to my annoyance, all I kept hearing was that I had to be patient. Not even a call-up to the first-ever England under-21 squad (replacing the previous under-23 format) could sway him, although that was a game that doesn't hold very good memories for me.

Initially it was a great honour to be named in the team alongside fellow up-and-coming players like Ray Wilkins, Andy King, Alan Sunderland and Brian Talbot, but on the night I just never did myself justice. The game against Wales was played at Molineux and for some reason my every touch was booed – maybe the home fans had not forgiven me being part of the Liverpool team that had sent Wolves down to the Second Division the previous season. I don't know. The jeers of the crowd echoed around the sparsely populated stands and it really affected my confidence.

Admittedly, I didn't have a great first half and it came as no surprise when I was later replaced by Peter Barnes. The game finished goalless and I returned home really frustrated.

When I reported back to Melwood my mood matched that of the entire club because on the same night I had endured a night to forget in Wolverhampton, the first team crashed to an emphatic 5–1 defeat just a few miles away at Aston Villa.

Christmas came and went and it wasn't until January, just six days after my twentieth birthday and not long after I'd scored twice for the second string in the New Year's Day fixture at Bury, that I played my first full ninety minutes of the season. I kept my place for the next game and, in front of watching officials from St Etienne, scored a late goal that rescued a point in a 1–1 draw at home to West Brom. Brian Kettle, in what was a rare first-team start for him, had unfortunately allowed David Cross to score Albion's goal and as I ran away to celebrate my equaliser he was first over, shouting how pleased he was because he'd now be able to pay his gas bill with the bonus we'd get for snatching a point.

My performance in that match, although I personally didn't rate it as one of my best, was a turning point in the season for me. Horace Yates in the Liverpool *Daily Post* was certainly backing my cause, stating in his match report that I had arrived, that I had outgrown the Supersub image and that Bob Paisley now had a real selection dilemma on his hands. With the European Cup soon to resume it was perfect timing.

My involvement in the competition so far had been limited to just a fifteen-minute cameo appearance in the second-round tie against Trabzonspor in Turkey. It was a trip that has remained long in the memory of those fans or players who made it, as the worst experience we had ever endured and the only time a Liverpool team were relieved to return home with just a 1–0 defeat. The flight was long and arduous, the hotel was best described by Bob Paisley as a 'doss house', the food wasn't edible, we couldn't sleep and come match-day the pitch was worse than a local park.

For the first leg of the St Etienne tie, which also ended in a 1–0 defeat, I was an unused substitute and would be on the bench again for the return. The boss announced his team the day before the game and, despite playing all ninety minutes of the previous weekend's 1–0 win away to Middlesbrough, I made way for the returning John Toshack. Little did I know at the time but in terms of what I'm now best remembered for it was probably a blessing in disguise.

*

DAVID FAIRCLOUGH

WEDNESDAY 16 MARCH 1977 BEGAN LIKE ANY OTHER.

I woke up around 7 a.m. From the view out of my bedroom window, looking out across the banked grassy verge at the back of our small council house, everything was peaceful. On the road out front stood my little three-year-old white Ford Escort, in the distance the tower blocks of Knowsley. With Radio One playing in the background, I sat down for some breakfast with my mum; just some cereal and a cup of tea before jumping into the car for the short journey to Anfield. Everything seemed normal.

Just a few miles away a loud army of green-clad Frenchmen were invading Liverpool. They had been coming over the Channel and converging on the banks of the Mersey in their droves since the day before. The city hotels were booked up and football fever had taken a stranglehold on Merseyside like we had never seen before.

There seemed to be a near unprecedented air of excitement around the city and it wasn't just the red half that was buzzing in anticipation. Our neighbours Everton were preparing for a similar date with destiny over in Yorkshire. Bringing the League Cup back to Merseyside for a first time was their aim and Aston Villa stood in their way at Hillsborough in the replay of a final that had finished goalless at Wembley the previous Saturday. Of course, that was the Mickey Mouse Cup in our eyes – until we reached the final for a first time the following year that is – and the only game that mattered from our point of view was the one taking place at Anfield.

We had been told to get to the ground for 10 a.m. and, rather unusually, informed that we'd be having a little warm-up session at Anfield. The normal routine was to train as a group at Melwood, then make the short journey up to Anfield, where we'd leave our cars and get on the coach for the short journey to the team hotel.

Did the manager have something special up his sleeve to tactically outwit the French champions? Well if he did, he certainly wasn't about to share it with us. As the coaching staff went about their business, getting everything ready for that night's match, the only instruction for us was to go out and do our own thing; have a jog and stretch the muscles. Nothing complicated, nothing planned. It was what we had come to expect and it typified the ethos of simplicity that ran right through the entire club. If St Etienne officials had been watching they'd have been amazed at how basic our preparation was.

Anyway, once changed I made my way out on to the pitch, along the corridor and down the steps where I paused momentarily to give the legendary 'This Is Anfield' sign its customary gentle tap. We might have been over eight hours away from kick-off but there was no harm in touching it in the hope it would bring us some extra good luck for the task ahead.

As I emerged into the morning sunshine the ground was eerily quiet, a far cry from raucous arena it was soon to become. I made my way on to the track that surrounds the pitch and John Toshack, who had just returned from injury to take my place in the team, asked me to race him down the touchline in front of the Main Stand. It was always going to be a bit of a mismatch. Pace was never Tosh's greatest strength and it was no surprise that he struggled to keep up in what was a short dash to the Kop end corner flag.

'I wish I could run like that without a warm-up', he said with an uncomfortable grimace on his face. The big man was obviously worried about his Achilles tendon. It was a problem that had kept him out of the previous game and I was left wondering how he was going to get through such an important game. Little did I realise then that his gnarled area of concern would pave the way for me to take centre stage later that night.

His attitude was typical of the times when all players would be reluctant to flag up an injury, thinking they could somehow coast through a game and at the same time somehow recover in their own way without giving up their valued place in the side. Once out of the team in those days you never knew when you might get back in.

When the warm-up was completed, all the lads got changed and we boarded the coach for the short trip to the hotel where we'd have lunch and rest for the remainder of the afternoon. Another change to the normal routine on this occasion was the choice of hotel. Usually it was the Holiday Inn, this time it was the Adelphi. For lunch we had the option of tomato or mushroom soup with toast – no bread was ever available – with the main course fillet steak or fish. After lunch some of the lads went for a little walk, normally for a look in the men's shop on Lime Street almost next to the hotel, before returning for the ritual of an afternoon sleep.

Pre-match tea and toast was served at around 4.30 and it came with the news that we'd be leaving for Anfield a bit earlier than normal due to unexpected numbers being up at the ground already. There were genuine concerns that it might take us some time getting there and they weren't wrong. The route from the Adelphi to Anfield took us along Great Homer Street, up Everton Valley and towards Anfield Road. As we edged up the hill it quickly became apparent that those early reports of crowd congestion were not exaggerated.

The streets were absolutely rammed, similar to the scenes outside Molineux the season before. We later found that supporters had been queuing at the turnstiles since around midday. Many feigned illness to leave work early and I've since heard countless stories about how kids bunked off school to make sure they were there. It seems every supporter at Anfield that night has a story to tell, whether they were one of the lucky 55,000 in the ground or among the reported 10,000 locked out.

The coach managed to slowly meander its way through the sea of bodies but, given the density of the crowd, it almost came to a standstill during the last few hundred yards. It was only thanks to a police escort that we managed to complete the remainder of the short journey and eventually reach the sanctuary of the dressing room. It didn't take a genius to sense that this was no normal Anfield night. It had the feel of something very different. Already the atmosphere was electric. And that was only on the outside.

When that dressing-room door slammed shut behind us though, we became totally oblivious to what was happening around the ground. As kick-off fast approached the normal routine clicked into gear; sorting out tickets for family and friends, then the process of getting changed. Each player had his own individual habits and some would be ready earlier than others. I was always quick to get into some of my kit even when I was only sub and would then warm up in the shower area. The last item to go on was always my shorts, and only when we were just about to leave the dressing room.

We'd not yet seen sight of the pitch or had chance to sample the cauldron of noise that was starting to bubble away on the terraces. All pre-match preparations back then were confined solely to the inner sanctum. It was unheard of for us to indulge in anything like a pre-match kick-about on the pitch. Of a weekend, some of the lads would often pop out to check the afternoon's racing results in one of the lounges but it was rare for a Liverpool player to set foot on the hallowed turf until kick-off time.

We waited until the referee's bell sounded and only then did we head towards the tunnel. It's common practice nowadays for both teams to enter the field side by side but only on European nights did it happen back in those days. As we came face to face in the tight corridor you could feel the tension rising. All thirty-two players lined up alongside each other. No words were spoken, just a few cursory glances and nods of the head, the look of steely determination etched on the faces of everyone. Not since Inter Milan in 1965 had Anfield played host to a European night as big as this. Forget the UEFA Cup finals, this was the competition that mattered most and, although only a quarterfinal tie, the general consensus was if we could overcome St Etienne then the path to glory would become a lot easier.

Although I had played no part in the first meeting, I saw enough during that frenzied ninety minutes in France to know that this St Etienne side posed a real threat to our European Cup aspirations. I was also well aware of how unlucky they had been when losing the previous season's final to Bayern Munich at Hampden. 'Les Verts', as they were known, were among the favourites to go one better in the competition this time around and of the remaining participants in the last eight when the draw was made I doubt we could have been handed a sterner task.

They were without doubt the most flamboyant team in Europe around this time. Among their star players were Gérard Janvion, Christian Lopez, Dominique Bathenay and Dominique Rocheteau, a quartet of players who would represent their country at the following year's World Cup. These sophisticated-looking foreigners, with their tight-fitting, fluorescent-green silk shirts, may have looked like they'd been beamed down from another planet but, as they were about to discover, the white-hot atmosphere of a fully charged Anfield really was something out of this world.

As Emlyn Hughes led us out, all those in a red kit reached up to give the 'This Is Anfield' sign another touch. Then came the first decibels of the Kop roar, three paces more and we were hit by a wall of sound that grew louder and louder as we climbed the final six steps towards the pitch. Once out into the open I was temporarily startled, the noise was deafening, and on a jam-packed Kop that was baying for victory there were more flags flying than I'd ever seen before. A red flare added to the sense of occasion, while clouds of smoke wafted their way across a goalmouth littered with masses of toilet roll. Whether as a supporter or player, I was no stranger to big occasions at Anfield but this all seemed new and so much more exciting. There was so much passion emanating from all four sides of the ground, it was almost frightening. As the two teams, including substitutes, lined up in the centre circle to applaud the crowd I was stood next to Brian Kettle and we both looked on in awe at the scene.

As was often the case for a European night it was a tight squeeze in the dugout that game. Not that I was complaining. I was used to sitting in there as the only substitute, so it was always nice to have a few extra bodies to keep me company for a change. It didn't make the view any better though. Given that we were sat below ground level it was never the best and the curvature of the pitch meant it was difficult to see the touchline on the opposite side. You'd also run the risk of banging your head on the roof if jumping up to celebrate a goal or contest a dubious refereeing decision. Still, it was what we were used to. They were unique to Anfield and would have been more of a culture shock to the opposition, especially those from Europe.

Strangely, with some supporters still trying to get into the ground, especially over on the Kemlyn Road side where there were still a large number of empty seats due to severe congestion at the turnstiles, the game kicked off early. Those still outside missed a dramatic start when Kevin Keegan cancelled out St Etienne's first leg advantage inside just two minutes. Was it a cross or was it a shot? Only KK knows that but we didn't care. Whatever it was, Ivan Curkovic in the visitors' goal was fooled by the flight of the ball that was floated in from near the left-hand corner flag and the tie was all-square. What a start.

St Etienne, to their credit, didn't panic and the expected onslaught from us failed to materialise. There was little to separate the teams for the remainder of the first half and the prospect of extra-time, or maybe even a dreaded penalty shootout, did get a mention among those watching from the bench.

Half-time arrived and I've no idea what was said in the dressing room because the substitutes were told to stay out on the pitch in order to stretch our legs, should any of us be called upon. If I'd have been a betting man my money would have been on it going the distance. Thankfully, I never was much of a gambler. Within six minutes of the restart the chance of penalties disappeared when Dominique Bathenay scored a stunning goal. It was a spectacular, swerving shot, struck from distance, and it had Ray Clemence clutching fresh air.

St Etienne suddenly began to justify their status as favourites for the competition and with the away goal in their favour it meant we now had to score two more. Our hopes of progressing were looking highly unlikely. It was the cue for Bob Paisley to leave his seat in the stand and as he cosied up to Joe Fagan on the bench I was ordered to warm up. I sprinted up the perimeter track, towards the Anfield Road end. The usual shouts of encouragement were mixed with some desperate pleas for me to 'go on and get a goal'. Ronnie Moran signalled for me to return to the dugout and just as I got there Ray Kennedy provided us with a lifeline by restoring our lead on the night.

As a renewed sense of hope surged through the ground I sat back down, but when another fifteen minutes passed without any further scoring the time had come for a change. The call came for me to get ready. I was given no specific instructions. I took off the old training jumper and adjusted my shorts. As the Dutch linesman inspected my boots, Ronnie Moran patted me on the backside and told me, 'Just go and make a nuisance of yourself.' By now any nerves had disappeared. I was raring to go and, as always, the great welcome I received from the fans gave me a massive lift. We needed a goal and, so long as an opportunity came my way, I was always confident I could deliver.

I joined the action in the 74th minute. Play was flowing from end to end and as a result the game became more stretched. If only a ball could be played through the middle I'd fancy my chances but the French champions were an experienced bunch and used to keeping it tight at the back in these situations. As time ticked by our hopes were fading. 'Liverpool are playing too many long balls into the box and look to be heading out of the European Cup,' stated Elton Welsby in his Radio City commentary.

Then suddenly, with just six minutes to go, a ball out of our defence fell to Ray Kennedy. With his first touch he controlled the ball on his knee then nonchalantly volleyed it over the top of St Etienne's back-line. I immediately chased after it but needed to outrun Christian Lopez in the process. I managed to reach the ball first and Lopez was struggling. He was on the wrong side of me from a defensive point of view and made a vain attempt to drag me back. With my left arm I forced him off and brought the bouncing ball under control on my chest. I took a touch with my right foot and, as the goalkeeper Ivan Curkovic came out, a gaping Kop goal beckoned.

All those years of playing football in the streets and parks, re-enacting great Liverpool goals of the past, and now here I was with the chance to score a goal every bit as memorable as those I had witnessed from Kop.

There was never any doubt in my mind that I would score. I just could not miss. The consequences if I did would have been too painful to bear. I stood on the verge of creating my own special niche in Liverpool history. It was a moment of immense magnitude and time seemed to stand still, as if I was in a bubble. If I'd have thought about it too much then maybe it would have affected me. Instead, I had just a couple of seconds to decide what I was going to do. I looked up, picked my spot and kept it low, stroking the ball home with the inside of my right foot.

As it nestled safely among the toilet paper in the back of the net, I ran off in celebration, turning towards the Main Stand with my fists clenched and arms waving in the air. I jumped for joy. A photographer behind the Kop goal caught the moment on camera to capture what has since become arguably the most iconic image of the night.

As far as celebrations go it mightn't be the most graceful. Maybe if I'd have known how many times it would be shown in future I'd have planned something more elaborate. Celebrating goals has almost become an art-form in recent times, whether it's a cartwheel, robot-dance or sucking of the thumb. Back in my day they were a lot more basic and I never went into a game with any preconceived ideas of how I might celebrate if I scored. Sometimes I would just clap my hands and casually run back to the centre circle. Thankfully, on this night, it was a bit more memorable.

It's hard to explain what goes through your mind in the immediate aftermath of scoring a goal as important as that. Everything just becomes blurred and for a split second you lose all sense of reality. I remember Jimmy Case was the first to hug me but very soon I was lying under a mountain of ecstatic Liverpool players. Amid the cacophony of noise I could hear Kevin Keegan shouting down my ear, 'Stay down, Supersub, and let's waste a few extra minutes.'

The outpouring of elation said everything about just what the goal meant but the game was not yet over. Six minutes remained. The atmosphere was now even more electric than it had been. The entire ground was bouncing and everyone was singing. I found myself struggling to breathe as the visitors pushed forward once again, searching for the one goal that would have turned this tie completely on its head.

As time ticked agonisingly by, another chance almost came my way. Kevin sent in a cross from the left and there I was unmarked on the edge of the six-yard box ready to head home until a St Etienne defender appeared from nowhere to clear the danger. In the dying moments I found myself with the ball in space out on the left but rather than take it to the corner flag with the aim of wasting some vital seconds I opted to cross in an attempt to set us up for a fourth goal that would have put the outcome beyond any doubt.

It was a nail-biting finish and there were a couple of nervy moments at the opposite end but for me it was at times such as this that the incredible passion, strength and character which existed in that Liverpool team shone through. Natural-born competitors like Emlyn Hughes, Tommy Smith and Ray Clemence, to name just three, were absolutely immense in those final minutes as we clung on to clinch one of Liverpool's greatest ever victories.

I've often been asked why we were so calm at the end of that game, and having watched the highlights back down the years I think only Emlyn showed any real emotion. Most of us just shook hands with the devastated St Etienne players and left the crowd to continue singing their hearts out as they wallowed in the joy of victory. There might have still been a semifinal to come but the supporters were celebrating like we'd reach the final already. A trip to Rome was in their sights. 'We're the Greatest Team in Europe and We're Going to Italy' was the chant that boomed loud and proud from the Kop.

A lot of the lads swapped shirts, as was the tradition after European games. We'd taken a prize scalp and they wanted a souvenir. I chose to keep mine. It had been such a special night and I just didn't want to part with it. I collected quite a few opposition shirts down the years, many of which I still have, but that iconic St Etienne top remains conspicuous by its absence in my collection. On this occasion, it was the red number twelve shirt that went straight in my bag and came home with me. What it is worth in monetary value I don't know but as a symbol of my career it's priceless.

Back in the dressing room the scenes were certainly a lot more animated than they had been at the end of the match and everyone was going around congratulating each other. We were well aware of just what a big result this was although I don't think its real significance hit home until much later. It must have been special because a couple of photographers were allowed in and the three goalscorers rounded up for a shot that would appear in most of the following morning's newspapers. Once I'd showered and changed it was out into the packed corridor where Europe's top press corps had assembled. They were queuing up to speak with me and I was really flattered, providing them with the words that would accompany the aforementioned picture.

After that it was off to find my mum, dad and sister in the player's lounge before they headed back home to Cantril Farm. I then met up with my mate Bernie Jones, who lived just a couple of doors down from us. Our plan was to grab a drink in the local pub. In those days last orders were 10.30 p.m. on the button. As I pulled up to the Bulldog pub in West Derby we glanced across the road – I looked at my watch and saw it was almost half past ten. The landlord Ted was pretty strict about his time-keeping, the pub was packed and we'd have struggled to get a drink in so we decided to head back to Cantril Farm.

Five minutes later I was parked up at home and got back in the house just as the highlights of the game were starting on ITV. My mum and dad were still up so we sat together and relived the best of the action from what had been one of Anfield's most dramatic nights. I don't remember any of us saying much about it and within minutes of it finishing my dad had fallen asleep on the couch. I went to bed not long after, totally oblivious to the wild celebrations that were going on elsewhere throughout the city, sparked, of course, by the goal I had scored.

My reward for scoring the goal that sent Liverpool into the European Cup semi-final was breakfast in bed. Well, sort of. Within minutes of me waking up the next morning, a photographer was on the doorstep wanting a picture of my mum serving me a cup of tea in bed – as if it happened every day. Not in the Fairclough house it never. But in those days all the lads would willingly take part in gimmicky photos, so I agreed and returned to bed to receive a first ever cuppa in my little single bed from my proud but shy Mum.

It was a strike that brought joy to thousands and still does to this day. I would never have imagined back in 1977 that it would have become this famous. It's only when you reflect on it later in life that you realise just how important it was. Without it our European Cup aspirations would have been over for another season and the future could have turned out oh so differently.

In France the goal is credited as being the one that started the demise of that great St Etienne team. The club never did reach those heady heights in Europe again and soon fell upon hard times. Because of it I found myself, years later, being playfully throttled by the country's most famous ever footballer, and boyhood St Etienne fan, Michel Platini. The current UEFA President was attending a football conference in Liverpool and chatting away to Phil Thompson when my face appeared on the big screen and he suddenly realised who I was. He immediately lurched towards me and put both hands around my neck before giving me a warm embrace. It was deeply flattering and he went on to explain how I had ruined the dream of an entire French generation. Everyone in France thought St Etienne were set to dominate European football until Liverpool knocked them out and the painful memories have still not faded.

Later in my career, when I was playing in Switzerland and Belgium, I regularly had to pass through French passport control and on a couple of occasions, I'd be greeted with the same reception. A shrug of the shoulders and huge, but friendly, Gallic sigh. 'Ah, Fairclough . . . St Etienne,' that's all that would be said before I was ushered through with a wry smile and nod of the head.

In the sporting psyche of a disappointed nation it was a goal that's assumed a sense of macabre notoriety. L'Équipe magazine consider it to be one of the top five sporting crimes against the French and for some St Etienne players of that time it became a stain on their careers. I bumped into Christian Lopez at a Masters Tournament a few years back and, similar to myself, he explained how he will forever be remembered because of it, albeit for the wrong reasons.

It is certainly something I'll never be allowed to forget. And nor would I want to. From a Liverpool perspective it's genuinely regarded as one of the most famous moments in the club's history and the mere mention of it, no matter how many times it crops up, fills me with immense pride.

It's with me every day. I've replayed it so many times. Even now when I hear the commentary it makes me shiver, whether it's the Gerald Sinstadt TV version or Elton Welsby on the radio. I can still hear the unmistakable noise of the crowd and picture the sea of fans surging across the Kop. It was a night that spawned so many stories. I must have been told over a thousand and will never tire of hearing more.

At the time it was difficult to take everything in because the focus quickly switched to the next game. I didn't even get the following day off. I might have been the hero of the hour but because I'd only played fifteen minutes that night I was back in for training as usual the next morning. When I got to Anfield I went for a walk around with a couple of the reserve lads and future Scotland coach Andy Roxburgh, who was spending time at the club studying our training methods. Compared to the pandemonium of the night before, a scene of serenity had now descended over the ground.

Greater challenges lay ahead and St Etienne was quickly consigned to the record books. What followed was just another routine day at the office as the chase for an unprecedented treble gathered pace. It was never going to live up to what we had witnessed less than 24 hours before. Then again, what could?

9

DOUBLE DISAPPOINTMENT

Sopwell House, Hertfordshire, 20 May 1977

IT WAS THE DAY BEFORE THE FA CUP FINAL, THE SHOWPIECE FIXTURE of the English football calendar. It would be watched by millions worldwide and was an occasion I'd dreamed about playing in since I first kicked a ball along the cobbles of Carmel Street.

I was in my room at the team hotel in St Albans. It was just after 9.30 in the morning and the sun was shining brightly through the big sash window. My room-mate Alec Lindsay had gone down for breakfast and I was getting ready to follow suit. Although a touch nervous, I was generally feeling good about myself. The season was shaping up to be the most momentous in the club's history. I'd recently scored one of the most celebrated Liverpool goals of all time and featured in all but three of the sixteen games since that incredible night against St Etienne. A massive few days of unprecedented importance loomed and I was more than ready to play my part as Liverpool prepared to take on Manchester United.

I opened the door to leave the room and, to my surprise, there standing right in front of me was Bob Paisley. I was momentarily startled. How long had he been stood there and what did he want? It all seemed a bit surreal. Straight away, I could sense something was not right. Deep down I knew what was coming. I feared the worst and my heart was racing. Time seemed to stand still and amid an awkward moment of silence a million thoughts flickered through my mind as to what I could possibly have done wrong.

SUPERSUB

*

ALTHOUGH IT'S MY EXPLOITS IN THE EUROPEAN CUP FOR WHICH
I'll always be best remembered in 1977, I more than played my part in helping
Liverpool reach the FA Cup final that year too.

The road to Wembley began at home to Crystal Palace, then of the Third Division but an emerging team under the guidance of a young Terry Venables. They were
to win promotion later that season and would soon be competing alongside us in the
top flight. On that January afternoon at Anfield they served notice of their potential
by holding Liverpool to a goalless draw.

I came on as sub to replace a limping Terry McDermott after just 38 minutes of
that game and went close to breaking the deadlock with my first shot. For the replay
at a jam-packed Selhurst Park four nights later I was handed my first senior start of
the season and we did enough to avoid an upset by running out 3–2 winners.

Although I warmed the bench for the next two rounds, at home to Carlisle and
Oldham, I then made a significant contribution in the last-eight tie at home to Middlesbrough. It was another massive day of football on Merseyside, one the few times
both Liverpool and Everton had been allowed to stage first-team fixtures on the
same afternoon. The Blues were in FA Cup action themselves, playing host to Derby
County, and the combined attendance at Anfield and Goodison was over 100,000.

We'd beaten Boro in the league at Ayresome Park just the previous Saturday and,
with home advantage, were clear favourites to reach the semifinal. Played just four
days after St Etienne, it was a tense, tough battle, with little to separate the teams
during the first half. As we came out after the break I could sense the pressure growing and, given the events of the previous midweek's European tie, a lot of people
were looking at me to pull something out the bag once again.

Something special was needed to break the deadlock. Within nine minutes I
collected the ball out on the right, about thirty yards from goal. I cut inside fullback Terry Cooper and with no one closing me down I took an extra stride. A gap
opened up and I hit one of the hardest shots of my career. As soon as the ball left
my foot I knew it was going in. It took Boro keeper Pat Cuff by complete surprise
and thundered past him. He had no chance of stopping it. I scored better and more
important goals for Liverpool but that is one of my personal favourites.

The referee on the day was the legendary Jack Taylor and he described it as the
effort of 'a freak or genius'. Tommy Smith often laughed about this and joked that I
had two sets of legs, my Charlie Chaplin legs and my Stanley Matthews legs. I could

be gangly and awkward, I'll admit. But no one was complaining that day and I took it as a great compliment. Jack had watched a lifetime of football, and took charge of the 1974 World Cup final – he must have known something even if he was only a referee. My goal set us on our way to another crucial victory. Seven minutes later it was from one of my crosses that Keegan made it 2–0 to put the result beyond any doubt.

The line-up for the last four was one of the strongest in years: ourselves, Everton, Manchester United and Leeds. Hopes of a first all-Merseyside final were high but when the balls were drawn out of the velvet bag at Lancaster Gate the following Monday lunchtime a collective groan reverberated around the city. And so it was to the neutral setting of Maine Road, Manchester, that the Scouse hordes converged for a last-four tie that, for once, lived up to the hype.

With so much at stake these games can often be dull, sterile affairs, where the fear of defeat eclipses the will to win. This, my first experience of playing in the white-hot atmosphere of an FA Cup semifinal, was nothing of the sort. What followed was a four-goal thriller laced with the most controversial of endings – one that, to this day, still ignites the ire of Evertonians.

Just before kick-off there was an incredible rainstorm. Half the pitch was underwater but the game went ahead as planned. The conditions were hardly ideal for a tie of such magnitude and the conditions actually prevented me from scoring an early goal. Straight from the start the ball was played out to me on the right wing. My spectacular strike against Everton the previous season was on my mind as I glanced up and accelerated past the first blue shirt. On I continued until I got to the edge of the penalty area, but just as I was about to shoot the ball held up in a big puddle and I comically fell over. I've often thought 'what if'. That was in the very first minute and from there on in things got a little bit tougher.

When I came off midway through the second half the score was one apiece and I was really disappointed not to have made amends. Jimmy Case put us 2–1 ahead just a minute later but Bruce Rioch restored parity five minutes from time.

I then watched from the bench in utter despair as Brian Hamilton scored what looked to be the winner. Fortunately, thanks to referee Clive Thomas my mood quickly switched to one of joy. The Welsh official had signalled that the goal wouldn't stand due to an alleged handball. The Everton players were incensed and I couldn't help thinking how lucky we were to have got away with it.

Even so, despite our relief, there was still a lot of disappointment among the lads that we had not completed the job at the first attempt. A draw was probably a fair result on the evidence of the ninety minutes but we knew we were a better side than Everton and back at the hotel in Sale, where a post-match reception had been arranged, an inquest was held into why we had performed in such a mediocre way.

There was no doubt among the lads that we'd come through the replay on the Wednesday. It was perhaps the strongest feeling of confidence I ever experienced. The belief within the team that we'd win was astonishing. Everton had made it difficult for us in the first game for sure but there was no hint of fear that they could do it again. We were never going to make the same mistakes again and, true to form, won the replay comfortably 3–0. Although our final two goals weren't scored until late on, the outcome was never in doubt and I was delighted to complete the full 90 minutes.

In terms of post-match celebrations that night was one of the greatest I can remember. It really was up there with the best of them. We celebrated long into the night at the Aughton Chase, a pub restaurant near Ormskirk. To beat Everton was always huge. For it to come in the semifinal of the FA Cup just made that feeling all the more special, especially because, for a lot of us, it was our first experience of reaching a FA Cup final.

Kids of my generation didn't dream about winning the league – they dreamed about playing at Wembley in the FA Cup final. Without any doubt it was the biggest day in the football calendar, one of the very few games to be covered live on TV, and everyone aspired to play in it. I was no different. There was something magical about the FA Cup back then. To play in it was the pinnacle of most players' career and here I was, still only twenty years of age, with a chance of doing so for my boyhood team.

My quarterfinal goalscoring heroics at the expense of St Etienne and Middlesbrough had earned me a prolonged run in the team. The newspapers were suddenly raving about me once again and the frustration I had felt during the first half of the season had long been forgotten.

Another memorable game during this period came in the league. It was a 3–1 win over Leeds on Grand National morning when, following a fifty-yard run that saw me beat five men, I won the penalty for our first goal, scored the second with a header and was named man of the match, all in front of watching England manager Don Revie. One match report even described part of my play as 'worthy of Greaves or Best'. But what thrilled me most about the performance was that I had produced the goods as a ninety-minute player. It was one of six successive games that I started – my best run in the first team yet – and it seemed like I was finally shrugging off the Supersub tag.

Given that it was also the second year in succession I'd scored on the morning of the big race at Aintree there were some inevitable tongue-in-cheek comparisons with the number one racehorse of the time. 'Anfield's very own Red Rum' was the headline in one newspaper, while Bob Paisley also used a racing analogy when telling the press: 'Some players are like horses – they prefer a particular part of the season and that applies with Davey. When he gets the sun on his back he seems to go faster. He also likes the big occasion.'

I don't know why, but there was certainly some truth in that. As the days got longer and the flowers began to bloom everything just seemed to be coming together for me once again. The spring was most certainly back in my step and it all seemed just like the season before.

After scoring against St Etienne I had started every game but was actually rested for the game that would clinch our place in the European Cup final for the first time. The semifinal tie against FC Zurich was something of an anticlimax following the drama of the previous round. Still, it was a fantastic achievement to finally banish the painful memories of 1965 when Liverpool has last reached this stage of the competition, only to be cheated out of a place in the final due to a couple of dubious refereeing decisions.

Every game we played was of massive importance and there was no let-up in the schedule. In addition to the progress we'd made in the two major cup competitions we were also locked in a battle to defend our league crown with Manchester City and Ipswich Town. Three games a week was almost the norm, so fortunes could quickly change.

Competition for places remained fierce and as the remarkable triple-pronged trophy chase gathered pace the jostling for position to remain a part of it was becoming more intense. I was pleased with my form in general and not overly concerned that my place in the team could be at risk. The only slight worry as the season's end approached was that my goals had dried up a little.

When I think back now, the alarm bells should have started ringing the night we played away to Coventry. It was right at the tail-end of the league season, a midweek game that had been rearranged due to our involvement in the FA Cup. As usual, after our pre-match nap in the afternoon, we assembled downstairs for some tea and toast. The boss asked if we could have a word and took me into a room off the main corridor. He told me I wouldn't be playing but explained it was nothing untoward, that I'd still be part of the cup final team so there was nothing to worry about. I was a bit shocked that he mentioned the cup final as there was no need to, but it did help reassure me because when someone says something like that you have to take it on face value.

I watched the game up in the stands. It was a vital match. A win would have seen us retain the title but we drew 0–0. Having played an integral part in the previous season's title run-in I'd have loved to have been playing, naturally, but I got over it. The boss wanted to keep it compact and perhaps played for the draw.

Three days later I was back in the squad and came on to replace David Johnson for the final twenty minutes against West Ham in the game that saw us crowned champions for the second successive season. That also finished goalless and compared to the previous year I suppose it was a slight anticlimax. Nevertheless it was still a great feeling to win the league, especially on home soil. Talk of a possible treble had been dominating the back pages ever since we reached the two cup finals and this was the first leg of what we all hoped would be an historic achievement.

*

THE BUILD-UP TO THE FA CUP FINAL WAS EVERYTHING THAT I EXpected. From the begging letters for tickets, to being fitted for our suits, the traditional cup final song and travelling south full of hope and expectation – it was an amazing experience.

We went down by train on the Thursday amid a lot of talk in the press about who was going to be left out. There was a core group of thirteen players battling it out for eleven starting places, plus a seat on the bench. One unlucky person was going to miss out altogether and I was praying to God that it wasn't going to be me. Much of the speculation centred on who would partner Hamburg-bound Kevin Keegan in attack, for what was to be his last game on English soil as a Liverpool player. Tosh had been out injured since the St Etienne game so basically, barring any late injuries to the other players, it was between myself and Davey Johnson, while also pushing for a place in the team, after recently returning from injury, was veteran midfielder Ian Callaghan.

My excitement about the prospect of playing in these two massive finals had been tempered slightly by concerns over my dad's health. He had suffered a mild heart attack just a few weeks before and spent some time in hospital, but the plan was that he would still come down for the final. However, earlier in the week he had been told by the doctors that they didn't want him to attend for danger of getting too excited. I therefore travelled south in the knowledge that the biggest influence on my career wouldn't be there on what I hoped would be my big day. My mum and sister were still coming, along with my auntie and uncle, and it was an emotional time for us all.

There was nothing else I could do about it other than fully focus on the massive week that lay ahead. It just didn't get any bigger than the FA Cup final followed by a first-ever European Cup final, both coming on the back of a tenth First Division Championship. For now though, all our thoughts were fixed firmly on the game against Manchester United at Wembley. I can honestly tell you that there was no talk of Rome whatsoever. The saying 'one game at a time' was not a myth. That's what we did.

Friday morning arrived and still there was no official word regarding the team. Everyone was talking about it. The word going around among the lads was 'don't get too close to the boss because he's going to deliver the bad news to someone soon.' I must admit the ongoing speculation was starting to make me nervous. Just like the situation I'd found myself in twelve months earlier I was still no nearer to being guaranteed a starting place but was confident that, at the very least, I'd be on the bench.

Then came that fateful moment when I opened the door of my hotel bedroom.

I assume he was about to knock but how long he'd been stood there for I don't know. I must admit I was totally taken aback by the situation. 'Can I have a word,' Paisley mumbled, then beckoned me to follow him, which I did. We went out into the corridor, turned the corner and headed towards his room. Subconsciously, I knew what was coming.

I went in and as soon as the door closed behind me, without another word being uttered, he came straight out with it. 'You won't be playing tomorrow,' he said. It knocked me for six and I struggled to compose myself, allowing him to add before I could get a word in: 'I know how you feel because the same thing happened to me in 1950.'

I remember reading his own reflections about his disappointment back then. He said: 'Probably missing out on a European Cup final is the only thing that matches being left out of the FA Cup final, it hit me so hard in 1950 that had any club come in for me and Liverpool wanted me to go I would have left. As a manager I had to tell players they were left out, and I when I say I understand how they feel, I really do and I'm patient when they fly off the handle as I was tempted to do in 1950.'

I was too stunned to fly off the handle. I knew the story of how he missed out on playing at Wembley all those years ago but his first sentence had left me numb. I was speechless and could feel myself welling up. I sensed he was a bit tearful himself and he later admitted that he could have cried for me. 'It's just about how I want to play it tomorrow,' he continued. 'What I'm going to do is start with David Johnson. Hopefully we'll get an early breakthrough. Cally will be sub and he'll come on later to replace Johnno and close things down.' It was the most definitive plan I ever remember Bob Paisley having. He was so direct in his thinking and seemed to know exactly what he was going to do.

In a way I could see where he was coming from in terms of introducing Cally from the bench. He could act as the calming influence if needed and also had the experience of having played in two previous cup finals. Now Ian was, and is, one of the nicest men you'll ever meet but I suspect that his inclusion was something of a sympathy vote, a decision made to ensure that the club's most respected and longest-serving player was somehow part of the big occasion. But he lacked match practice, having been out injured, and had made just two appearances since March.

I suppose Paisley's more important decision was who to go with up front. There was little between myself and Johnno in the scoring stakes that season. He'd scored eight. I'd scored five. But he had played more games and only netted once since Christmas, as opposed to my four. In my opinion, this should have been enough for me to be given the nod. Johnno will of course no doubt argue the opposite and claim that he fully deserved his place in the team. In the end, what may have slightly edged it in his favour was the goal he scored earlier in the week at Bristol City. It was our last league game of the season and with nothing resting on it the boss made a few changes. We started up front together in a 2–1 defeat. The result didn't really matter. For some of us, including myself and Johnno, it was more a case of seizing this one last opportunity to stake our claim for a place in the FA Cup final team. Without either of us knowing at the time, his goal at Ashton Gate was probably very significant.

Paisley later confessed that selecting two from myself, Cally and Johnno was one of the hardest decisions he ever had to make as manager. I'm sure it was but the disappointment I felt was unbelievable. Like nothing I'd experienced before. I was absolutely devastated and I'm not ashamed to say that I wanted to cry. As I left the room his final words were: 'Don't worry, I'll definitely need you on Wednesday in Rome. You'll be a part of it and play over there.' That was scant consolation at the time but deep down at least I had that to look forward to.

I turned and walked away, re-entered my room and had a moment to myself. At this point the tears flowed. My dream of playing in the FA Cup final had been dashed and I was distraught. I eventually managed to compose myself, washed my face and went downstairs to report for training. Nobody knew. It was so difficult to hide my disappointment but no one sensed it and as we left for training I remember everyone was still joking about staying away from the boss because the first player he collared would be the one that wouldn't be playing the next day. The mood among the rest of the lads was very upbeat. Everyone was laughing and joking. Everyone apart from me, that was. I did my best to maintain the pretence that I knew nothing and it seemed to work, even though I was very subdued.

The news finally broke about lunchtime and I had to phone home to tell my mum and dad. Letting them know I'd been left out was extremely hard and there were more tears. I could tell how upset for me they were and as I sat on the bedroom floor talking to them I was inconsolable. It was a very emotional moment, perhaps even more so I think because of the concern surrounding my dad's health. It had been building up and this was a release of it all.

I've thought about it many times since. I know a manager has to be bold and that difficult decisions are part and parcel of the job but I think it's how they are made that defines a person and I believe Bob Paisley hid behind excuses. I've often used the analogy that if I didn't buy one of my kids something for Christmas I wouldn't say I'd then buy them it for their birthday. Paisley used the carrot of playing in Rome to try and soften the blow of being left out at Wembley. He might have had a genuine intention of using me at some point against Borussia, I don't know, but unless he was naming me in the starting eleven, he could never have been 100 per cent certain that I would play a part. I felt it was a cowardly way of letting me down, just as he had done in the hotel at Coventry.

If he'd have just come out and said he didn't think I had been playing well enough to make the team then I'd have respected him more. To use the European Cup final as a sweetener was pathetic and it certainly left a bitter taste, particularly after it turned out to be a false promise. I'd like to think that if I'd ever gone into management I would never have let a player down in that way. Paisley was a great manager, rightly hailed as one of the best ever – and with the trophies to prove it. But when it came to the art of man-management I lost a lot of respect for him that day.

I think the timing could also have been better. If Paisley had put off telling me until the Saturday morning I don't think I'd have felt as bad. By being informed on the Friday I had too much time to stew on it and it just killed the whole cup final experience for me. It was like being cut off at the knees. In addition, anything could have happened between Friday morning and kick-off the following afternoon. One of the lads could have gone down ill overnight or suffered an injury in training, so it would have been in the manager's best interests to have helped try and keep my spirits up.

One slight moment of light relief, during what was a harrowing 48 hours, came later in the day when we went for a walk through the High Street in St Albans. I remember going into Woolworths, having a little meander about and then standing by the sweet stall when a lady came up to me and said: 'You're David Fairclough, aren't you? Are these other two gentlemen footballers as well?' I looked around and alongside me were Ray Clemence and Phil Neal. I remembered what Kevin Keegan had told me the previous season and I gave a wry smile. To be recognised above the England goalkeeper and right-back meant I must have been doing something right. If only Bob Paisley could have thought the same.

To rub further salt into the wound our pre-match interviews, which were to be broadcast on Cup Final Grandstand the following day, were to be recorded that afternoon. I'd spent many cup final mornings glued to the television watching all the build-up from the players' hotel and always thought they were live but here we were before the cameras to pretend it was now Saturday morning. We all had to get dressed up in our new match-day suits and toe the party line. For me it all felt so hollow.

It was John Motson's first FA Cup final as commentator and I remember him being at the hotel to conduct the interviews. I did mine and it was put to me that I must have been desperately disappointed at being the player to miss out. I can't re-member what I actually said but if I'd have told the truth I might never have played for the club again, such was the strength of my anger. I kept trying to tell myself that there were more important things in life, which of course there are. At least my dad was out of hospital and on the mend. That was the only crumb of comfort I had.

Motson was, in fact, one of only three people who offered any words of sympa-thy regarding my plight, Joey Jones and David Johnson being the others. Team spirit is something that really only exists out on the pitch, when the players are all in it together and fighting for the same cause. Off it, there wasn't much compassion for me and that was what first really opened my eyes to the cut-throat world of football at the top level.

I know that the small matter of an FA Cup final against Manchester United was uppermost in the thoughts and the obvious number one priority but at that time I just needed a reassuring arm around my shoulder; to be told to keep my head up, that I was still an important part of the group, and to channel my energy into the next game, which of course was the European Cup final in Rome.

Instead I felt cast aside and cut adrift from everything else that was taking place. Left to wallow in my own despair, my emotions were all over the place. Having played such a big part in the run-up to Wembley it was so hard to accept. There's a picture of me, taken as I'm looking out over the balcony at the team hotel on that Friday afternoon. I didn't know it was being taken and I'm just staring into space, looking all reflective. A more apt caption would have been 'absolutely gutted'.

If Friday was bad, Saturday was even worse. Try as I did, I just wasn't feeling the cup final excitement and Wembley was the last place I wanted to be. It was only the wise words of my dad that kept me there. A similar thing had happened to Phil Boersma prior to the FA Cup final in 1974 and his infamous response was to storm off. I now knew how he felt and probably would have contemplated doing likewise if it hadn't been for a conversation with my dad. He told me to take it on the chin, stay strong and stand tall. 'Show them you're a man,' he said, 'and don't be running off.' He was right, of course, but it failed to lighten my mood at the time.

I wasn't the only one hovering around on the periphery. My room-mate Alec Lindsay also had no part to play on the big day but that had come as no surprise to him and at least he had sampled the cup final experience before, having played in 1971 and '74. I got a great cheer from the fans pre-match when I walked along the side of the pitch, which was nice, but my mind was elsewhere and when I took my seat on the bench alongside the other players not involved, I cut a pretty vacant-looking figure. I was really on edge, locked away in my own little bubble.

Amid the haze of my anger and frustration all sorts of things were running through my head. The Liverpool–United rivalry is one of the biggest in world foot-ball and, although it perhaps wasn't quite as intense back then as it is now, the stakes couldn't have been higher. It was the most important game ever played between the two clubs – and I know my fellow Liverpool supporters will find this hard to comprehend – but to me the result was now irrelevant. I was hurting so much and no matter how hard I tried I just couldn't shake off what had happened.

I was in turmoil and battling with my emotions. It's hard to admit even now but there were moments when I wasn't sure if I actually wanted things to go our way. I was never a good spectator anyway. I would always be thinking about what the best outcome would be for me; what needed to happen for me to get on or give me a better chance of playing in the next game. Clearly if we had won that day there would have been no chance of me starting in Rome.

Deep down, as a dyed-in-the-wool supporter, I wouldn't have wanted the team to lose. It was unthinkable to want anyone to beat Liverpool in a cup final, least of all Manchester United. But this was a unique situation. I was emotional. I was angry. I wasn't thinking straight. And I wanted Bob Paisley's decision to somehow backfire on him. At the same time I wished nothing bad on the lads and wanted only the best for them. I couldn't help how I felt. My head was a mess and I'm sure I would have made a terrific case-study for a psychologist that day.

No matter who you are, once you've tasted life in the first team it's very dif-ficult to cope with not being in it, even more so for a match of this magnitude and especially when you'd been led to believe you'd be involved.

Of course, football is a team game and in the eyes of those on the outside, including the supporters, all that matters is that the team wins. I can fully understand that view. To say otherwise can be perceived as showing a lack of respect for those supporters and your team-mates. Only those who have experienced being in this position will appreciate how I felt and I defy them to argue otherwise.

In these situations every player's number one concern is not for the team, even the most team-spirited of them. It's about you as an individual player. It's also about your family, your friends, and the effect it also has on them. I knew how much they were looking forward to this day and I felt as disappointed for them as I knew they were for me, that I'd let them down. And for that I felt sick.

As for the game itself, I remember nothing apart from the goals going in. The two we conceded were very poor and they took the shine off Jimmy's equaliser, which many people still say is one of the best cup final goals ever scored. Other than that, everything was just one giant blur. Even when the goals were scored I just sat there and didn't move a muscle. It was a horrible experience from start to finish. Paisley stuck to his word about taking Johnno off but unfortunately we were 2–1 down at that stage and there was to be no way back. Whether I'd have made more of an impact is hypothetical but I always had the utmost faith in my own ability, so obviously I'd like to think that I could have done.

On the journey home everyone was devastated. We travelled by train but first had to get a coach to Watford Junction where we'd catch the connection back to Lime Street. I'll always remember Joey Jones' comment that 'the cat better watch out when I get back home'. That was typical Joey and it lightened the downbeat mood somewhat, while Ray Clemence also did his best to lift spirits on the way back to Merseyside.

For me the pain was double-edged and it hurt like hell. Our hopes of becoming the first team to win a treble had been cruelly dashed and so too had my boyhood dream of playing in the FA Cup final. The manager later revealed that his tactics on the day were heavily influenced by the fact that if the game had been drawn the replay would not take place until late June, slap-bang in the middle of Wimbledon fortnight. With the end of season Home International's being followed by England's tour to South America this was deemed to be the earliest suitable date for any possible rematch. It was a ludicrous ruling by the FA and as a result he also later admitted that his team selection that day was a mistake.

Never once though, either at that time or in the future, did Bob Paisley concede that he should have played me. I've no doubt that his decision was made with the best interests of Liverpool at heart. But in my opinion it was the wrong one. And I'll forever stand by that.

*

THAT FA CUP FINAL WEEKEND WAS, WITHOUT DOUBT, MY LOWEST point in football. I openly admit that it still hurts. But back then, with Rome and a first-ever European Cup final on the horizon, there was no time to dwell on it. On arriving back in Liverpool my only thought was to get back home and put the experience of the last couple of days behind me. A letter I received from a fan in Yorkshire made me smile. After hearing the team news on Friday he successfully predicted the outcome, which pretty much summed up my own feelings. However, come Monday, for the time being at least, it was forgotten about.

I pulled myself together and managed to get the bitter disappointment of Saturday out of my system. When we left for Italy on the Tuesday, I went in great spirits like everyone else. The treble might have been no more but this Liverpool squad still stood on the cusp of history and it was a fantastic feeling to be part of it.

The European Cup had really captured the imagination of the Liverpool supporters. The club had been on a crusade to win it ever since that first-ever game in continental competition back in 1964 and my quarterfinal winner had heightened the belief that this was going to be our year, while our 6–1 aggregate victory over Zurich in the semifinal was as emphatic as they come at that stage of the competition. The final would be a much tougher task. Borussia Mönchengladbach had succeeded Bayern Munich as the dominant force in German football and could boast a star-studded side. What they didn't have was the incredible backing of 30,000 fans in Rome.

It seemed as though the entire red half of the city had been transported en masse to Italy and the intrepid tales of how they got there are now legendary. Some embarked on a train journey that took the best part of a week. The stories we later heard made us wince but such dedication came as no surprise. Such is their love for the club, nothing is ever too much or beyond the Liverpool supporters when it comes to backing the team. This trip was a true pilgrimage and on the night they played their part as much as the players. To know that so many fans had travelled gave everyone a massive lift and added to what was already an unmistakable air of confidence within the camp.

When Bob Paisley named his European Cup final team we gathered for the announcement in a small anteroom near the restaurant of the team hotel. 'Just one change from Saturday,' he said. A sudden surge of expectation came over me and my ears pricked up. 'Cally is in for Dave Johnson.' I quickly sank back into my seat, named as one of the five substitutes but deflated once more. I'm sure Johnno was disappointed to be left out having played against United but I was equally downhearted to just be on the bench. Had the manager conveniently forgotten our conversation on the Friday morning? It certainly looked like he had and this time there was no one-to-one explanation.

The only consolation was that at least there was a chance I'd still play a part. It slightly cushioned the blow of not starting and I kept repeating, over and over, in my head what Paisley had said to me prior to the FA Cup final; that I'd be needed in Rome. I prepared for the game firmly believing that I was going to be used at some point on the night and everything continued as normal. I've since read the manager's autobiography and gather that he had chosen the team for the Rome final on Saturday night on his way home from Wembley.

On the Wednesday morning, while the travelling fans bedecked the Trevi Fountain, Spanish Steps and Coliseum with their Liverpool flags, we took part in a light training session that consisted of just a few sprints, a little passing exercise and a short small-sided game. Then it was back to the hotel for lunch and a team-talk, followed by a sleep. Even ahead of Liverpool's first appearance in a European Cup final, there was no break in the usual routine.

For the journey to the Olympic Stadium the team coach was flanked by police outriders and they guided us through the streets of Rome at breakneck speed. The tension was building but the mood remained relaxed. Into the bowels of the stadium we headed, a quick glimpse of the sparse dressing room and then outside into the arena for a pre-match walkabout. This would be the first time we'd set eyes on the pitch because there had been no chance to train on it beforehand like they do before Champions League finals nowadays.

What greeted us as we emerged from the deep tunnel was a sight to behold and one that will live with me forever. At the far end of the stadium, where the majority of Liverpool supporters were housed, a kaleidoscope of colour lit up this particular part of the Eternal City. It was amazing. There must have been no one left at home and everyone it seemed was waving these thousands upon thousands of red-and-white chequered flags. Though Borussia Mönchengladbach were a very good side, once the boys saw that crowd there was never ever any doubt in our minds who would win the cup that night. And so it proved.

The first half played out well. Terry McDermott put us ahead and we looked in control until Allan Simonsen drew the Germans level not long after the break.

At 1–1 the game could have gone either way, and the longer it stayed like that the more hopeful I was of getting into the action. I was expecting to come on at some stage but the sooner the better from my point of view. I was ready and waiting in the wings, eager to get on, help us win the European Cup and prove to the manager that he was wrong to have left me out of his plans against United.

With the score deadlocked I got the call to warm up. I was immediately lifted and set off on my usual routine, down the side of the pitch we were attacking. It had been a long hard season, even more so for those who had endured a full ninety-minute run-out on the wide-open spaces of Wembley on Saturday. My fresh legs could have given us some added impetus up front. Then Tommy Smith, on what was supposed to be his last appearance for the club, headed us back in front. We celebrated, then I was told to sit back down and wait a few minutes to see how things progressed.

There was still just under half an hour left, plenty of time to come on and still make an impact, I thought. And if I was sent on now at least I wouldn't be under as much pressure to deliver. Another goal would make it safe and I was hoping I could be the man to get it.

Kevin Keegan, on what was definitely his last appearance for the club, was then fouled in the box by Berti Vogts and Phil Neal made no mistake from the penalty spot. There was only eight minutes remaining now and my hopes of getting on were fading fast. Surely, with the game safe, the boss would be true to his word. Again my fresh legs could have proved crucial in the closing stages. Unfortunately, Paisley wasn't thinking the same. I wasn't needed in Rome after all. I couldn't believe it.

It wasn't the time or the place to be crying about my ill-fortune though, so I cast my personal feelings aside and managed to put on a brave face. Back at the team hotel after the game I was glad to see my mum and sister for the celebration banquet, which is best remembered for the hundreds of Liverpudlians who gate-crashed the planned party. Italian security were powerless to stop the delirious Scouse hordes from celebrating this greatest of nights with their heroes. Like a swarm of locusts they devoured the banquet that had been laid out for the players, staff and their families. It was that packed we struggled to get a seat but to witness those scenes was magical. It was the moment everyone connected to the club had been striving for since 1964 and no one will ever forget the glory of Rome.

Deep down though, I was still hurting like mad. The manager had let me down again, gone back on his word that he'd use me at some point in the final and it cast a shadow over what should have been the greatest moment of my career. The only consolation I could take, and it felt very scant at the time, was that if hadn't have been for my goal against St Etienne, none of this would have been possible. I'd played my part in this most historic of triumphs, that's for sure, and have the medal to prove it, but on the night of 25 May 1977 it didn't feel that way.

We returned home to a fantastic reception. As the entire red half of Merseyside partied I must have been the only Liverpudlian with mixed feelings. My club, the one I had supported all my life, had been crowned champions of Europe. As a supporter, yes of course, I was delighted and proud. As a professional footballer? No. It was difficult. I had missed out on playing in what would have been two of the biggest games of my career and justifiably felt hard done by. What a week it had been, one of so many contrasting emotions.

Bob Paisley took the plaudits, and rightly so. He had just become the first English manager to win the European Cup, after all, and narrowly missed out on leading us to what at the time would have been an unprecedented treble. I'd never try to undermine his achievements in the game – how could I? His record speaks for itself. He went on to become the most successful manager in the history of the European Cup and in the space of just nine years won it more times than any other manager before or since.

For that he has my utmost respect and always will. But as the curtain came down on the club's most successful season yet, my relationship with him seemed almost beyond repair. It had been a harsh lesson. I wouldn't go so far as to say that it moulded me as a person but it certainly instilled a sense of cynicism in me. And, sadly, a lingering mistrust of the manager.

10

EUROPEAN CHAMPION

'I THINK YOU'RE GOING TO HAVE TO ACCEPT IT SON, YOU'RE always going to get the rough end of the stick at Liverpool.' So said my dad in early summer, 1977.

It was not long after the curtain had come down on the most epic of seasons. The party which had engulfed the red half of the city since that historic night on 25 May was still in full swing and would continue unabated until the start of the following season. You could spot a Liverpudlian a mile off during that summer. They were walking taller than ever before and sported smiles as wide as the Mersey.

In the living room of a house in Cantril Farm, the mood was a little mixed. I was still reeling from the double disappointment of having been brutally cut from the picture for two of the most important games this club would ever play. The pain of being left out of the FA Cup final at Wembley then missing out on the European Cup final in Rome remained raw, while my dad's health was also still a concern, even though we hoped he was now on the mend.

It was time to take stock and think a little about which way my career was going. So over a cup of tea one morning I sat down for a chat with my dad. As he was still recuperating from his recent heart attack I'm sure he could probably have well done without the stress of seeing what I was going through but there were no agents in football back then, not unless you were a superstar in the Kevin Keegan bracket. Like most young lads, having my dad alongside me was the strongest form of support I could have. He was my sounding board and the person I went to when in need of advice over anything football-related.

As always, he was totally honest in his assessment of the situation. He had taken great pride in seeing his only son rise through the ranks to play for the club he had followed all his life and I'm sure it was now hurting him to see how the situation was developing. In no uncertain terms, he was telling me that the writing was on the wall for me at Liverpool.

They weren't the words I wanted to hear and it was hard to accept. In his eyes he couldn't see how it was going to get any better for me. Deep down I knew he was right but I just didn't want to admit it. My boyhood dream, everything I had worked so hard for since I'd first kicked a ball, was in danger of slipping away. Above all else I wanted, and needed, to be playing first-team football. I was desperate for that to be at Liverpool but on the back of me not featuring in the team in those finals my name was now linked with a couple of clubs elsewhere, the likes of Aston Villa and Anderlecht. I had to think about what was right for me. Granted, it was mostly paper talk, but my mind was in a state of flux and I had no idea in what direction my career was heading.

My dad would eventually be proved right. But before it got worse it did actually get better. Much, much better. Despite what he'd said and how I felt, the 1977–78 season was to offer a temporary reprieve and a glorious silver lining. Sadly, my mentor, the man I looked up to more than anyone else in the world, would not be around to see my Liverpool career scale its highest peak.

THE PAIN, ANGER AND FRUSTRATION THAT I HAD FELT OVER MISS-ing out on the previous season's cup finals was put totally into perspective when hearing that my dad had suddenly passed away. It was early July and after enjoying a summer holiday with friends in Benidorm we'd only just returned to pre-season training. We always went back on a Thursday and this was the second day. My mum, dad and sister were due to go on a week's holiday that Friday morning, so as usual my dad was up first and went for a newspaper with the dog – but never returned. On what was a beautiful summer's day my mum answered the phone to receive the news from her friend that my dad had collapsed outside her house. She dashed out to him and told me to follow the ambulance to hospital. Obviously he had been ill, having suffered the heart attack, but it still came as a massive shock. He was only fifty, having celebrated his birthday a week before. As I arrived at the hospital we were informed he'd already died. The devastation was numbing and I just didn't know how we were going to cope without him.

I might have played for Liverpool but we were still just a normal family living in a council house in Cantril Farm. My mum and dad had never had much money and worked hard just to live day-to-day. It was just as well I now had some security from the contract I was on. Because of all the win bonuses, 1977 was, at the time, the most fruitful year of my career financially and we had talked about moving from the estate, but all that suddenly paled into insignificance.

I was only twenty, just a kid really, and still living at home; my sister was fourteen. As anyone who's been through it will know, to suffer the pain of losing one of your parents at any age is a traumatic experience. All our friends and family rallied around but none of them had been in this situation before, so no one really knew what I was going through.

A week's compassionate leave was all I had off but I suppose that was probably the best thing for me personally. I was still in mourning when I returned to training and I remember thinking to myself that it was going to be really tough to pick myself up off the floor and start playing again. Given the events at the tail-end of the previous season and the discussions I'd had with my dad just before he passed away, I really had no idea what the future held. I'd lost someone who I could confide in implicitly and someone I looked to for guidance. All of a sudden I now couldn't really see beyond the next day. It was like living in a vacuum and I just seemed to be going through the motions on a daily basis.

There is no way of describing how tough a time it was but this was an era when you were just expected to get on with things, your problems were your own. There was no sympathy in football. Certainly not from the manager or coaches, who were from a time when, perhaps, because of their wartime experiences, just thought, 'That's life – move on'. It wasn't that they didn't care or were being mean. That's just how it was. Clubs didn't offer any form of counselling and I don't even remember anyone ever mentioning the loss of my dad.

One thing clear in my mind was that looking for another club was now out of the question. There was no way I could leave my mum and sister. We all needed each other more than ever so I quickly had to forget about moving. In a way, I think that eased the pressure slightly. I had no other option but to focus all my energy into training and playing for Liverpool again. Gradually, it would get easier and life slowly returned to some sort of normality but it took a while.

I figured in all three pre-season games and started in the Charity Shield, which was perhaps just the lift I needed at the time. Knowing what I'd been through, maybe it was Paisley's way of giving me a little gee-up because contrary to what he'd said a year before about this fixture being a reward for the players who'd finished the previous season, there were three players missing from the side that had won in Rome.

One, of course, was Kevin Keegan, who had now completed his move to Hamburg. Replacing him in the iconic number seven shirt was Celtic's Kenny Dalglish. He arrived with the reputation as Britain's best all-round footballer and more than justified what was then a record-breaking £440,000 fee. Apart from having seen him on television playing for Scotland against England I must admit to not knowing too much about Kenny before we signed him. From his first training session at Melwood though, it was plain to see just what a class act he was.

I had the honour of partnering Kenny in attack on his debut against Manchester United and was excited to be playing at Wembley for the first time. Unfortunately, it wasn't the glorious type of day you associate with games beneath the twin towers. It was a hot and humid day, but overcast. There'd been a lot of rain, which affected the pitch, and in keeping with the weather the game was something of a damp squib. I don't remember playing particularly well, which probably explains why I didn't start the following week, but I wasn't alone and we had to be content with sharing the shield after a goalless draw.

Ahead of our first league game of the season away to Middlesbrough I received another, rather unexpected, boost to my confidence. Ron Greenwood had recently succeeded Don Revie as England manager and he came to our team hotel prior to the game. It had been agreed that he could have a brief meeting with Liverpool's England contingent in order to talk them through his plans. Having had no international involvement since the previous year's under-21 fixture I had no reason whatsoever to believe I'd be involved, so it came as a big surprise when Ronnie Moran pulled me to one side and said Greenwood would like me to attend. At the briefing he made no secret of his admiration for Liverpool and explained how he wanted his England team to be based around a strong spine of players from Anfield. It made perfect sense. After all, we were the best team in the land.

Greenwood kept his promise and, in what was an unprecedented move, his first game in charge saw him field a total of six Liverpool players in the team for a friendly against Switzerland (seven if you counted the recently departed Kevin Keegan). Unfortunately, a dour goalless draw at Wembley drew widespread criticism of his tactic and probably made him think twice before picking so many members of the same club side again. Still, it gave me hope that if I could manage to hold down a regular place at club level then there'd be every chance of being called up by my country.

That was easier said than done and I found myself back on the bench for that league opener at Ayresome Park. Tosh started and the closest I got to the action was running out of the tunnel directly behind our new number seven. It was early September before I made my first start, against Birmingham at St Andrews, and I played well enough to retain my place for the following game, a 2–0 win at home to Coventry in which I opened the scoring.

As European Cup holders we received a bye into round two but I again watched from the bench as we made a successful start to the defence of our crown, hammering Dynamo Dresden 5–1 at Anfield. It was a result that should have made the second leg a mere formality but, despite eventually completing a comfortable aggregate victory, our passage into the last eight never looked safe on a chilly night in East Germany.

A super-charged Dresden subjected us to a barrage of pressure. They were simply unrecognisable from the first meeting. It was one of those rare occasions when Ray Clemence had to be absolutely on top of his game. Thankfully he was. A series of stunning saves meant it was goalless at the interval but two goals for the hosts inside the first seven minutes of the second half had us rocking. On the bench, even Joe and Ronnie feared that we wouldn't hold out. If Dresden had netted another at this point then we might well have fully capitulated. Their second goal was the cue for Bob Paisley to send me into battle. With our aggregate advantage reduced to just two, a game-plan based around containing the opposition was jettisoned. Snatching an away goal was suddenly our priority and, during a rare break forward, it was from a cross of mine that Steve Heighway delivered just that. It killed the tie and we all breathed a huge sigh of relief.

Some pundits reckoned that Dresden performance was one of the best ever seen against Liverpool in Europe and it didn't augur well for our next continental excursion: a return to Germany, albeit the Western version, for the first leg of our first-ever European Super Cup tie. Adding a touch of extra spice to these games was the identity of the opposition and, in particular, their number seven.

A fortnight before Liverpool won the European Cup in Rome, Hamburg had lifted the Cup Winners' Cup with an impressive 2–0 victory over Anderlecht in Amsterdam. Since then they had, of course, strengthened their ranks by signing former King of the Kop Kevin Keegan. It made for an intriguing contest. It wasn't the first time we'd faced KK in his new colours: we'd met Hamburg in a pre-season friendly just a few months previous. I scored in a 3–2 defeat that was neither unusual for that time of year nor worried us.

This was a different matter altogether and although the competition is, admittedly, nothing more than a glorified Euro-version of the Charity Shield there was genuine excitement about it among our players. No one was thinking, 'This is only the Super Cup'. It didn't matter what level you played at for Liverpool Football Club, no competitive game was ever treated half-heartedly. The fact that no English club had won the trophy before was an added incentive for us to go and put another piece of silverware on the Anfield sideboard.

The Volksparkstadion, where Hamburg played their home games, had been one of the venues used for the 1974 World Cup but on a terrible night weather-wise a crowd of just 16,000 braved the ice, sleet and freezing temperatures. It was a complete contrast to the full house that had witnessed our pre-season fixture there. Such a sparsely populated arena might have lessened the sense of occasion slightly but it didn't dim the will to win of the teams. KK would have been desperate to get one over on us, that's for sure, and we faced no easy task against a side that was among the strongest in the Bundesliga at the time and included stars of the international team like Manny Kaltz and Felix Magath.

We treated the game as we would a normal two-legged European tie, with the aim being to make sure we brought something back to Anfield. And that's exactly what we did. Despite falling behind in the first half, I equalised with a far-post header in the 65th-minute. It was the first headed goal of my career. A 1–1 draw was never a bad result away in Europe and it gave us the edge going into a second leg that was expected to be similarly tight.

The return meeting two weeks later proved to be one of those unforgettable European nights at Anfield. It might have lacked the electric atmosphere of St Etienne or the nail-biting drama of Bruges but it was as emphatic a performance against a top-ranked continental side that I was ever part of at Liverpool. All the focus was on Keegan's first return to the club where he'd made his name and how he'd compare to the new Kop favourite, Kenny. But on the night both were totally overshadowed by Terry Mac's treble in a stunning 6–0 win. I netted our fifth goal and was thrilled to be part of a cup-winning team once again.

I find it strange that a lot of people tend to disregard this as being 'only the Super Cup'. To beat Hamburg so convincingly was a fantastic achievement and further proof of just how dominant a side we were becoming in Europe. I know for a fact that their players were devastated to have lost, especially so heavily. For poor old KK it was a nightmare return and those fans who once adored him took great delight in letting him know that he'd left a team that was in the ascendancy and for whom more glory beckoned.

Despite having deposited another item of silverware into the rapidly filling Anfield trophy cabinet, the team continued to evolve. Emlyn was nearing the end, as was Smithy. Cally had gone to Swansea with Tosh. Alan Hansen had arrived the previous May and in January 1978 we signed Graeme Souness.

Souey's first game was away to West Brom. He hadn't brought his usual shin pads with him so I was asked to lend him mine. They were Lispro pads and although they probably only cost about £3 they were considered to be top of the range at that time. Souness then proceeded to cut them down. They ended up so tiny it was hardly worth him having them on. Anyway I never did get them back and I think he ended up wearing them for years. Luckily it was his opponents who more often than not found themselves on the receiving end of a crunching tackle rather than him because those shin pads would have offered no protection whatsoever.

Like Kenny, Souey settled in immediately. He actually took my place at the Hawthorns but I could have no complaints as he turned in a majestic performance. From the moment he found a red shirt with his first pass from thirty yards away the fans were won over; when he burst the back of the Anfield Road net with his first goal in a red shirt against Manchester United a few weeks later it was clear for all to see that we had a truly great player in our midst.

Unfortunately, Souness was ineligible to play in League Cup, having already featured in the competition for Middlesbrough earlier in the season. For him, and for us, this was a shame because for the first time in the club's history Liverpool were heading to the final and it was only now that we stopped referring to it as the Mickey Mouse Cup. Previous to this, it had not been a competition that anyone had placed too much importance on. In 1978 it suddenly started to be taken a lot more seriously, especially when we reached the semifinal and played Arsenal.

I was in really good form at the time this game came around. I'd recently enjoyed a mid-season run of fifteen straight first-team starts, the best I would ever manage with Liverpool. During that, I got myself on the score-sheet in five successive games. I was flying and it was enough to attract the attention of the England selectors.

Ron Greenwood had already confided in me that I was a player he admired and explained that he saw me as the natural understudy to Steve Coppell on the right wing. In November I had been selected by him to play for an England XI in a testimonial at Villa Park for referee Jack Taylor. On the back of that game I received a call-up for the first B team international in 21 years. It was Greenwood's decision to re-introduce the B team. He had played in it himself back in the 1950s and looked upon it as an international reserve team, a bridge between the under-21s and full team.

Bobby Robson was in charge and also included in the team to play West Germany were my Liverpool team-mates Phil Thompson and Terry McDermott. Before flying out we trained at Bisham Abbey and I remember Don Howe saying to me

My childhood was one blessed with happiness and for that I have my parents to thank. Here we all are, including my baby sister Lesley, during one of our regular family holidays at Butlins. *(Personal collection)*

Showing off my skills at young age. I've been football-daft from as far back as I can remember and as long as I had a ball at my feet I was always happy. *(Personal collection)*

It was for my school team Major Lester that I first began to show promise. As captain of both the 'A' and 'B' teams I'm pictured here holding the ball at the centre of the front row. *(Personal collection)*

I first got to play at Anfield as a 14-year old in 1971. It was for Liverpool Boys against London and although a young Ray Wilkins inspired the visitors to victory it was a thrilling experience. *(Personal collection)*

Left: Venturing into enemy territory. Myself and future Liverpool reserve team-mate Alex Cribley at Goodison Park for national penalty prize competition with Everton goalkeeper Gordon West. *(Mirrorpix)*

Below: In training with the Liverpool Boys team at Penny Lane, the year we reached the semi-final of the ESFA Trophy. I'm second to the end, one of the smallest in the squad. *(Personal collection)*

The Liverpool youth team of 1974/75 – Back row (left to right): Brian Kettle, Max Thompson, John Higham, Joe James, Derek McClatchey, Jon Laisby, me, Mick Branch. Front row (left to right) Chris Tansey, Colin Williamson, Tommy Tynan, Kevin Kewley, Jimmy Case, Jeff Ainsworth. *(Getty)*

The Liverpudlian 'Likely Lads': taking a walk in the shadow of the Kop with fellow Anfield hopefuls Max Thompson and Brian Kettle during the autumn of 1975. *(Personal collection)*

The press attention that greeted my first team breakthrough was a real eye-opener but the people around me made sure I never forgot my roots, including the kids in Cantril Farm. *(Personal collection)*

Casually stroking home the first of my 55 goals for Liverpool. It came against Real Sociedad in a UEFA Cup tie at Anfield in November 1975. I'd made my senior debut just four days before. *(Steve Hale/ Liverpool FC)*

Derby debut delight: Grand National morning 1976 and I come off the bench to score a dramatic last-minute winner versus Everton. *(Personal collection)*

'We Are The Champions', the celebrations that followed our title-clinching victory at Molineux in 1976 are up there with the best I ever experienced. *(Getty)*

At just 19 years of age I got my hands on the UEFA Cup, a competition that was perhaps even tougher to win than the European Cup back in the day. *(Steve Hale/Liverpool FC)*

Bringing home the silver in the spring of 1976. What a way to end my first season as a senior player. *(Adrian Killen)*

The moment that defined my career. Scoring the decisive goal in the 1977 European Cup quarter-final against St Etienne. I've never been allowed to forget this one and nor would I want to. *(Steve Hale/ Liverpool FC)*

Friday May 22

Friday May 20th. 1977.

Mr. Fairclough.

I have just seen on T.V. that you have

been left out of the F.A.Cup Match tomorrow.

If you don't play tomorrow as advertised then

Liverpool WILL NOT win the Cup.

And if they leave you out of next weeks game in

Italy Liverpool WILL LOOSE that one also.

By the time you get this letter it will all

be over Liverpool will have lost the Cup,

unless at the last minute they let you play.

I can see a great future for you David so if

you do have to miss tomorrows game don't be too

downhearted you will live to see the backside

of most of those who are playing in the future.

D.DOBB
9 Cavendish St.
MANSFIELD, NOTTS.

Missing out on the 1977 FA Cup final remains the biggest disappointment of my career. I received this letter a few days later. If only Bob Paisley would have thought the same. *(Personal collection)*

Three months later I did get to play against Manchester United at Wembley. It was my first game beneath the twin towers and it ended in a goalless draw, meaning we shared the Charity Shield. *(Steve Hale/ Liverpool FC)*

A proud moment as I celebrate scoring a goal for the England 'B' team against West Germany in a snowy Augsburg, February 1978. *(Personal collection)*

The Anfield dug-out seemed like a second home for me at times. This picture was taken during the European Cup tie against Benfica. To my right is Liverpool's record appearance holder Ian Callaghan, to my left the Boot Room brains trust. *(Steve Hale/Liverpool FC)*

A banner at the 1978 League Cup Final against Nottingham Forest asks the prevailing question of the day. *(Colorsport)*

'We hate Nottingham Forest…' so sang the Liverpool supporters and this game, a frustrating goalless draw in the 1978 League Cup final, was one of the reasons why. For a three-year spell Cloughie's men were our bogey side. *(Steve Hale/Liverpool FC)*

10 May 1978. In action at the European Cup final at Wembley. After missing out on the glory of Rome the previous season I savoured every moment of this occasion. *(Colorsport)*

King of Europe: celebrating with Sammy Lee on the train back to Liverpool the day after beating Bruges. Feelings in football don't get much better than becoming a European champion with your hometown club. *(Offside)*

The second goal of the hat-trick I scored away to Norwich in February 1980. The game ended 5-3 to Liverpool but is best remembered for Justin Fashanu's 'goal of the season' strike. *(Personal collection)*

In action against Finland's Oulun at Anfield in the 1980 European Cup. Liverpool won 10-1. *(Steve Hale/Liverpool FC)*

Seven years after overlooking my claims for a place in the team that played Manchester United in the 1977 FA Cup final, Bob Paisley sends me into action against the same opposition in the Milk Cup final, which we won 2-1 in extra time. *(Colorsport)*

TORONTO BLIZZARD SOCCER CLUB

Front Row--Left to Right: Duncan Davidson #18, Pasquale Deluca #12, David McQueen #28,
Frank Ciaccia #14, Paul James #15, Cliff Calvert #10.
Middle Row--Left to Right: David Turner (Assistant Coach), Jomo Sono #11, Juan Carlos
Molina #21, Sam Lenarduzzi #4, Patrick "Ace" Ntsoelengoe #8, Bob Houghton (Coach),
David Bryne #19, Bruce Wilson #2, Alan Merrick #23, Jim Panno (Equipment Manager).
Third Row--Left to Right: Gary Kraft #30, David Needham #26, Neill Roberts #6,
Clyde Best #17, Jan Møller #00, Victor Kodelja #7, David Fairclough #20, Randy Ragan #16,

A move to Toronto Blizzard in the North American Soccer League was just what I needed in the summer of 1982 and it helped me regain full fitness after my recent knee injury. *(Personal collection)*

The schedule in the NASL could be hectic at times but the Blizzard still managed to squeeze in a high-profile friendly against Juventus, a game I was sent off after just 90 seconds. *(Personal collection)*

I thoroughly enjoyed my solitary season with Tranmere Rovers. The team spirit was fantastic and I would have loved to have extended my stay at Prenton Park. *(Personal collection)*

My time in Switzerland may have ended on a sour note but there were some good moments, including this goal for Luzern against FC Aarau. *(Personal collection)*

The style of football at Beveren was much more to my liking and, in the first season especially, we gave the bigger clubs in Belgium a run for their money. *(Personal collection)*

Happier times. My lovely wife and soul-mate Jan. Tragically and prematurely taken from us but forever in our thoughts.

A portrait in my life after playing. *(Offside)*

With my son and daughter, Tom and Sophie. I couldn't have wished for two better children and I'm so proud of how both have turned out.

that he thought international football would really suit my style of play. He also added that he fancied me to score by coming in at the far post and his prediction was proved right.

The game was played in the Bavarian city of Augsburg on 21 February 1978 and two inches of snow covered the pitch. Conditions were difficult but following a goalless first half the game burst into life. Terry Mac opened the scoring before a rare mistake by Thommo gifted the Germans an equaliser. Just a few minutes later I headed in a cross from future Anfield team-mate Alan Kennedy and that was enough to clinch an impressive 2–1 victory over a team that hadn't lost for twelve months.

It had been a much more memorable international experience than my previous one and, although not getting carried away, I was hopeful that a full cap wouldn't be too far away. With a trip to Wembley also on the horizon and the resumption of the European Cup to look forward to, the season was going way better than I could have anticipated back in those dark days of the summer.

In the League Cup semifinal first leg against the Gunners I laid on the winning goal for Ray Kennedy at Anfield. With a 2–1 advantage we travelled to London for the return with high hopes of completing the job. Unfortunately, I was forced to sit it out through injury but in what was a first for me during my time at the club, I was invited to go and watch despite not being in the team. Myself and Souey took the train down to Highbury where the lads ground out a goalless draw that was enough to clinch our place in a first-ever League Cup final.

Razor's goal in front of the Kop had proved decisive so I was pretty satisfied with the part I had played in getting us to the twin towers. Furthermore, I had also scored some crucial goals in the earlier rounds, the importance of which don't dawn on you until these latter stages of the competition. A third-round tie at home to Derby County in October saw me don my Supersub outfit for the first time since St Etienne as I came off the bench in the 70th minute with the score tied at 0–0. Within five minutes I'd scored two and booked our place in the last sixteen, where I netted again in a 2–2 draw with Coventry.

In the dressing room at Highfield Road before the replay, Bob Paisley stood up to announce the team and talk us through how we were going to play. His idea was to play me in a more isolated role up top with Kenny withdrawn into a deeper-lying position. But in trying to explain that I would be the lone striker, he got a bit muddled up and proceeded to tell everyone, 'Davey will be the lone star ranger.' It had the lads rolling around in fits of laughter and for a short time the nickname stuck. It's one of many I've acquired down the years and every now and again when we get together at a former players' function someone will remember it.

With our interest in the FA Cup having ended at Stamford Bridge in the third round and the league title already looking beyond us, the League Cup was now one of only two trophies realistically left to play for. Standing in our way beneath the twin towers were our new nemesis. It's not for nothing that in 1978 Kopites started a new chant. You may remember it. It's still sung to this day and it goes something like this . . .

> *We hate Nottingham Forest,*
> *We hate Everton too,*
> *We hate Man United,*
> *But Liverpool we love you.*

Everton and Manchester United – fair enough. Both age-old rivals. Why such hatred though, for a medium-sized club from the East Midlands you may think? As a kid growing up in the 60s, Nottingham Forest to me had been nothing more than a run-of-the-mill club. There was nothing remarkable or glamorous about them. I recall that they had a decent year around 1967 and at one time I was a big admirer of their winger Ian Storey-Moore. Other than that, they weren't a club that had featured too prominently on my radar. Until now.

The men from the Trent had come from nowhere to clinch promotion the previous season, scraping through in third place by a point. No one was predicting that they'd make a big splash in the First Division so what manager Brian Clough went on to achieve deserves a lot of credit.

Following a great start to the 1977/78 campaign Forest topped the table, but most people, including myself, were expecting that they'd fall away. We met them for the first time on Boxing Day when I set up a goal for Steve Heighway in a 1–1 draw at the City Ground. We realised there and then that these were the real deal. They looked the finished article and would soon become, without doubt, our most fierce rivals. The next day we played Wolves at Anfield and worked hard for a 1–0 win – imagine the screams there would be these days, playing twice in as many days. I played ninety minutes in both and thought this might begin to dispel the theory I could only play as a substitute.

Publicly, the Liverpool backroom staff were never overly glowing about Forest but I knew from spending time around them that there was a deep-seated acknowledgement that they were a good side. There might have been a supreme air of confidence about the Liverpool team of the late 70s but Forest suddenly emerged on the scene and, for a while, threatened to disrupt that. They posed a genuine threat to our dominance and, although none of us would have admitted it at the time, we did fear them slightly. No other team during my entire time at the club did that to us.

Arsenal, we knew, would always be liable to cause us trouble and we'd have some epic games with them too, especially in the cup. Manchester United was another team that thwarted our cup ambitions on more than one occasion during this era but there was never a fear factor about them. Each season would also throw up a different challenger in the league, be it QPR, Manchester City, Aston Villa or Ipswich Town. And it was the same with them. Good sides on their day, yes, and occasionally capable of getting one over on us. But there was never a concern that they possibly had what it takes to usurp us as the country's number one club. Unlike Forest.

To prove the point, they ended up succeeding us as champions and beating us in the final of the League Cup. Similar to Liverpool, there was an unmistakable swagger about Cloughie's team. People often accused them of being just a workmanlike eleven but they were set up well by the manager and his assistant Peter Taylor. They were a solid unit and possessed quality in every area. It proved very effective and you had to respect them.

This League Cup final was the start of our rivalry. It was a massive game and over the course of 120 minutes at Wembley there was nothing between the two teams. I came on as a sub for Ray Kennedy at the start of extra-time. A Forest fan who I met on holiday a few years ago remembered being there that day and told me that my introduction really panicked their supporters. I'd never really thought about the effect I had on opposition fans when coming off the bench. It's flattering to know they feared me. Unfortunately on this day I was unable to deliver, although I still believe I was denied a blatant penalty when, late on, I was taken out throat-high inside the box by former Liverpool defender Larry Lloyd.

It wasn't the last controversial refereeing decision of the final. Four nights later we met again at Old Trafford and it was the man in black, Pat Partridge, who made the headlines. First he wrongly awarded Forest a penalty for a foul that took place outside the box and then disallowed a perfectly good goal by Terry McDermott. If that wasn't enough, he also did the unthinkable and booked Ian Callaghan. It was the first time in a previously unblemished eighteen-year career that Cally's name had been taken by the ref. I only played the last 25 minutes but we just couldn't find an equaliser. It was one of those frustrating nights when, no matter how long was played, I doubt we would have scored. In the dressing room afterwards, everyone was outraged at the injustice of it all, so much so that in his post-match interview Tommy Smith even joked that the ref should be shot.

The disappointment at missing out on a first League Cup triumph was huge but, for now, it was back to being known as the Mickey Mouse Cup. Fortunately, there wasn't much time to dwell on it. We had our sights set on a much bigger prize. One that also had big ears. The European Cup had reached the semi final stage.

I had played no part in the quarter final victory over Benfica and I also had to be content with a seat on the bench for both legs of the last-four tie as a return ticket to Wembley was secured at the expense of Borussia Mönchengladbach. Luckily, I forced my way back into the team during the run-up to the final and was playing really well, scoring two at home to Norwich, the winner against Arsenal and another at West Ham the following week in a game that saw us relegate them. I then laid on a couple for Kenny in what was our penultimate league game against Manchester City, by which point our title had been surrendered to Forest.

Liverpool's final league game was, ironically, against Brian Clough's side and although nothing rested on it there was still a crowd of over 50,000 inside Anfield to witness the latest instalment of English football's newest rivalry. It was not the fixture we'd have chosen to play just six nights before the European Cup final and I remember Ian Bowyer winding me up by saying: 'You best be careful not to get injured if you want to play at Wembley next week.' I tried to pay no attention but I must admit it did make me think about what was at stake. No player wants to risk losing his place by suffering a needless injury in what, apart from pride, was a meaningless game. Thankfully I came through unscathed and we saved a bit of face by holding the new champions to a goalless draw.

I considered myself to be in really good form and saw no reason why I wouldn't play against Bruges. Then, in the days leading up to the final, Bob Paisley announced to the press that he still hadn't decided on his team and that he would be making a late check on the fitness of Steve Heighway before finalising his plans. After what had happened a year before you can imagine how I was feeling. When I read the quote I could feel the muscles in my stomach starting to tighten. 'Oh no, not again' was my immediate thought. I was furious.

The omens weren't good. Our pre-match base was again Sopwell House, scene of my lowest ebb. On the morning of the game I still didn't know whether I'd be starting or if history was about to repeat itself. After a light training session I went for a walk with Colin Irwin, who I was rooming with, and Joey Jones. All sorts of things were running through my mind and I couldn't help but keep remembering the events of twelve months earlier. I got myself so wound up that when we got back to the hotel I went to my room and wrote a letter, which was effectively a transfer request. If Bob Paisley left me out again, I would hand it in. The prospect of possibly missing out again was almost making me sick with worry. If I didn't play that would be it. My mind was made up. I put the letter in the inside pocket of my suit jacket and we left for the stadium.

We got to Wembley and made our way out on to the pitch for the traditional pre-match walkabout. It was a lovely sunny evening and you could tell even then that the Liverpool fans were going to vastly outnumber those who had made the trip from Belgium. There were pockets of red everywhere, just as there had been on the coach journey in, and an unmistakable air of supreme confidence about the place. The official attendance at Wembley that night was 92,000 and at least 80,000 of them must have been Liverpool fans. It really was like a home game for us.

Yet still, we didn't know the team. That meant I couldn't fully enjoy the build-up and it's a good job I didn't catch sight of the match programme because in that I was listed on the team sheet as number thirteen. Only when I got back inside the dressing room and saw that my boots were out did I know I'd be starting. It was a massive relief and I could feel the weight literally dropping off my shoulders. Suddenly my mind was focused solely on the game but again it left a bit of a sour taste because I don't think there was any need to delay naming the team for so long. Knowing what I had gone through before the FA Cup final, Paisley must have been well aware that I'd have been on tenterhooks to find out. Maybe he thought it was the best way of keeping me on my toes but I don't agree.

It was not as if I'd just forced my way back into the team and presented him with a selection headache. I'd played in every one of the previous six games and scored four goals in the process, so my form could hardly be in question. And with Johnno out injured there was no other obvious striker to play up front alongside Kenny. So what he was thinking I don't know. To be left to worry about whether I'd play or not until an hour and a quarter before kick-off was completely unnecessary and I considered it another slight on the boss. I think I deserved to have been treated with a bit more respect. Maybe he could have just pulled me to one side in the days leading up to the game and put my mind at ease by giving me an indication that my place in the team was safe. Again, it led me to doubt Bob Paisley's man-management capabilities.

That aside, to be named in the starting eleven for Liverpool in a European Cup final, no matter how late I found out, was a moment of immense pride. Better late than never and as highlights of my career go this was it. The feeling around the city throughout the previous few weeks had been pumped. You just couldn't get away from it and, living where I did, I'd been breathing it every day. Liverpool Football Club ruled Europe and the pride that instilled in everyone, be it players or supporters, was huge. I was so desperate to play my part and it felt great to know that I was going to be involved from the start.

Despite the magnitude of the occasion I had no nerves. Playing at Wembley now held no fear for me. It was a great stage on which to play but I'd now been there a few times before. During the warm-up I was flying and couldn't wait to get started. I remember just looking up in awe at the mass of red and white that filled almost the entire stadium and trying to read what was on all the banners.

The game itself wasn't the worst in the world, whatever some people seem to remember. Granted, it was no classic, but that wasn't down to us. The tactics Bruges adopted spoiled the spectacle: they chose to play with a blanket defence and continually kept trying to catch us offside, especially in the first half.

After the break they became a little more adventurous but continued to sit deep and tried to steal a goal on the counter-attack. We tried our best to open it up but it was very difficult when coming up against such negativity. We were always on top and once we finally took the lead through Kenny Dalglish's 65th-minute goal I never felt we were going to lose it. There was one little scare at the back, involving Thommo and Alan Hansen, but other than that we were home and dry.

Why Bruges opted to play that way I don't know because Belgian football was quite strong at the time. Anderlecht had reached the last two finals of the European Cup Winners' Cup, while the national side would go on to finish runners-up in the European Championships two years later. Bruges were without two key players, in Paul Courant and Raoul Lambert, but still they could boast nine internationals in their side, including René Vanderycken.

With continental teams you never knew what to expect. They would approach each game differently and alter their tactics accordingly, depending on who they were up against. In contrast, Liverpool's philosophy was to treat every game the same and I think that was proved to be the correct way. They came with a plan and in denying us more than just one goal, I suppose they could say that it almost worked. It wasn't pretty at times but if a few of our early chances had gone in there could have been a completely different outcome. A couple of those opportunities fell to me and on another night I would have scored. One chance came from a Terry Mac through ball; I tried a little Kenny-style dink over the keeper but he did well to save it. Just before that, from another Terry Mac pass, I managed to beat their offside trap and was clean through on goal. I stumbled, which allowed the defenders to close the space, but I regained my footing and continued to race towards the penalty area only for Jensen to rush off his line and thwart my effort.

When the breakthrough did finally arrive I couldn't have been any closer to it. As Kenny chipped the keeper I was running in at the far post and would have been handily placed had the ball come back off the woodwork.

Bob Paisley would often tell me to hang on the outside of Ray Kennedy if he ever ghosted in as an extra centre-forward. That was the position Ray played in at Arsenal during their double-winning season in 1970/71, and although it was on the left side of midfield that he proved so effective at Liverpool he'd often push up into attack and provide us with an added threat. The defenders would be too preoccupied in trying to stop myself or Kenny that Razor could sometimes move into the danger zone almost unnoticed and he got many of his goals that way. The boss would say to me, 'Hold that position.' I would do and then Ray would pop up in his own time – a bit like what you'd describe as a false number nine in the modern game. It was a tactic that suited me because, don't forget, I was traditionally a left-winger. I could play inside but rather than a main striker, a more apt description of me would be 'a winger who scored goals'.

When I look back on games there are some where I know I didn't do myself justice but on that night I was really satisfied with how I played. I would have loved to have scored, that goes without saying, but other than that I was really pleased with my performance. I've got a tape of the game at home. I've watched it back in full a couple of times and I know I played well. My only regret is not scoring but I'm safe in the knowledge that I played a big part. I'd have hated to have played in the European Cup final and just let the entire occasion pass me by, as can sometimes happen in big games. I earned my medal that night and it's something I look back on with great pride.

Towards the end of the game I remember being close to Ray Kennedy when he asked the ref how long there was to go. 'Two minutes,' came the reply. I was gutted because I could have carried on playing all night. Normally with just a slender lead in a cup final you'd be willing the ref to blow his whistle and let the celebrations commence but for some reason I just wanted the greatest night of my footballing life to continue. I was enjoying it so much and was feeling no signs of tiredness. There was no way they were going to stop us from winning and I just didn't want it to end.

When the whistle went the first player I embraced was Souey. I would later become a next door neighbour of his and, despite the shin-pad incident earlier in the season, we were fast becoming great friends. It was from his pass that Kenny had scored and it was a great way for both of them to cap their first season at the club. The post-match party that night was at the Swiss Cottage Holiday Inn. Souey was famously pictured there with the Miss World of the time, Mary Stävin. That was typical Souey. He always enjoyed the good things in life.

In defeating Bruges, Liverpool joined an elite band of clubs to have won back-to-back European Cups. Again, credit had to go to Bob Paisley. When it came to this competition he was proving beyond doubt that he possessed a Midas touch. No British club had ever won it twice. And as both Celtic and Manchester United could attest, defending it was an extremely difficult task. Paisley had gone all the way and won it in each of his first two attempts. How many managers can say that?

We might have had our differences of opinion over my inclusion in the team – and that would continue – but there's no doubt in my mind that he deserves all the praise that comes his way for doing what he did. In the short space of just four years he had assembled the most successful side this country had ever seen. Had the club twice not declined the invitation to contest the World Club Championship (or the Intercontinental Cup as it was then known), then he might also have led Liverpool to global domination. We were certainly good enough and it would have been a great experience to have tested ourselves against the best South America had to offer at that time.

In 1977 and 1978 that would have been Boca Juniors of Argentina. Imagine what those games would have been like? In those days it was still a two-legged affair and history had shown that the trips to South America could be quite brutal. Still, I'm well aware of just how passionate they are about their football in Buenos Aires and would have loved to sample the atmosphere inside the famous La Bombonera. It would have been fascinating to see how we'd have fared, especially home and away over two legs unlike the one-off contests in neutral Japan that later Liverpool teams competed in.

The decision not to participate was typical of how Liverpool Football Club was run at the time. It wasn't due to any inferiority complex. It's just how it was back then. Anything out of ordinary that might have disrupted the normal routine and they just weren't interested. Long gruelling flights and the increased possibility of picking up needless injuries in what were traditionally highly physical encounters just didn't appeal.

To be crowned the best club team in the world may bring untold riches in a commercial sense nowadays but attitudes were a lot more insular back then. Of much greater importance to the suits upstairs in the boardroom and the coaching staff downstairs in the bootroom was ensuring Liverpool stayed top of the tree domestically and in Europe. In order to do that they just didn't see the point in risking the so-called 'bread and butter' by hot-footing it across the Atlantic to chase glory in a competition they viewed as nothing more than glorified friendlies.

This was a prime example of the so-called Liverpool Way. It's something that I'm often asked about and it's so difficult to explain. The one word that can best be used to describe it is simplicity. From the way you played on the pitch – doing the basic things right – to how the club was run off the pitch. There were never any visions of grandeur around Anfield or Melwood. No egos. No showbiz. It was just an extremely modest football club. Even after winning back-to-back European Cups nothing changed.

Every player became indoctrinated into the Liverpool Way. It not only influenced how you played on the pitch, it also had a huge bearing on how you lived your life. The origins of it can be traced back to Shanks and how he shook things up at the club in the early 60s. This was carried on by Paisley, together with the chairman John Smith and chief executive Peter Robinson. These were the true guardians of this concept and they were a pair that complemented each other well; it was a coming together of like-minded souls and it's no coincidence that their reign at Anfield was also the most successful era in the club's history.

Whether Liverpool's class of 1978 was better than the one in 1977 or those that would follow is a futile debate. What is for sure is that Liverpool under Bob Paisley became a byword for success. Our fame stretched way beyond these shores and the borders of Europe. We were renowned throughout the world for being the best.

In Brazil there's a big display at the Flamengo club museum, celebrating the time they defeated the mighty Reds to lift the World Club Championship in 1981. It just shows the high level of esteem in which Liverpool was held. It was the type that very few clubs could command and it initially came about because of our success in Europe in the late 70s. It elevated us to the loftiest of heights and because of this our reputation went before us. To be part of that meant we walked around with our chests puffed out and heads held high.

I mentioned in the previous chapter how my boyhood dream had been to play in the FA Cup final but nothing could have topped playing for Liverpool in a triumphant European Cup final. There are few higher accolades in football than a winners' medal in that competition and I was now the proud owner of one. How many of my fellow Scousers can say that? Not many. Dennis Mortimer, Kenny Swain and Peter Withe won it with Aston Villa in 1982, while Steve McManaman helped Real Madrid lift it twice. I, however, am one of only nine players to achieve it with Liverpool; Ian Callaghan, Tommy Smith, Jimmy Case, Terry McDermott, Phil Thompson, Sammy Lee, Jamie Carragher and Steven Gerrard are the others. Not bad company to be in, I'm sure you'll agree.

Just a year after I almost walked out on Liverpool Football Club here I was: a European champion. From my lowest ebb to the highest peak in twelve months. I might have enjoyed more memorable personal moments in a red shirt but to have that medal in my collection was something special.

For the right reasons this time, it had been another unforgettable season. My only regret was that my dad had not lived long enough to experience it with me. If he was looking down on me that night at Wembley he'd have no doubt been beaming with pride, that's for sure. He certainly hadn't predicted it, but dads aren't often wrong and, as would be proved in the long-run, neither was he.

11

THE PARTY'S OVER

THREE MONTHS AFTER PARADING AROUND WEMBLEY WITH THE European Cup I was back at Anfield doing what came naturally to me; scoring in a comfortable Liverpool victory. My first goal of the 1978/79 season though, was greeted by just a slight ripple of applause.

After watching from the bench as the first team kicked off their campaign at home to Queens Park Rangers four days earlier I found myself back in the reserves for their season-opener against Bury.

That summer I had been feeling more part of the main group than I ever had. But still a nagging worry remained that my place was never assured. I played against Bayern Munich in the Olympic Stadium. Myself and Karl-Heinz Rumenigge scored in a 1–1 draw. The next game I was on the bench against Austria Vienna, all very confusing, I never did know where I stood.

Those games might only have been pre-season friendlies but it was different back then. Not many changes were ever made. The summer was more a case of building up match fitness and fine-tuning for the coming campaign rather than giving everyone in the squad a run-out like today. No matter what I did I never seemed able to convince Bob Paisley that I should be an automatic starter. Even after being part of the team that had conquered Europe, I was having to constantly prove myself, over and over again.

The closest Paisley came to putting my mind at ease came on the eve of the season. 'I'm going to start off with Stevie Heighway, let him play the first half-dozen or so games. After that he'll have tired himself out. That'll be it for him then. You'll come back and the shirt will be yours," Paisley explained. Given that I'd just been in the team that had won the European Cup I obviously wasn't best pleased to be told I wouldn't be starting the season in the first team, but Stevie had recently turned thirty so at least there seemed to be grounds for optimism.

What happened next? Heighway and the team started like a house on fire. He scored the winner on the opening day, played in every one of the first 23 games and Liverpool stormed to the top of the table on the back of an incredible run that saw them lose just one league game before December. I couldn't believe it. The goals were going in for fun. It was the season Tottenham were hit for seven at Anfield and the football was breathtaking.

League games very rarely stay in the memory. When players or supporters recall their most memorable matches of days gone by it is often a cup final or European tie that gets the vote. Never a league game. That win over Tottenham is an obvious exception. Like Liverpool's famous 5–0 victory over Nottingham Forest in 1988, it's remembered as one of the most clinical footballing displays seen in this country.

It goes without saying that it was one of those games I would have loved to have played in. It was a beautiful sunny, early September afternoon. There was a big crowd and a huge sense of anticipation. Liverpool had made a winning start to the season but if you believed what the London-based press corps had been writing, recently promoted Tottenham, with their new Argentine imports Ossie Ardiles and Ricardo Villa, were the team to end that run.

What followed was a footballing masterclass, served up by a Liverpool team in which every player was right on top of their game. The quality on show in this total annihilation of the Londoners had the majority of the capacity crowd drooling. I was sat up in the Main Stand kicking my heels. For me, it was terrible to watch because I knew that it meant, for the foreseeable future at least, there was no way back. And there was simply nothing I could do about it.

I managed a couple of run-outs as sub during this time. Unfortunately, they coincided with two of Liverpool's lowest points of the season. First was a humiliating League Cup defeat away to Second Division Sheffield United, for which I played the final twenty minutes, and then the game that ended our reign as Kings of Europe.

*

FOR ABOUT A FOUR-YEAR PERIOD, EVERY GAME WITH NOTTINGHAM Forest was huge. I'd liken the rivalry to the one that's existed between Liverpool and Chelsea in recent years. We met so many times in all the different cup competitions that we became a thorn in each other's side.

The previous season's League Cup final defeat was still fresh in the memory, as was the fact that they'd taken our championship crown. It was almost inevitable then that we'd be drawn together at some point in the 1978/79 European Cup. What I don't think any of us expected was to be paired at the first hurdle. There were audible gasps from both sides when news of the draw filtered through. I'm sure they wanted to avoid us as much as we wanted to avoid them, but I bet there wouldn't have been too many tears shed at the UEFA headquarters in Switzerland.

Playing in the European Cup should have been all about visiting glamorous cities: the likes of Rome, Paris, Madrid or Munich. A trip to Nottingham was definitely not what it was supposed to be about. I remember driving towards the City Ground on the bus that evening for the first leg and it was such a strange sensation. It just didn't have the feel of a European tie. Because of this, our approach maybe wasn't what it should have been and we eventually came unstuck.

I was an unused substitute that night. We fell behind to a first-half Garry Birtles goal and I could only watch on helplessly as we pushed for an equaliser when normally we'd have been content to take a 1–0 first-leg deficit back to Anfield. Three minutes from time Forest hit us on the break and full-back Colin Barrett plunged a dagger into our hearts.

We always felt capable of overturning any deficit, especially at home, with the power of the Kop behind us. It wasn't as if we hadn't done it before. Rekindling the spirit of St Etienne was inevitably mentioned in a number of interviews prior to the return with Forest but the task facing us this night was much sterner. At the time, no Liverpool team had ever turned around a 2–0 first-leg defeat in Europe and it was clear from the outset that goalscoring chances were going to be very limited.

What Nottingham Forest did that night was 'park the bus' in a style very reminiscent of Chelsea when they came to Anfield for that infamous game which derailed Liverpool's bid for the Premier League in April 2014. The tactics employed by José Mourinho on that day were nothing new. Thirty-six years earlier Brian Clough's side just sat back and invited us to pump long balls into their box.

When I went on in the 71st minute the aggregate score remained 2–0 in Forest's favour. My brief was to try and get in around the back of their cast-iron rearguard and cause as much trouble as I could. Try as I did, it just wasn't happening. They were absolutely resolute. The centre-back pairing of Kenny Burns and ex-Red Larry Lloyd were cited as being a possible area of weakness due to their obvious lack of pace but they were a great partnership, one based on good old-fashioned defensive solidity, and there was no way past them that night. We were restricted to the odd shot from distance and with the formidable Peter Shilton between the sticks it was always going to take something special to beat him from that range.

When the final whistle sounded a shroud of utter desolation came over us. We were Kings of Europe no more. Phil Thompson had to be dragged up off his knees. He looked how the rest of us felt. The supporters did their best to lift our spirits but they were hurting too. It had been a massive blow just to be drawn against Forest. To go out against them at the first stage of the competition was simply devastating.

The first European Cup win in 1977 was like the Holy Grail. The hardest thing was to then defend it and once we'd done that we harboured high hopes of going on to create a Real Madrid-style dynasty. Or, at the very least, emulate the more recent achievements of Ajax and Bayern Munich, who had won three in a row. This was the level we were at in the autumn of 1978. While we didn't take success for granted that year, having won it back-to-back the previous two seasons, we certainly expected to go a lot further in the competition than we did.

Maybe it was only another English team who'd have been capable of ending our run. Perhaps UEFA thought that way too, hence the reason that we were pitched together so early in the competition. Or am I being too cynical?

The Forest result was one that certainly pleased most of the so-called neutrals. Like those at local TV station Granada, for example, who, at the end of that night's highlights show, cruelly played out with Frank Sinatra's version of 'The Party's Over'. Not surprisingly it didn't go down too well on Merseyside and has still not been forgotten.

It might well have had something to do with the fact that the studio was based in Manchester and those Mancunians must have been sick to the back teeth of our success. In truth, it was probably nothing more than a bit of fun, but we didn't appreciate it being at our expense. In our eyes, Liverpool, as the country's standard-bearers in Europe, had earned the right to be treated with a bit more respect than that.

It was symptomatic of the attitude to success in this country. I never have understood the peculiar British pastime of knocking those that succeed. It happens all the time, especially in sport. Just as quick as the media are in building someone up, they are then only too quick to gloat when that particular individual or team start showing signs that they are on the way back down. It's the same with the general public. They revel in supporting the underdog and take gallant losers to their hearts more than proven champions, although I have to say I don't think we were ever universally hated, except maybe in Manchester. I've heard so many fans down the years say we were their second team and I think that's because at Liverpool we never gloated about our success. I believe we were always gracious in victory and defeat.

Of course, contrary to the words of the song, Liverpool's European Cup exit to Nottingham Forest did not signal the end of an era, even though it felt like it at the time. It would be just a temporary blip and – as the critics were soon to discover – you wrote that Liverpool team off at your peril. It did usher in a new period of dominance on the continent as Forest went on to emulate our feat of winning successive European Cups, but Bob Paisley's team would be back.

Unfortunately, for me personally, while the party was not yet exactly over, chucking-out time seemed to be drawing closer. In the immediate aftermath of our European exit I dropped completely out of the first-team picture. There were repeated calls in the letters page of the *Football Echo* for me to start but they fell on deaf ears. For the next two months I didn't even get a sniff of the first team. On most days I still trained with the lads but when it came to match day I was nowhere to be seen, not even as sub. No matter how many goals I banged in for the reserves – and during October I enjoyed a run of scoring in five successive games – there seemed to be no end to the nightmare. To be back plying my trade in front of just a few hundred spectators for the reserves, so soon after being a European Cup winner, was soul-destroying.

I had no option other than to confront the manager. I'd never done this before but I plucked up the courage and went in to see him. I'd had enough and told him I wanted to go. There was always a string of clubs linked with me whenever I was out of the team. Manchester City and Anderlecht were just two that seemed to be constantly cropping up alongside my name in the transfer-rumour columns of the sports pages and it was no different this time around. So I said my piece and explained how I felt. He sat there, listened and nodded in agreement. It was a Thursday afternoon and I came out of his office happy in the knowledge that the situation looked to be heading towards an amicable conclusion. Jeff Ainsworth and one of the other reserve lads I used to knock about with were waiting outside in the car park. 'He's going to let me go,' I said, 'it's over for me here.'

I was deeply saddened that it had come to this but at the same time it felt good to have voiced my feelings. In my mind the future was now clear and it was like a huge weight had been lifted. Three days later, on the Sunday, a story appeared in the News of the World in which Paisley was quoted as saying: 'I had a chat with Dave earlier in the week, he's happy here and willing to fight for his place.' I was flabbergasted. That's not what was said at all. The truth was that he just didn't want me to go. Maybe he was worried that I'd come back to haunt him. I don't know. What I did know was that there was nothing I could do. There were no agents back then who I could call on to try and force through a move.

To make matters worse, I was also still going through a tough time off the pitch. It had now been over a year since my dad had passed away and the pain of losing him did not seem to be getting any easier. My mum was also still struggling to cope with our loss and I can only imagine how extremely difficult it must have been for my fifteen-year-old sister. We were all struggling with our own particular form of grief and all needed different help. Maybe if there had been more male figures in the family, especially an older brother, then it might have been a bit easier, but within the family circle it was down to me to help my mum and try and assume some responsibility.

I know as well as anyone that there's a huge amount of support available these days for anyone going through the grieving process. It's so vital. Back in the late 1970s there was just nothing like that about. Throw into the mix the fact that my career was seemingly heading towards a crucial crossroads and the suffocating stress of it all was really starting to take its toll. But while football was one part of my problems, it also offered me an escape route from the pressure that was building. A few good games and all of a sudden I'd have a much brighter outlook on life.

Thankfully, having so far endured a season to forget, I was about to enjoy a mini-revival. My next start was against Anderlecht, one of the teams I'd recently been linked with. It was the second leg of the Super Cup final. I'd been an unused sub in the 3–1 first-leg defeat a fortnight earlier in Brussels, a match we had struggled in, and this was a big opportunity for me.

As we knew from our games with Bruges, Belgian football was on the rise and Anderlecht had a more than decent team. Francois Van der Elst and Franky Vercauteren were two of their high-profile home-grown stars in a talented squad that could also boast the celebrated Dutch international duo Arie Haan and Robbie Rensenbrink. The weather in the run-up to the game had been icy. It was the start of a severe arctic spell that would disrupt the English football calendar for the next month or so. As a result the pitch was rock hard but then, as kick-off approached, the weather threw another obstacle in our way – dense fog.

It got so bad that you couldn't see from one side of the pitch to the other. The game was in severe jeopardy. There was inspection after inspection and I think the general consensus was that it would be called off. The only problem was that if it couldn't be played that night there were question marks over when it would ever take place because neither side nor UEFA could agree on a rearranged date.

We were sat around in the players' lounge waiting to be told if it would be played and I was probably more anxious than most for it to go ahead because it was going to be a rare start for me. The conditions were far from ideal and the tricky pitch wasn't conducive to how I played but I felt I did OK. I think the best players in the world would have struggled to shine that night. It was quite treacherous underfoot and at times it was a struggle to see the opposition in front of us, such was the thickness of the fog. It was a bizarre game, the type I'd have loved to play in when out on the streets as a kid, but for the final of the European Super Cup it was a bit farcical.

Emlyn opened the scoring for us early in the first half only for Francois van der Elst to all but kill our hopes with a goal on the counter-attack midway through the second period. I did what I'd hoped to do, scoring at the Kop End five minutes from time and making my point. It proved to be the winner on the night but not enough to overturn the first-leg defeat. As finals go it's probably not one that will have lived long in the memory of those who were there. It's a game best remembered for the fog, but while the European Super Cup may not have figured high on our list of priorities it was always disappointing to miss out on silverware.

My goal that night was significant only for the fact that in the record books I remain the only Liverpool player to score in three separate Super Cup final games. Of greater importance to me personally was whether that goal would be enough to keep me in the team. Given my previous experiences that season I wasn't too hopeful so it came as a pleasant surprise when I was handed the number nine shirt again for the Boxing Day trip to Old Trafford.

Now this was a match that will occupy a more prominent place in the memory banks of those Liverpudlians lucky enough to be there. Unfortunately, the game wasn't televised and therefore the masses missed out on a performance that must rank as one of Liverpool's all-time finest at this particular venue.

In pure footballing terms United, at the time, were not one of our strongest rivals and so we probably were expected to win. Nevertheless, there was always an added competitive edge to this fixture and so to come away with a 3–0 win was a more than notable achievement.

Goals by Ray Kennedy and Jimmy Case saw us cruise into a 2–0 lead inside the opening 25 minutes. It was nothing less than we deserved. The home fans were stunned and Ray Clemence was a virtual spectator as we threatened to run up a cricket score. Had our overall superiority on the afternoon been mirrored in terms of goals scored then this would have been a performance to rival the annihilation of Spurs earlier in the season. As it was, we must have been feeling a bit generous because it was Christmas and took our foot off the gas slightly for a brief spell in the second half. All it did was lull United into a false sense of security. Just when they started to believe that they somehow had a chance of dragging themselves back into the game I proceeded to take centre stage.

It was the 67th minute. We were attacking the scoreboard end and I netted with a solo effort to make it 3–0. According to the reports it was a 'brilliant' goal and I'm often reminded about it by the Liverpool fans who were there. I recall that it involved a 'Cruyff' turn past Gordon McQueen, out towards the right corner of the penalty area, followed by a jinking run that saw me cut a swathe through a further three defenders before flicking the ball past Gary Bailey. It must have been good because according to the match report in the *Liverpool Echo*, even a section of the home crowd stood up to acknowledge it. When has that ever happened to a Liverpool goalscorer at Old Trafford? I must admit I was too busy celebrating to notice but it is there in black and white, written by the man in the press box, so I assume it's true.

Because there were no major TV cameras present the goal has rarely been seen since and has therefore become even more special among those who witnessed it, similar to the famous Jan Molby strike against the same opponents in the 1980s. I'm not sure if my memory is playing tricks on me here but I do have a vague recollection of it being shown on the news that night. If it was then I just hope the tape hasn't been scrubbed because these things do have a tendency to somehow resurface, like what happened with Jan's goal. Nowadays, social media and the likes of YouTube are perfect for this sort of thing and I've seen a lot of my old goals this way in recent years.

So if anyone does have a copy, please put it out there. If it does one day appear then fingers crossed it's as good as I've made out. If it doesn't, then I've still got the memories.

It's always enjoyable to look back on victories over United, especially at Old Trafford, and because of the size of our win it's remained a big personal favourite. It would be another three decades before a Liverpool team was able to celebrate an equally emphatic win away to Manchester United.

After the match Bob Paisley told the press that the goal would do my confidence the world of good and he was right. Frustratingly, just as I found myself on a roll again, the fixture list was decimated by the weather and my good run of form slithered to a halt. With most of the country covered in a blanket of snow we managed to play just two games over the course of the next four weeks, both against Third Division Southend United in the FA Cup.

The first meeting was at Roots Hall and it had 'giant-killing' written all over it. The tie had already been postponed once and when we travelled back down there in the midweek it was again freezing cold. More snow fell while we slept during the afternoon and we woke to the news that it was again in doubt. I think the only reason it went ahead was because it was scheduled to be the main game on Sportsnight.

The record books show that we were held to a goalless draw but in reality it was a lucky escape for us. Apart from being relieved to have still been in the competition I remember the game for two curious reasons: playing with a white ball on a snowy pitch, and wearing my shorts back-to-front without realising for the entire ninety minutes.

The replay was a lot more straightforward and a comfortable 3–0 win secured a fourth-round tie at home to Blackburn. Again, that fell foul to weather at the first time of asking and instead we set off for a friendly in North Wales. It was arranged to provide us with some much-needed match practice. The Bangor City manager had convinced Bob Paisley that his club's Farrar Road ground was free of snow so off we went down the A55 and across the border. It quickly became clear that this particular part of North Wales had been affected by the weather as much as everywhere else and when we got to this tiny little non-league ground it came as no surprise that a layer of snow covered the sloping pitch. The boss struggled to get his words out as we arrived and realised how he'd been duped.

Now that we'd arrived there was no point in turning back. We were all desperate for a run-out and didn't want to disappoint the expected full-house that was hoping to catch a rare glimpse of the previous season's European champions. The game was little more than a light training session for us but, for the record, we won 4–0 and I kept my goalscoring run going, so everyone went home happy. I think it was the only match played anywhere in the UK that day, and credit to the forward-thinking Bangor boss who had pulled off a major coup.

It kept us ticking over and a few days later we continued our progress in the FA Cup, courtesy of a late Kenny Dalglish winner against Blackburn. By now the weather was starting to show signs of improvement and in early February we played our first league game for nearly six weeks. During that time Ron Atkinson's West Brom had moved a point ahead of us at the top of the table and it was they who we lined up against at Anfield.

There might have still been a long way to go in terms of the title race but this was being billed as a championship decider. In reality it was always going to be more a barometer of Albion's progress than anything else and, to be fair, they made it tough for us. They were a genuinely good side. Atkinson had assembled an exciting team that included a young Bryan Robson and the so-called 'Three Degrees' – Brendan Batson, Laurie Cunningham and Cyril Regis – who had recently hit the headlines by becoming three of the first high-profile black players in English football.

Despite the poor state of the pitch, which was showing the ill-effects of the recent big chill, Albion played with a lot of confidence and it made for an enthralling game, one that lived up to the pre-match hype. Luckily for us, Kenny was on top form that afternoon. Sadly, I couldn't say the same for myself. I wasn't having the best of games and, for the first time ever, I was aware of the crowd starting to get on my back. It was one of those matches when the little things just weren't coming off for me. We'd taken an early lead through Kenny but I'd squandered a couple of chances to double the advantage and the longer the game wore on, with the destiny of the points still hanging in the balance, and West Brom coming back into it, I could sense the anxiety starting to creep in, on and off the pitch.

There was one particular moment when an opportunity came my way. My usual instinct was to shoot at first sight of the goal but for some reason I hesitated. What had been a promising move broke down and the frustration of the fans began to boil over. It was nothing malicious and I probably should have ignored their disappointment completely because no one was more down than me when I missed a chance. I must admit, it knocked me sideways for a short spell.

I was suddenly paying too much attention to the crowd's reaction and picking up on any murmurs of discontent, because previously they'd always been very supportive towards me. Thankfully I managed to regain my focus; when a chance, similar to the one I'd wasted earlier, came my way shortly after half-time I reverted to type and manoeuvred the ball on to my right foot to hit a low shot into the left corner of Tony Godden's net right in front of the Kop.

In the act of celebrating I tried to let the crowd know how I felt. Apart from the really important goals, like St Etienne, my celebrations were normally quite understated. On this occasion I acted as though I'd just scored a winner in the cup final. It was probably a touch overzealous on my part – I allowed my emotions to get the better of me and my own frustration spilled out. Describing the goal later, BBC commentator John Motson says, 'Look how excited he is,' totally unaware of my reasons. Maybe I'd been too sensitive. West Brom managed to pull a goal back to ensure a tense finish but we hung on to secure the points that took us back to the top of the table.

It was a vital win. But by the time an eleventh league title was wrapped up in May my chances of claiming a medal had long since been dashed. In them days you had to have figured in at least 14 of your teams 42 games and I was to finish the season having played in only four. Following a home draw with Everton in mid-March I was ruled out for a prolonged spell with a thigh injury that took longer to heal than originally thought.

I had come off the bench with sixteen minutes remaining and had not been on long when I felt a twinge after attempting a long-range volley. I think it was a case of not warming up sufficiently and because of it my season was all but over, just as it was starting to get going. Knowing it was an injury that could have been prevented made it even more frustrating and with the team chasing a coveted League and FA Cup double, the timing couldn't have been worse.

Still, I belatedly managed to regain my fitness just before the campaign was out and returned for the final game, a rearranged fixture away to Leeds on a Thursday night. Although Manchester United had ended our cup interest at the semifinal stage, the title had been clinched with two games to spare. Yet this was not your normal end-of-season dead rubber.

As we headed across the Pennines there was still plenty to play for. A certain national newspaper had offered a £50,000 prize for the team that could average two goals a game over the course of the 42-game league season. With one game left to play Liverpool were just two goals shy of the target. There was a determined mood within the camp and although I was only named as substitute, having missed out on the title celebrations I was hoping to finish the campaign on something of a high by helping us to cash in.

By half-time the jackpot had been claimed with ruthless efficiency, although there was an amusing incident during that first half, when it was still 1–0. Graeme Souness had the ball in the back of the net for what should have been the goal that clinched the prize, only for it to be promptly disallowed for offside. Normally the lads were quite well disciplined when it came to matters such as this. We were instructed not to argue with the officials but I'd never seen a reaction as vehement as on this occasion. They went absolutely berserk, as if they were the victims of daylight robbery and the money had been snatched from their grasp. The Leeds fans sat around us by the dugout were bemused but a second goal quickly followed to ensure the money was banked and we were all happy.

With mission accomplished in terms of goals scored, I was looking forward to getting on and stretching my legs for the final time that season during the second half. There was now a carnival atmosphere inside Elland Road and when David Johnson, with his second of the night, made it 3–0 shortly after the break I assumed that the call to get changed would come any minute. But I waited and I waited until it was too late. When the final whistle sounded to bring the curtain down on what had been a quite remarkable league season for the club there was plenty of back-slapping and hand-shaking but I was left frustrated. I just couldn't understand the logic of not giving your sub a run-out in such circumstances. It wasn't the first time, and nor would it be the last, that I found myself in this type of situation.

In the eyes of many pundits the Liverpool class of 1978/79 is one of the greatest in the club's history. The league stats alone back it up. A record number of points gained (68) with an all-time high goal difference (plus-69) recorded in the process. It was certainly a championship won in style. But having made just four league appearances I couldn't claim to have played any meaningful part.

Winning the European Cup should have been the springboard for me to go on and finally fulfil my vast potential. Instead, it had been the prelude to the worst season yet of my professional career.

12

NO CHANGE
AT THE KOP

AS I'D ALREADY EXPERIENCED ON SEVERAL OCCASIONS, FORTUNES can quickly change in football. Whether you're a manager, player or supporter, it's a fickle business. From zero to hero and back again, it can all happen in the blink of an eye. And I was becoming well accustomed to it. With this in mind I prepared for the 1979/80 season hoping for a change of luck.

Unfortunately, although I returned to training fully fit and recharged, I found myself still paying the price of the previous season's thigh injury. In my absence David Johnson had established himself as Kenny's regular strike partner and it was he who started the 1979/80 campaign in possession of the number nine shirt. I'd slipped down the pecking order and faced an uphill battle trying to win it back, especially with Johnno in the form of his life. Added competition came in shape of Frank McGarvey, a summer recruit from St Mirren, of whom big things were expected.

After opening my account for the season with our final goal in a comfortable League Cup victory at home to local minnows Tranmere Rovers, I started a game for the first time in seven months when another quest for European success kicked off at home to Dinamo Tbilisi. The Soviet champions were something of an unknown quantity but at least this time we'd avoided our now all too familiar foes from the City Ground.

For some reason I wore number six that night. We were hoping to make amends following the previous season's painful first-round exit but Tbilisi shocked us. They looked like world-beaters, with Aleksandr Chivadze and Ramaz Shengelia the pick of a very talented bunch. Although we scraped through the first leg with a 2–1 win it was never going to be enough. I was on the bench for the return in Georgia and when I finally got on three minutes from time our European aspirations were over for another season.

The trip to Tbilisi had been an ordeal from start to finish. From the moment we were forced to travel by Aeroflot and go via Moscow, it seemed as though some crafty tactics were already in play. Once in Georgia they used every trick to unsettle us. In the middle of the night we were woken by a demonstration right in front of the team hotel, which led to most of the boys throwing fruit out of the windows to try and silence the noisy gathering. It was clear that they viewed us as fearsome op-ponents and we encountered many other obstacles in the lead-up to the match itself. Such dirty tricks were nothing new, especially when travelling to Eastern Europe, but on this occasion they certainly worked. The 3–0 defeat was Liverpool's heaviest in Europe for thirteen years and another damaging blow to our pride.

It sparked calls for a revamp of the squad and I've no doubt that in the modern era there would have been serious repercussions. Thankfully, Liverpool, under the wily watch of John Smith and Peter Robinson, continued to be a well-run ship and they were more than aware of the fine margins that defined success and failure in the old-style European Cup.

The two-legged defeat to Tbilisi proved that teams just couldn't afford an off-day in this competition. Under the modern rules of the Champions League it's a fair bet that we'd have recovered from that loss and still have been able to qualify for the latter stages. In that respect, the do-or-die nature of the competition under its previous guise certainly offered more in terms of excitement, especially in the opening rounds.

It was a risky business, that's for sure; for those in the corridors of power at Anfield, going out so early for the second season running must have been a concern. The amount of money at stake back then was nothing like it is today but the club had not long signed a ground-breaking shirt sponsorship deal with Japanese electri-cal manufacturers Hitachi and a continued presence in Europe was becoming a necessity.

Nothing much changed though. It never did. They saw no reason to rip up the system that had served them so well. They knew the players were good enough to get them back to the top and so kept faith in what we had. When it came to wheeling and dealing in the transfer market Bob Paisley and his scouting team made very few mistakes. Players were only released if deemed to be past their sell-by date and – with the exceptions of Larry Lloyd and Jimmy Case – hardly any ever came back to haunt us. At the same time, there was no point in just buying new players for the sake of it. If Liverpool signed a player it had to be the right player. Paisley's captures of celebrated Scottish trio Dalglish, Souness and Hansen, for example, are up there with the most inspired this club has ever made.

Of course, no manager can boast a 100 per cent success rate in the buying stakes and there were more than a few who failed to make the grade, including the afore-mentioned McGarvey, who returned to Scotland within a year after failing to make any sort of impact. Some might simply not have been good enough to succeed at Anfield but others were the victims of circumstance. As I knew only too well, and was constantly finding to my cost, breaking into this all-conquering Liverpool team and staying in it was no easy task.

It's interesting to note that between winning the European Cup in 1978 and claiming it for a third time in 1981, the playing personnel at Liverpool changed very little. Only my old reserve team-mate Sammy Lee broke through and established himself as what you would class a regular member of the side. The likes of Richard Money, Colin Irwin and Avi Cohen all came in from time to time to provide defen-sive cover but none could ever claim to be regulars.

With no European Cup dream to chase in 1979/80 the focus switched back to domestic matters and, while it might have been no consolation at the time, exit-ing continental competition at such an early stage left us free to launch an assault on total supremacy at home. By Christmas we were top and stayed there for the remainder of the season.

There was little festive cheer where I was concerned. In terms of my Liverpool career I was back in a dark place. Since the Tbilisi game I'd made just one appear-ance, albeit a two-goal match-winning one as a second-half substitute that saved us from embarrassment against Exeter City in the fourth round of the League Cup. With Kenny and Johnno enjoying such a prolific season together in attack I just couldn't get a look in. To be fair, the team's remarkable run of form would have made it difficult for any player to break in.

However, certain things continued to rile me. Like the manager's attitude in not giving me at least ten minutes off the bench when the lads were coasting to victory against Grimsby in the FA Cup. It was like the Leeds game all over again. Serious self-doubts over my Anfield future began to resurface and I was starting to question whether the boss really did rate me.

My mind was slightly put at ease on that matter after I went in to see him over these concerns. He explained that he'd been offered the chance to re-sign Kevin Keegan from Hamburg at the end of the season but had turned it down because he felt more than happy with the striking options already at his disposal. To have brought KK back to play up front alongside Kenny would have been a massive coup for the club so I felt reassured that Paisley did still have some faith in me.

With that in mind I was hopeful that another opening would soon come my way, so in readiness I started to stay behind at Melwood to do some extra training. We didn't get too much shooting practice during the normal sessions as they were based mainly on passing. As I'd been spending most of my time with the reserves, a few of us, including goalkeeper Steve Ogrizovic, went back to the training ground one Wednesday afternoon to do some finishing work on our own.

The practice went well until we were packing things up and moving the portable goal. I collided with the frame and in doing so cut my head. I had to go to hospital to have it looked at and the next day the incident was reported to the training staff. Ronnie Moran went berserk and gave us a right bollocking. 'We'll tell you when you need shooting practice,' he roared, while telling the groundsman never to allow any more DIY after-hours training sessions.

At that point I thought any hopes of a recall for the time being would be gone but in early February, totally out of the blue, an injury to David Johnson saw me handed a surprise start, my first in four months. It was against Norwich at Carrow Road and it was one of those games that only seem to come around once in a while. It was also an afternoon when my extra shooting practice would prove vital. We fell behind to a Martin Peters goal in the first minute but I drew us level almost straight away. Following a one-two with Sammy Lee I cut in from the right to drill a shot past the Norwich goalkeeper Kevin Keelan.

Before the game Bob Paisley had sidled over to me and said, 'We were watching their keeper on Wednesday and noticed that when he dives to his right he's got short arms!' In truth I wasn't entirely sure what he meant, but it proved to be a valuable piece of information. I took on board what he said and kept trying to place my shots to that side. It worked for the equaliser and I did it again for the goal that put us 2–1 ahead: a first-time strike from the right edge of the area following a great run by Alan Hansen.

After Kevin Reeves made it 2–2, I restored our advantage in the 75th minute with a simple tap-in at the far post. It didn't immediately dawn on me that I'd just completed my first senior hat-trick. My only concern at the time was that we now held on to our lead and saw the game out to clinch maximum points. At 3–2 though, and with me having scored all our goals, I was on course to be the hero. What better way to announce my return to the first team, I was thinking. Unfortunately, although we did go on to win the game, Justin Fashanu stole my thunder somewhat with his famous 'goal of the season', a spectacular dipping volley from the edge of the box that had Clem well beaten. Many years later I watched a re-run of the game and, although I enjoyed watching the three goals, I didn't sleep that night thinking of the chance I'd missed that could have made it 4–3.

Thankfully, two late goals from Jimmy Case and Kenny Dalglish completed a memorable 5–3 victory. All the talk afterwards was of Fashanu's goal and at the final whistle it didn't even cross my mind to grab the match ball, like you see players do nowadays. It was only after I'd showered and changed that someone came into the dressing room and handed over what they claimed to be the ball we'd just been playing with. It was an old tatty thing, with the leather peeling off it. All the lads signed it so it would have been a nice souvenir to keep but it was in danger of falling to pieces even then. Although I've kept many mementoes from my career that one didn't last too long and a few years later it ended up on the tip.

Normally I'd have had good reason to celebrate and, although the manager had said nothing of note to me on the long journey home, I was confident that my performance at Carrow Road would be more than enough to keep me in the team. Arriving back in Liverpool, a few of us did go to Sammy Lee's 21st birthday party but were very aware we were in a busy period fixture-wise. It was one that would see us play seven times in just under three weeks, so the focus quickly switched to the next task in hand as we prepared to resume hostilities with Nottingham Forest in the second leg of the League Cup semifinal three nights later.

It was a big game, the type I thrived on and was eager to play in. We'd lost the first leg 1–0 so there was everything still to play for. Wembley was in our sights once again and a capacity crowd packed into Anfield to witness the latest chapter in this now well-established rivalry. To my amazement I was a spectator for much of it myself; back on the bench despite my hat-trick heroics at the weekend. I could not believe it. If scoring three goals couldn't guarantee me a place in the starting eleven I didn't know what could. In one way, it didn't surprise me because I was getting used to being treated like this and it only reinforced my feelings of frustration. It was clearly evident that I was now fighting a losing battle.

From the dugout I watched our aspirations of reaching the final all but disappear halfway through the first half when John Robertson scored from the penalty spot, just as he had done in the first leg at the City Ground. I was summoned to enter the fray shortly before the hour mark and had a goal disallowed for offside before I finally managed to draw us level on the night in the 89th minute. It was too little too late, and for the second time in three seasons Forest had thwarted our hopes of winning the League Cup for a first time.

Although it was no consolation at the time, my goal had helped preserve our proud unbeaten home record that stretched back to February 1978 and would continue for almost another year. But again, it was not enough to earn me a starting place for the next match. Third Division Bury were the visitors to Anfield for a fifth-round FA Cup tie and for the opening hour a major shock looked very much on the cards. I came on in place of David Johnson at half-time and before the full-time whistle sounded I'd scored twice to spare our blushes.

I knew straight away what the headlines would be in the following day's papers. Supersub was back. It had been a decent week and despite starting just one of three games my six-goal haul was enough to earn me the Observer newspaper's 'Sportsman of the Week' award. It was the prelude to a spell of three successive starts, during which I netted the opening goal in another important match, my seventh in five games. It was at home to fellow title-challengers Ipswich, a game best remembered for the controversial incident in which Frans Thijssen threw mud at the ball as Terry McDermott ran up to take a penalty kick. It happened four minutes from the end and Terry's subsequent effort was saved, thus denying us maximum points.

Two weeks later I was back on the bench as our number ten hit the headlines again. Thankfully it was for the right reasons, his stunning long-range volley settling a tense FA Cup quarterfinal away to Tottenham. It set up the famous long-running semifinal showdown with Arsenal – four epic games that remain so vivid in the memory.

With the league becoming something of a procession, a bit boring even, when the FA Cup ties came around, especially in the absence of European football, they seemed so much more glamorous. Saying that, the first meeting at Hillsborough was a non-event. Semifinals were always the most nerve-racking of games to play in and I came on ten minutes into the second half of what was a typically cagey affair. The tension of the occasion got the better of both sides and neither of us could manage a breakthrough.

The replay at Villa Park four nights later was the complete opposite, an absorbing contest that flowed from end to end. I played from the start and broke the deadlock in the tie after 51 minutes. I really thought it was going to be the goal to put us in the FA Cup final and if it had I'd have rated that strike right up there alongside my most memorable because it would have meant so much. Unfortunately Alan Sunderland equalised about ten minutes later. There was a touch of controversy about it because we thought it looked offside and come the end of extra-time, with no further goals having been scored, we certainly felt hard done by.

Before the second replay, again at the home of Aston Villa, we met in the league at Anfield and even that game ended in a 1–1 draw. So intense was our focus on the FA Cup at this time that my memories of that game are vague. What I do know is that there was just nothing to choose between the two teams. We may have been ahead of them in terms of places in the First Division but when it came to the FA Cup Arsenal could raise their game. They were renowned cup battlers and aiming to reach the final for a third successive season.

In Alan Sunderland they possessed a man for the big occasion. He'd scored a dramatic winner in the previous year's final and after cancelling out my goal in the first replay he was at it again in the next meeting, netting one of the quickest goals in FA Cup history. Arsenal kicked off and before any Liverpool player had touched the ball he'd put it in the back of our net. To say we were stunned would be an understatement. When I was introduced at half-time we still trailed 1–0 and as the minutes ticked by our efforts were becoming more and more frantic.

It was in the midst of a desperate goalmouth scramble near the end that I suffered a nasty cut to my head after colliding with David Johnson. We both hit the floor and were in a pretty bad way. There was blood pouring from the wounds but Johnno was in a worse state than me and was stretchered off, meaning we were temporarily down to ten men. I could do nothing but soldier on with just a bit of Vaseline applied to a cut that later needed three stitches. A goal down and now a man down, we'd reached desperation stakes, but because of the break in play while treatment was administered, about four minutes of injury-time was added on and it was deep into this that Kenny finally got the ball past Pat Jennings to sensationally hand us a lifeline.

The relief was palpable. There was barely time to restart the game and another exhausting half-hour of extra-time ensued. It was like two heavyweight boxers going toe-to-toe. We might have been getting more sluggish by the minute but the entertainment on show was compelling. Yet again, come the final whistle, there was still nothing to separate us.

Coventry's Highfield Road was the chosen destination for the next instalment of what was now developing into a marathon-sized saga. How the supporters were able to finance all these away trips I don't know. It was no doubt hitting them hard in the pocket but they too were gripped by the drama and full credit to them, because they were there in their thousands at each one. While no doubt rubbing their hands together at the prospect of their cut of the extra gate receipts, the Football Association was now probably starting to get a little worried. There seemed to be no end in sight for this tie and, with the third replay taking place just nine days before the scheduled date of the final, contingency plans were being drawn up should any more replays have been needed.

Unfortunately, on Thursday 1 May the final curtain came down on the longest-running FA Cup semifinal of the twentieth century. And for Liverpool it was a tear-jerking finale. The goal that eventually settled the tie came via the head of Brian Talbot after just eleven minutes following a rare slip by Ray Kennedy. We were well aware of the threat posed by Talbot because Bob Paisley had singled him out at the start of every one of these four games, even though he got confused and kept calling him 'Osborne', in reference to Talbot's former Ipswich Town team-mate Roger. I came on to replace David Johnson for the last quarter of an hour but there was to be no more drama. The FA Cup dream was over for another year and with it our hopes of becoming only the third team that century to complete the double.

It was a cruel conclusion to an epic battle and I think it's sad that we'll never again see the likes of that famous quartet of games. I can understand the reasons for scrapping multiple replays nowadays but it was all part and parcel of what used to make the FA Cup so magical. People still talk about them now. Semifinals are the hardest and most nerve-shredding type of games to play in anyway but those four tension-fuelled games really were something else and I became a stronger player for the experience of being involved in them. Had it been decided on penalties after the first game, like they are now, then I'm sure it would have been long forgotten.

It's right what they say about the pain of losing in a semifinal. It really is one of the worse feelings in football. To have lost the first game against Arsenal would have been hard to get over but to lose after four games as gruelling as those absolutely floored us. They not only sapped us of our energy, they were also so mentally tough that our emotions were all over the place. When it was all finally over the mood in the dressing room at Highfield Road was one of total despair. Our sights had been firmly set on ending the season with a day out beneath the twin towers. Since beating Newcastle at Wembley in 1974 the club had won almost everything but we just couldn't get over the line in the FA Cup. That was a major source of frustration and disappointment for this otherwise magnificent Liverpool team.

Fortunately, the small matter of wrapping up a twelfth League Championship helped ease the pain and when Liverpool welcomed Aston Villa to Anfield just two days later there was a party atmosphere as a 4–1 victory sparked what were now familiar title celebrations. I didn't feature that day, having made Ronnie Moran aware that I was feeling a pain in my thigh. It was nothing too serious but it was thought best not to risk it. In hindsight I shouldn't have been so honest. I know plenty of players who carried injuries into games and it remains a big regret of mine that I denied myself the chance of being involved in another famous title-clincher, even if I'd have only probably started on the bench.

Dressed in my civvies I managed to play a small part in the post-match pomp and ceremony when, together with Alan Kennedy, I helped carry the trophy out on to the pitch ready for the official presentation. A second-half appearance in the final game of the season away to Middlesbrough the following midweek then ensured I had played just enough games to qualify for a championship medal, unlike the previous campaign when I missed out.

The following season would be Liverpool's worst in the league for ten years. Aspirations of a third successive title faded early but in the autumn of 1980 I found myself revelling in the hottest scoring streak of my Anfield career. Seven goals in six starts proved once and for all that I wasn't just an impact player. It had taken a while but I felt as though I'd finally convinced the doubters. I was enjoying my football more than at any point since I'd first broken into the team. I was still only 23 and the future looked bright once again.

My purple patch in front of goal began with two in a 4–0 win at home to West Brom. It would have been three had Bryan Robson not denied me my second senior hat-trick by deliberately punching my goal-bound header over the bar midway through the first half. I then scored with a header that earned us a point in a 2–2 draw against Southampton at the Dell, netted in a 5–0 League Cup defeat of Swindon and completed the scoring with my right foot at the Kop end as Brighton were defeated 4–1.

It was towards the end of that game against the Seagulls that I became aware of some discomfort in my knee. It locked on me and the pain was terrible. I somehow managed to unlock it but having seen a few of my friends from the reserve team suffer something similar I feared the worst. I didn't mention anything to the coaching staff afterwards and decided to see how it went.

That night I was having a house-warming party, having finally moved out of my mum's and bought a house in Sandfield Park in West Derby, close to the club's Melwood training ground, but as the evening wore on the pain in my knee became more severe and my concern grew. First thing the next morning I headed up to Anfield for treatment. Nothing untoward was diagnosed and even though I was still in agony I didn't admit to it because that would have seen me immediately ruled out of the next game – a midweek European Cup tie against the hapless Finns Oulun Palloseura. I'd learned my lessons from previous occasions and the fear of losing my place in the team was enormous.

On a night when it rained goals at Anfield I scored two with my head, our eighth and ninth in a 10–1 rout. My knee still didn't feel right but I was scared of discovering the truth so I just tried to carry on as normal. I was hoping that I could maybe run the injury off. It was a foolish train of thought. Without seeking any further treatment I played again on the Saturday, away to Manchester City.

It proved to be one game too many because my movement was severely restricted and as I found it harder and harder to get around the pitch my knee finally gave way on me. I was forced to limp off in the 69th minute, replaced by Howard Gayle who, in coming on for his debut, became the club's first-ever black player. I was pleased for Howie. I'd played alongside him in the reserves and we always got on well. But as I sat out the remainder of the game in the dugout both Joe and Ronnie said they suspected that I'd torn my cartilage.

As the news sank in that I required an operation I cursed my bad luck – to this day I can't remember how the game ended. I wouldn't play again until January. It was a devastating blow, especially given the form I was in. An increasingly familiar but frustrating pattern was emerging. Every time my career seemed on the up, a cruel twist of fate was lurking just around the corner, waiting to knock me back down. This time it hung around for a bit longer than expected.

Of all places it was back at Maine Road that I made my comeback in January. It was the League Cup semifinal first leg and after claiming a 1-0 win we had one foot in the final. The job was completed at Anfield a few weeks later but I played no part in that or the final. My return had been cut short – it lasted all of four games.

In an attempt to build up my match fitness it was thought that an extra run-out for the reserves might aid my recovery, but away to Derby County in mid-February I found myself on the receiving end of a high tackle by Keith Osgood. The pain in my knee was incredible and I knew straight away that I'd be sidelined again, only this time my absence would be a much longer one. My season was over and, having only just come through the recovery process, the thought of going through it all again was gut-wrenching.

It was the first major injury of my career. I'd been relatively lucky up to this point but now it was my turn to experience the anger, frustration and fear that comes with being seriously injured. It was an absolute nightmare time for me, the worst of my entire career.

I did everything in my power to get back to full fitness. I trained morning, noon and night, for hours and hours, on my own in the gym at Melwood, continually doing weights in an attempt to build up the muscles around my knee. I wouldn't leave until old Eli, the groundsman who had seemingly worked at the club forever, kicked me out when he was locking up. The discomfort was constant whenever I tried to move. I couldn't run or turn without a sharp pain shooting through my knee. The advice from within the club was that it would eventually heal itself but I was seeing no sign of that. There were no investigations or X-rays. All I was hearing in the treatment room was, 'Do you not think it might be all in your head?' That was a favourite old adage at Liverpool and I was just left to get on with it.

I remember being at home listening to radio commentary of the European Cup ties away to CSKA Sofia and Bayern Munich. The lads were on their way to another final in Paris, while I was left behind at Melwood feeling despondent, with no prospect of being involved in their quest for glory. I was walking freely, even running, but twisting and turning was now my big worry. I started reading up on what could be possibly causing the problem and, off my own back, even arranged to go and see various specialists.

However, the injury was not clearing up. People were queuing up to tell me what wasn't causing the pain but no one was able to tell me what was. I was reaching a point where I didn't know what else I could do and started to feel myself sinking, deeper and deeper, into a state of depression.

Were the club right and was the problem more psychological? Or was it much more serious and would I ever play again? These were the contrasting thoughts that were constantly spinning around my head as the 1980/81 season drew to a close.

As if that wasn't bad enough, on a rare gym-free afternoon I wasn't even able to relax in the comfort of my own home. It was a relatively overcast spring day and the new daytime television schedule seemed the best option for a lazy few hours on the couch. That was until the tranquil silence was pierced by the unexpected sound of the telephone ringing, the type that would normally have made me jump off the couch in panic had it not been for the pain in my knee.

On the other end of the line was Everton captain Mick Lyons. I always got on well with Mick. He was blue to the core but a great lad whose company I always enjoyed. While it was good to hear from him, his call came as a surprise. With the telephone in one hand I got myself comfortable on the big window seat in my living room and gazed out into the front garden as we exchanged pleasantries for a few minutes. Once that was over we got down to the real reason for him ringing. 'Our boss has asked me to give you a call,' said Mick. 'He's been made aware you will be available at the end of the season, how would you fancy coming to our place?'

'What?' It took a moment to fully comprehend what he'd just said. Everton want me. Liverpool don't. I was temporarily stunned and didn't know what to say. 'Would it be OK if he gives you a call?' Mick added. I was still trying to take it all in and wasn't thinking straight at all. 'Suppose so,' I muttered.

I thanked Mick for his call and put the phone down. What he made of my reaction I never did find out. For the rest of that day I was in a complete daze and didn't know what to do. Should I immediately confront Bob Paisley over this or was it best to wait and see if Everton followed up their interest? Could it be a wind-up? I didn't know what to think but I immediately dismissed the latter because I had no reason to disbelieve Mick – he was as honest as the day is long and too much of a professional to joke about something as serious as this.

I tried putting it to the back of mind, which was obviously easier said than done. I just couldn't shake it off. If Gordon Lee, the Everton manager, knew that the Anfield exit door was being opened for me, then other clubs must have known the same. The reality started to sink in that this was the beginning of the end for me at Liverpool.

In bed that night I tossed and turned. All manner of thoughts were going through my mind and I couldn't sleep. I eventually did but when I woke the next morning the pain in my knee acted as a timely reminder that this was my pressing concern. Until it was resolved I would be of no use to anyone.

While Liverpool supporters were being swept along by the romance of a third European Cup win in Paris, I was starting to believe that I'd kicked my last ever ball.

13

THE SECOND BEST TEAM ON MERSEYSIDE

AS A GREAT MAN ONCE SAID, THERE ARE ONLY TWO TEAMS ON Merseyside. I was lucky enough to play for them both and would spend almost the entire 1981/82 season turning out for the one he dubbed the second best.

The call from Gordon Lee never did materialise. Just a few weeks after Mick Lyons rang me, Everton sacked their manager in response to a league campaign that had seen them narrowly avoid relegation for the second time in successive seasons.

Whether I'd have made the move across Stanley Park is immaterial now but, despite the frustration I was feeling at Anfield, I honestly don't think I would have. No player had switched directly between the age-old rivals since Johnny Morrissey two decades before and although other boyhood Reds have played for the Blues and vice versa, I'm not so sure I could have done the same.

That's no disrespect to Everton as a club. I've got a lot of good friends who are of a blue persuasion. However, my relationship with my fellow Liverpool supporters is one I've always valued highly and I wouldn't have wanted to jeopardise that.

Of course, you shouldn't let sentiment cloud your judgement in football and if I'd believed the move would have been beneficial to all parties then I'd have had to consider it. As it was, I'm not convinced that it would have been the right move at that particular time.

At the start of the 1980s, Bill Shankly's famous quote about the best two teams in the city being Liverpool and Liverpool reserves had perhaps never had more foundation. Plying my trade for the second string of the European champions might have seemed like a step backwards in terms of my career but for once I wasn't complaining. I was just grateful to be playing again.

AS THE SUMMER OF 1981 APPROACHED, MY FOOTBALLING FUTURE hung precariously in the balance. There still seemed no end in sight to the injury nightmare that had curtailed my involvement in Liverpool's first League Cup win and third European Cup conquest.

It got to a point where I was getting quite desperate and exploring all options. From acupuncture to homeopathy, I was willing to try anything. One doctor even drew up a special diet plan that advised me to cut out all red meat. I must admit, it left me feeling great everywhere else but it wasn't able to cure the pain in my knee. I genuinely feared that I was finished.

Finally, after eleven weeks of worry and desperation the club accepted that there must be a reason for the constant pain I was suffering and agreed to look into it. I'd read about a procedure called arthroscopy, a type of keyhole surgery used to diagnose and treat injuries connected to joints. It was a relatively new procedure so I told Bob Paisley about it; he then found a guy who was pioneering some research into this and arranged for him to examine my knee.

It turned out that I had what they call 'roughening of the knee', caused because there was a crack in my femur and there'd been some rubbing going on between that and the back of my kneecap. It needed tidying up and so I was booked in to go under the knife on 23 June. It meant I had to cancel my summer holiday but that was a small price to pay if it meant my career would be saved.

I remember it being a lovely hot summer's day when I checked in at the Park House Nursing Home in Crosby for the op. Thankfully, everything went well, although I got the fright of my life when I came round after it. The first thing I saw was a nun standing at the end of the bed. I was still a bit groggy but for a moment I thought I hadn't pulled through.

Within a month I was training again. I successfully came through a couple of pre-season reserve team friendlies and was chomping at the bit to resume my career. I knew there was still some way to go before I'd be fully fit so I didn't want to rush things. This was going to take time. I had come back too soon in January and paid the price and I wasn't about to make the same mistake again. Fighting to regain my place in the first team could wait. For the time being I was focused solely on regaining my sharpness and getting myself fully match fit.

It felt great to be playing again and it was good to be back among old friends in the reserves. There was always a familiarity about pulling on the red shirt for Roy Evo's team. Other players who dropped out of the first team might have felt there was a stigma attached to 'slumming' it in the 'ressies'. For the likes of myself who'd been there before it was a case of stepping back into my comfort zone. True, there had been times earlier in my career when I might not have embraced the situation so readily but I now appreciated how precious a football career is and was determined to make the most of it.

If I'd have acted like a big-time Charlie and sulked because I thought reserve team football was beneath me then I'd have got no sympathy from the rest of the lads. I know, because that's what used to happen when I was an up-and-coming youngster in the reserves. We didn't take kindly to the 'bigheads' dropping down from the first team and not possessing the right attitude. Like everyone at the club, as a unit we wanted to win every game and the last thing we needed was a disruptive influence. It remained the same.

There were no shrinking violets in that reserve team dressing room either and if someone wasn't putting in a shift they'd be told in no uncertain terms. The stick that could be dished out by the first team might have been legendary but the same attitude ran through whatever team you played in at the club. No one was immune to being put in their place.

The team spirit and general camaraderie fostered by Roy was great and it was always good fun playing under him. I was always of the belief that a game for the reserves beat sitting on the bench for the first team. It's just that there wasn't the same buzz surrounding these second-string fixtures. Training all week without a big game at the end of it often felt hollow. Having experienced the highs of winning trophies with the senior side, strolling to another two points in the Central League just didn't stir the emotions quite so much.

Reserve team football had been good to me in the past though, and I'd never knock it. It helped launch my Liverpool career back in 1975 but life at Anfield had now seemingly come full circle for me. I was still only 24, an age when I should have been approaching my peak years. Had everything gone to plan I'd have been a long-established regular in the Liverpool first team at this point and well on my way to becoming one of the club's leading goalscorers. I'd have had a cabinet full of England caps and been preparing to take part in the forthcoming World Cup in Spain.

Instead, it felt like I was starting from scratch. Six years' experience at the top level, a glittering medal collection and raft of important goals now counted for nothing. The fame and fortune of being a first-team star doesn't wash when running out in front of one man and his dog in the Central League outposts of East Lancashire or the West Midlands. If these multimillionaire foreign players of today think the proverbial 'wet Tuesday night at Stoke' is a chore, I'd like to see their reaction to experiencing it in a near-deserted stadium with virtually nothing at stake.

It could be soul-destroying at times and was not how I had anticipated my career panning out, that's for sure. But I knew I was there for a purpose – to get back fit – and, of course, I needed no reminding that things could have been worse. Just a few months before, trying to walk was a struggle, never mind running around for ninety minutes against defenders whose only aim for the entire duration was to try and kick the living daylights out of me.

I was now the proverbial big fish in a small pond. The player young lads looked up to for advice and guidance. That felt strange but having been through it all before I knew what it was like for them. Most of the time, I was also the most well-known face in the team and therefore the obvious target for abuse from supporters when playing away from home.

There'd always be at least one bigmouth in the crowd and, though I tried not to let it wind me up, the shouts of 'You're rubbish, Fairclough' sometimes did get to me at places like Burnley and Blackburn. Equally, it sometimes helped inspire me and I have plenty of memories of scoring goals to temporarily silence them, which was always nice.

Because the grounds would be virtually empty, the abuse could be heard loud and clear. Sometimes it was funny and we would all have a good laugh about what was being directed at us. Other times it could annoy me to the point where I was left thinking, 'Just what the hell am I doing here?'

DURING MY ENTIRE ANFIELD CARER THERE WASN'T ONE SEASON when I didn't play for the reserves. I actually made more appearances in the Central League than the Football League and I'm proud of my association with the all-conquering teams managed by Roy Evans. But when I look back on my time at Liverpool, I consider myself, first and foremost, a former first-team player.

I was fortunate enough to make my breakthrough early and, if not always a regular in Bob Paisley's match-day squads, up until this point I had always been seen as more part of the senior group than a member of the reserves. The fact that I regularly dipped in and out of the first team (albeit more out than in for my liking) meant I maintained my connection with the reserves.

Since I first played for them back in 1974 nothing much ever changed. From the way we trained and played, which was a carbon-copy of the first team, to the amount of games we won and the craic among the lads in the dressing room. The only noticeable difference was in the playing personnel. Opportunities to progress were so few and far between that not many players hung around in the reserves for too long. Those who did tended to be the local lads, in particular ones who supported the club. They were reluctant to let go of their boyhood dreams and I could fully empathise with them over that. I still felt the same.

Players such as my old mate Brian Kettle instantly spring to mind as a prime example. Kets and I made our first-team debuts within a few days of each other back in 1975 but he managed only a further three appearances with the 'bigheads' , the last of these coming in 1977. Still, he clung on to the hope that his fortunes might change and remained at the club until 1980. Though he was 'thirteenth man' on a couple of occasions, in those days that counted for little. In the modern era, where the use of extra substitutes are allowed, it does present far more opportunity for young players to perhaps gain a chance. But as I've already explained and, as I knew only too well, breaking into the Liverpool first team of our era was an extremely difficult task.

Having briefly sampled the big time it must have been demoralising to play out the remaining three years of his Liverpool career in the reserves. To his credit, he didn't let his frustration show on the pitch and captained them to a couple of Central League titles before finally conceding defeat and signing for Wigan.

It was a similar story for other mates of mine, lads I've mentioned on previous pages. Colin Irwin made his reserve team debut before me and had to show the patience of a saint before finally making his senior bow on the opening day of the 1979/80 season. To be fair, his persistence was then rewarded with an extended run in the team, but others weren't so lucky. Max Thompson and Kevin Kewley are another two who had worked their way right through the ranks with me. Both can look back and say they played for Liverpool's first team but between them they figured in less than a handful of games before later moving to the US.

It must have been even worse for players such as Jeff Ainsworth, who eventually left the club without even making an appearance on the subs bench for the first team. As a schoolboy, Jeff's services had been courted by Don Revie's Leeds United and he was tipped for big things. Unfortunately, he suffered a serious knee injury at a crucial time. It severely hampered his progress and he eventually drifted out of the game. There are many more. Alex Cribley, who beat me in the penalty shoot-out at Goodison all those years earlier, is another one. The list is endless and it would continue well into the 1980s and beyond. When I think of all these lads I played alongside in the reserves I realise I was one of the lucky ones.

With such limited prospects, life as a Liverpool reserve could certainly be frustrating but, as the majority of those who failed to make the grade would discover when trying their luck elsewhere, adapting to life away from the club could be equally problematic and some found it difficult. Their quality was obvious for all to see but the comedown that came with leaving Anfield meant their heart was sometimes no longer in the game and they quickly drifted away. That happened to a lot of lads.

Of course, some found their level in the lower leagues and blossomed. Tommy Tynan, for instance, went on to be one of the most prolific scorers outside the First Division during the late 70s and early 80s. In later years other highly talented players like Bobby Savage, Mick Halsall, Steve Foley and Tony Kelly, all team-mates of mine in the reserves during this 1981/82 season, eventually left Liverpool without making that step up from the second string, yet each of them made names for themselves at a variety of clubs lower down the ladder.

There'll be many players who believe they were harshly treated at Anfield and deserved a chance but, if the truth be told, I believe that the coaching staff at Liverpool generally got it right when it came to promoting players from within. By and large, the ones for whom opportunity knocked were the ones who earned it. In my time at the club I can't think of many players who went on to prove themselves at the top level after failing to break out of the Liverpool reserve set-up.

One exception has to be Alan Harper, who went on to enjoy a successful stint at Everton during their glory years of the mid-80s. People may say that he slipped through the net, but think of who was blocking his path to the first team at Anfield – only Mr Consistency himself, Phil Neal, the man who made 417 consecutive appearances and became the club's most decorated player of all time. That's how stiff the competition was.

Another player who established strong links across Stanley Park after learning his trade on the red side was Kevin Sheedy. Kevin was actually given his chance on the left side of midfield before Ronnie Whelan. It came about because of a rare injury to Ray Kennedy. Unfortunately for Kevin, he then got injured himself, which paved the way for Ronnie to come through and establish himself.

As well as natural ability, a lot of it is also down to getting the breaks. The problem at Liverpool during this period was that first-team players were rarely injured and many were allowed to have the odd 'off day', meaning it was a virtual closed shop. As I've explained, I discovered this to my own cost and found it to be a very annoying aspect of life at the club. It also stifled the progress of anyone else coming through the ranks; but then, more often than not, when the trophies were totted up at the end of each season there could be no arguments. The management was almost always proved right.

Given that the strength in depth at Liverpool was so outstanding, it's no surprise that the standards within the reserve team were also consistently high. That might have brought with it high expectations but there was never a problem fulfilling them. The balance within the side always seemed to be right and whether it was a talented youngster, highly rated new signing or experienced professional, Roy Evans constantly had a vast array of talent at his disposal and his teams got used to winning comfortably almost every week. Between 1969 and 1985 Liverpool were champions of the Central League 14 times. How many other teams, no matter what level they're playing at, can boast consistency like that?

It begs the question – could any of these Liverpool reserve teams have held their own in the lower divisions of the Football League if given the opportunity? The success we enjoyed in the Central League certainly suggests that we could. My only doubt would be in terms of how the lads in the reserves would have coped with the physicality of lower-league football. Given the ease with which we won most games it was clear that we needed to be playing in a more competitive environment. While winning is a good habit to get into and one that breeds confidence in players, when playing at this level it's also important that you are constantly being tested.

The standard of the Central League was quite decent. Other teams had good players and there'd be some decent match-ups among the reserve teams but Liverpool's superiority reflected the overall dominance the club was enjoying at every level around this time.

Although nothing could beat playing for the first team, if you couldn't be one of the lucky eleven selected by Bob Paisley, this wasn't a bad alternative. The gulf in class between the two wasn't as big as it is now. Back in my day the step-up from A-team to reserve team football was the biggest. That's when lack of space and time on the ball was most noticeable.

There was also no age limit back then. Sixteen-year-old apprentices could be up against seasoned professionals twice their age. It certainly did us no harm. It helps to toughen young players up. Nowadays, players are playing within their own age group right through to under-21 level. It's said this is done to protect the individual, but surely there comes a time when a young player with potential needs to be thrown in at the deep end to see if he'll sink or swim. It's the only way to find out if they have what it takes.

*

DESPITE THE OBVIOUS DRAWBACKS TO PLAYING FOR THE RESERVES, during the first few months of the 1981/82 campaign I was really enjoying my football once again. As my knee grew stronger and the fitness levels increased, the goals started to flow and the confidence returned. It was like the old days. But although I've explained how I was delighted just to be playing again, once the New Year came I was starting to question why no first-team opportunities were coming my way.

Secretly, I had also started to do some extra training away from the club, working with an old-style weight-trainer in his gym near Sefton Park. 'Johnny Fitz' was an inspiration; he built up my confidence mentally and with his training methods I felt I had never been stronger. I thought it showed in my performances but despite doing well the manager stubbornly felt I was still not back to how I'd been before the injury.

In the twelve months since I had last appeared, the make-up of the side had changed significantly. It was a rare period of transition at the club, which meant saying goodbye to some more of the old guard in the shape of Ray Clemence and Jimmy Case. Ray Kennedy, Terry McDermott and David Johnson would also soon follow suit. New faces included Bruce Grobbelaar, Mark Lawrenson, Ronnie Whelan, Craig Johnston and, last but not least, a young striking sensation whose imperious form in front of goal would eventually have a direct impact on my own future at the club.

Amid the fanfare that had greeted Liverpool's title triumph of 1980, Ian Rush, a teenage capture from Chester City, slipped into Anfield almost unnoticed. Although he'd obviously been bought with a view to one day challenging myself and Johnno for a place alongside Kenny in attack, he was deemed to be one for the future, so his presence at the club did not unduly concern me at the time.

A year on and this was still the case. He hadn't exactly made a big impression during his first season at the club. He struggled to settle initially and on the few occasions that I played alongside him in the reserves that year he showed nothing to suggest there'd be such a goal-laden future ahead of him. He really didn't stand out in those first few months and I just didn't see him as a threat to my own ambitions. Frank McGarvey had been and gone without ever really challenging for a first-team place and, at this stage of his career, there was no guarantee that Rushie wouldn't go the same way.

While I'd been out injured the previous season though, Rush had come in for his first-team debut and then made several more appearances but failed to score in any of them. Around September 1981 we again played together for the reserves away at Wolves and, although the game ended 2–0 in our favour, I remember it as a turning point for him because afterwards the coaches were quite vociferous in their belief that he should be doing better. It was just a few days after Rush had scored his first senior goal so maybe he'd fallen into the trap of thinking he'd made it. That type of attitude was never tolerated at Liverpool and harsh words were exchanged. It certainly didn't do him any harm. Another opportunity in the first team quickly came his way. He scored two, then another two in the next match and didn't look back, embarking on a life-changing scoring spree.

It reminded me of the impact I had made back in 1976 and, while I never once begrudged him the success that was coming his way, it made me reflect more on my own fall from grace. I'll be honest, it could get me down at times and people would pick up on this. Our chief scout Geoff Twentyman, for example, would always do his best to try and keep my spirits up. I had a lot time for Geoff and I knew he had a soft spot for me; he had been instrumental in my joining the club. So when all the talk was of this new goalscoring machine from North Wales, a player Geoff himself had scouted, he would constantly be reassuring me that I possessed qualities Rush couldn't offer. 'He's good but can he go both ways?' was one of his familiar refrains.

A lot of people believed that the emergence of Rush was bad news for me but I didn't necessarily see it that way. We were different types of players. He played through the middle and nowhere else. I don't know what the general perception of me was among the fans but I'd imagine they saw me as an out-and-out striker similar to Rushie, probably because of the type of goals that I scored and because when I did come on as substitute it was often a forward that I replaced.

However, it was never the position I saw myself in at Liverpool. In my mind it was out wide where my long-term future lay at Anfield. That was the position I had started out in, where I felt I was always at my most dangerous and where I most enjoyed playing. Perhaps I was wrong in thinking it but I didn't want to be just a goalscorer. I enjoyed being involved in general play and always loved running with the ball, and the wide areas allowed more opportunity to do that.

I'D DROPPED WAY DOWN THE PECKING ORDER AT LIVERPOOL. SO much so that I didn't even make the substitutes bench in 1981/82, not a single appearance. I was even overlooked for the European games, when a much larger squad was required. I also missed out on a trip to Tokyo for the World Club Championship clash with Flamengo. That was a big disappointment; I had been desperate to be part of that. When Rushie dropped out through injury it meant there was one remaining place in the squad up for grabs and it was touch and go who filled it. It was the first time ever that the players had to wear shirts with their names on the back and the fact that one was made for me increased my hopes of getting the nod, but in the end the last seat on the flight went to Kevin Sheedy. As a souvenir I was given the unworn shirt with 'FAIRCLOUGH 20' on the back!

With respect to Kevin, that decision told me everything I needed to know. The top and bottom of it was that Bob Paisley didn't think I was yet back to my best, that I'd lost some sharpness. What was frustrating was the fact that he wasn't prepared to give me even the slightest chance to prove myself. Until he threw me back in, even as a late sub – as was usually the norm – he wouldn't actually know how match-fit I was.

An old friend of mine, Bob Rawcliffe, who ran a garage not far from Melwood, was also mates with Bob Paisley. The boss would regularly call in for a cuppa with Bob and, inevitably, football played a big part of their conversation. Whenever I found myself out of the team Bob Rawcliffe would always try to canvass on my behalf. The message that kept coming back throughout that year though was always the same: 'He doesn't believe you're back to your old self yet – he wants the old you back.' So did I.

In fairness I had lost that burst of pace. The injury had taken it away. One of my biggest strengths in the past had been my speed off the mark. That's what got me away from defenders, so without it I had a problem on my hands. I was aware of that and doing my best to try and put it right. What I hadn't lost was my eye for goal. I was leading scorer in the reserves for large parts of that season. Yet that still wasn't enough to convince the manager that I was worthy of a recall. I was at a loss to think what else I could do.

The writing was on the wall for me. That fact was becoming louder and clearer by the day. It was clear Bob Paisley lacked confidence in me and had for some time now. The club had moved on in the two years since he had outlined his reasons for not bringing Kevin Keegan back to Anfield. I got the impression that he considered me to be no longer part of his first-team plans. Since getting off the mark, Rushie had quickly established himself in the number nine shirt and was already starting to show glimpses of the goalscoring form that would eventually see him surpass almost every record there is. Whelan had made the left-side position his own and Craig Johnston, signed from Middlesbrough at the tail end of the previous season, was becoming an automatic choice on the right. Paisley was looking to the future.

His third great Liverpool team was taking shape and it seemed as though it didn't include me.

It was hard to accept. In my heart I wanted to stay and I still maintained a belief that I was good enough to be playing in the first team. When I'd be training with Roy and the reserves at Melwood I'd often glance over to the other pitch. Ronnie Moran and Joe Fagan would be putting the senior lads through their paces and I'd see players who were no better than me. That was the frustrating aspect of it all. I knew I could still do a job for Liverpool but persuading the manager to give me another chance was proving impossible.

There was no sign of the situation changing and that was so disheartening. At this stage of my career, playing for the reserves is all well and good when you're coming back from injury. Having regained my match fitness though, anything beyond that was doing me no good. It was all old hat to me. I had nothing else to gain. With respect to those I was playing against, it was all too easy. I was simply going through the motions, and with that comes the danger of stagnating.

The more it went on, the more difficult it was becoming to give 100 per cent each week. In one newspaper interview at the time, I explained that I wouldn't be able to stand another season of it. One way or the other, something had to give.

TWELVE MONTHS HAD PASSED SINCE THAT PHONE CALL FROM Mick Lyons and still no one at Liverpool had spoken to me about my future. I had just over a year left on my contract and it was clear that they were prepared to let me go. Nothing was ever made public but reports linking me with a move away resurfaced in the press around this time. Brighton & Hove Albion was one of the clubs to have allegedly shown an interest. Some journalists even wrote that I was on the verge of putting pen to paper on a deal at the old Goldstone Ground, but that was news to me and I had no contact with them whatsoever.

What I did know was that Middlesbrough and Portsmouth both made offers to take me on loan. Neither held much appeal for me. If I was going to move to another club in England it had to be one that was going places. Middlesbrough, struggling at the foot of the First Division and soon to be relegated, certainly didn't tick that box. Nor did Pompey, who were mid-table in the old Third Division at the time. When told of the approach from Fratton Park I was at such a low ebb that I did almost consider it.

On reflection, I made the right choice in not pursuing it any further. I might not have featured in the Liverpool first team for over a year but I still felt I was better than that. I was clinging on to the hope that somehow I still had a future at Anfield and trudging through the backwaters of the Football League's lower reaches did not strike me as being the ideal place to prove my worth to Bob Paisley. The standard was probably no better than the Central League. I needed to be testing myself at a higher level.

In March 1982 Liverpool were back at Wembley to play Tottenham in the final of the League Cup. It was just the type of occasion I'd have relished being part of but I was now further away from the first-team picture than I'd been at any point since breaking into the side as a teenager. To emphasise these changing times two members of the new brigade, Whelan and Rush, were the goalscorers in a 3–1 victory.

I continued to live in hope that the situation would change and that I'd soon be experiencing the big-match atmosphere again but there seemed no end in sight to the frustration I was again feeling. I had no idea what the future held and was slowly coming round to the fact that a loan move might be the only way of saving my Liverpool career.

I decided that I'd give it until the summer and then reassess my options. In the meantime I just got my head down and continued to try and do my best for the reserves. Again, we were way out in front at the top of the table and another title was a mere formality.

It would be the seventh time in eight years that I'd contributed to a Central League triumph. The novelty had worn well thin. I'd outgrown the reserves and it was time for a change.

By the time the winners' tankards were handed out in May I'd got my wish and was 3,500 miles away, trying to relaunch my stuttering career on the other side of the Atlantic.

14

SUMMER
BLIZZARD

FROM A WET AND WINDY NIGHT ON THE BANKS OF THE MERSEY, slugging it out in a Liverpool Senior Cup tie at Prenton Park – to a warm spring evening in San Jose, strutting my stuff among the star-spangled glitz and glamour of football California style.

The contrast could not have been more appealing and it all happened in such a short space of time. It was just what I needed. I'd been going nowhere at Liverpool. Out of favour with a stubborn manager and stuck in a rut playing for the reserves.

My name had been linked with a few clubs in England when suddenly this opportunity to head overseas for the summer arose. It might not have been the World Cup in Spain, which would soon be the focus of everyone's attention, but it excited me all the same. It was a no-brainer. An offer I couldn't refuse.

One minute I was helping Liverpool reserves to yet another comfortable victory, scoring one of the goals in a 7–0 victory away to Tranmere. Next, I found myself looking forward to going supersonic on a transatlantic flight, preparing to open a new chapter in my life. One I felt immediately reinvigorated by.

IT WAS TOWARDS THE BACK-END OF THE 1981/82 SEASON THAT THE first seeds were sown for this move. Bob Paisley approached me. We hadn't spoken much for a while and he came straight to the point. 'How would you fancy spending the summer on loan with a club in Hong Kong?' he asked.

I thought about it for all of two seconds. 'Erm, no thanks,' being my immediate reply. It was a move that just didn't appeal to me. I knew nothing about Hong Kong and didn't bother taking time to look into it. Maybe I was too quick to judge, because I visited the place in later years and enjoyed it. Back then though, my gut feeling was telling me that it just wasn't right for me.

Another reason for snubbing the move to Hong Kong was that, with all due respect, I believed that I deserved to be plying my trade at a higher level than that. But if the club was prepared to let me go, which they now clearly were, then I wanted to be in a position to choose where I'd be going. Having given it some thought a move abroad was starting to seem a more and more attractive proposition. The only sticking point was the timing. It was March and all the top leagues in Europe were drawing to a close. There was only one other destination that captured my imagination. One that I'd heard a lot about but only ever saw snippets of on the Saturday lunchtime football shows – the North American Soccer League.

The likes of Pele, Best, Cruyff and Beckenbauer had all been out there. If it was good enough for some of the world's best ever players then it was good enough for me. Soccer, as they like to call it, might have peaked Stateside in the late 1970s but it still had something to offer. A lot of British players had also played there, including a fair few from Liverpool – some of my old mates from the reserves (Max Thompson, Brian Kettle and Kevin Kewley), and Roy Evans, Tommy Smith and Steve Heighway had all sampled what football had to offer across the pond.

So I went back to the boss and explained that if he could find me a club in the NASL I'd consider a loan move for the summer. 'Leave it with me,' he said. A day or two later he returned. A couple of teams were mentioned but there was one in particular that he seemed to be pushing more than the other. It was Toronto Blizzard. Similar to the Hong Kong situation, I knew nothing about Toronto and I'd never been to Canada, or America for that matter. But this time I was prepared to give it a go.

By getting away for a few months I hoped I could raise my profile and prove to Bob Paisley or, failing that, another top-flight manager, that I still had something to offer. I'd already proved that I could play at the top level and supposedly still had my best years ahead of me.

Clive Toye, a former English journalist who had been instrumental in helping to set up the NASL and an influential figure at New York Cosmos, was now overseeing with Toronto. It generally seemed to be a club on the up, a strong franchise as they used to say. Dennis Roach, one of the first big-name agents in English football, was involved in the move. He travelled up to Liverpool from London to go through the finer details. The prospect of trying my luck out in North America was starting to excite me and, rather naively, I signed without fully examining the terms of the contract. Ironically, it was April Fool's Day. I assumed that I'd agreed to join Toronto on the premise that it was a loan deal but, as I'll explain later, that wasn't quite the case.

Still, a new adventure beckoned, and it was with a mixture of trepidation and excitement that I set off across the Atlantic, determined to enjoy every minute of the experience.

Due to complications with my visa I left England a day later than originally planned. Disappointingly, that meant I now had to fly to Vancouver to meet up with my new team-mates instead of California, where the Blizzard were due to play George Best's San Jose Earthquakes in the season-opener. Despite his connections to Manchester United, Best was a schoolboy idol of mine and someone I admired immensely. I used to try and imitate his dribbling style as a kid and to have played against him would have been a dream come true.

Another disappointment when I reached the check-in desk at Heathrow was the news that if I'd have travelled the day before I'd have been booked to fly on Concorde. I was beginning to think this experience was not starting well, but by way of compensation I flew first class for the first time in my life.

I arrived in Canada 24 hours ahead of the team and was to starting feel a bit nervous. There was no one to meet me at the airport, just a letter containing directions to a hotel in downtown Vancouver. It was my first time in this part of the world and I was totally alone. I couldn't help thinking that maybe it was all one big joke!

Come the next day I felt a whole lot better. The team flew in from San Jose and I discovered that the game against the Earthquakes had been postponed at the last minute, so I hadn't missed out on playing against Bestie after all. I was delighted because I thought there'd be another chance when the game was rearranged; sadly, the great man had cut his losses with the NASL and hung up his boots by that point.

Still, it was great to meet up with all my new team-mates and the coach, Englishman Bobby Houghton. He was the man who had guided Malmo to the European Cup final in 1979 and he'd been brought in to help revitalise the club. It was the start of a new era for the Blizzard and I was one of his many new signings. Houghton was a very thorough type of guy, his training could be quite intense but he was always meticulous in his preparation for games and post-match debriefs.

When I met the team for the first time I really didn't know what to expect but there were a few familiar faces in the squad and I quickly struck up a rapport with former Manchester United defender Jimmy Nicholl. We'd obviously played against each other on a number of occasions back in England and we became the best of pals out in Canada. From the first moment, we just clicked. We were the same age and shared the same attitudes towards life. During those initial few weeks of what was my first time living in a foreign country it was a real blessing to have someone like that as a team-mate. Without him that summer would have been a lot tougher for me. He was also an excellent player, a lot more versatile than I thought, and for six weeks in the middle of the season we missed him due to his commitments at the World Cup with Northern Ireland.

Throughout the team we had a good mix. David Needham, of Nottingham Forest fame, was another player I'd come across before. Also among the British contingent was ex-West Brom midfielder Alan Merrick, while Colin Franks and Cliff Calvert had both played for Sheffield United. As for the rest, other players of note included Bermudan forward Clyde Best, once of West Ham. What a lovely guy he was, his laugh alone would always make me smile. We had a very good goalkeeper from Sweden called Jan Moller and two talented locals: Bruce Wilson and Randy Ragan, both of whom would go on to represent Canada at the 1986 World Cup in Mexico.

Then there was a quartet of highly rated South Africans, among them striker David Byrne (the son of West Ham legend and former England international Johnny Byrne), Neil Roberts, Jomo Sono and last, but certainly not least, Patrick 'Ace' Ntsoelengoe, who was undoubtedly the most naturally gifted player in the squad. It was once said on BBC Radio 5 that 'Ace' was the best player you never saw and he is rightfully regarded as one the greatest ever South African footballers. What that lad could do with a ball was just unbelievable. These days all the young lads can do tricks and are always practising but back then no one really showcased extravagant skills. Sometimes the coach would pull 'Ace' out at training, get him to do a trick and say to the rest of us to copy what we'd seen. None of us could ever imitate him. 'Ace' would stand there, cool as you like, with a big smile on his face, looking like he could do it in his sleep. With him in the team we certainly didn't lack flair.

So it was a real eclectic mix of players I first encountered at Toronto. They were also a good bunch of lads. Everyone was very easy-going, we all got on and it was a very relaxed environment in which to meet new friends. I quickly settled and was impressed with the set-up. Toronto Blizzard was a very well-run club and everything about it was ultra-professional.

There was a perception among some in England that the North American Soccer League was not 'real football'. That it was just an opportunity for us to go and earn a few extra quid during the summer. While I wouldn't exactly go along with that – and

I definitely didn't treat it as a holiday – I did look upon it as a working break. It was never my intention to stay there and make a career of it in North America but for the next five months I had a serious job to do and, as I was to discover, it wouldn't be all plain sailing.

The games might not have been as intense as back home but they were highly competitive. There were at least a couple of star players in every team and while the standard wasn't akin to playing in the European Cup, it was comparable to the bottom half of the First Division in terms of quality.

Ahead of the 1982 season the NASL had suffered an exodus of major stars and seven clubs had folded, meaning the number of participants was reduced to fourteen. It was the start of a decline that would eventually lead to the league's demise two years later. Those that remained were reorganised into three regional divisions, from which the top sides would advance to a knockout-style play-off system that would eventually determine the 'Soccer Bowl' champions. Toronto played in the Eastern Division, along with the previous season's winners Chicago Sting, Montreal Manic and New York Cosmos. We played each other four times and then everyone else twice.

Travelling could be arduous at times, especially when we hit the road and were away for anything up to ten days, sometimes playing three games back-to-back before returning home. At the same time, the trips could be great fun and I loved visiting all these big cities in America and Canada. We'd always stay in the best hotels and I couldn't believe the sheer size of them. I'd never seen skyscrapers such as these before and I thought I must have landed on a different planet when waking up in Chicago one morning. I looked up out of the window from what must have been the sixtieth floor only to be greeted by the sight of the Sears Tower opposite, which continued to rise at least another fifty floors higher. When it came to flying, Toronto might not have had their own plane – like the Cosmos famously did – but our trips were well planned and we were always well looked after. An added bonus was that we'd often have enough downtime to go out and explore these cities, which for a first-time visitor to the country like myself was amazing.

More often than not we'd arrive the day before a game and the first thing we'd do was get out on the local golf course. The attitude, while still very professional, was so much more relaxed. After a game there'd always be a party. Restaurants would be hired and the hospitality was quite lavish. Almost every team had a fair contingent of Brits in their squad so I tended to know at least one opposition player each time we played. Against Edmonton I came up against former Liverpool reserve full-back John Webb, who had been at the club just before me, while Montreal's star man was

Gordon Hill, who I had played alongside for the England 'B' team. There were a whole host of others: Steve Hunt (New York), Archie Gemmill (Jacksonville), Willie Donachie and Ron Futcher (Portland), Terry Yorath and John Wile (Vancouver), Brian Kidd and Keith Weller (Fort Lauderdale), while Seattle's team contained a number of Midlands-based players. If we didn't get to see each other at the hotel beforehand we'd always meet up at the post-match bash.

*

ON THE FIELD I MADE A GOOD START. AGAINST A HIGHLY FANCIED Vancouver Whitecaps team, managed by Johnny Giles and featuring a young Peter Beardsley, we pulled off an impressive 3–1 win. The feedback was that I'd done well. I didn't score but I made two of the goals and was surprised to discover that a lot of fuss was made about assists. Stats were a big part of the game over there and it was all new to me. I'd always be keen to create opportunities for my team-mates but I'd never counted how many goals I'd made before. American sport is all about facts and figures, and although I think too much emphasis is placed on such details in the game these days, I wasn't complaining back then because it endeared me to my new team-mates from day one.

There were quite a few other notable differences between the NASL and the football I was used to in Europe. In an attempt to make it more interesting for the American and Canadian audience there could be no draws. If the score was level after ninety minutes, overtime would be played, similar to the 'golden goal' rule by which Liverpool famously won the UEFA Cup in 2001. If there were no goals during this extra half-hour then a shoot-out was required to determine the winners. Six points were awarded for a win in regulation time or overtime, with just four points the prize if winning in a shoot-out. To complicate matters further, bonus points were on offer for goals scored, but only in regulation time and up to a maximum of three per game. No surprise then that it took time for me to get my head fully around the format.

Then there were the little things, like extra stoppages in play to accommodate ad-breaks when games were televised live, the cheesy music that greeted every goal and the presence of cheerleaders pitch-side. It was all a million miles from what I was used to back home. And years before they were introduced in English football, every player was also given his own designated squad number. If you guessed that I wore number twelve though, you'd be wrong. Although the now stereotypical Supersub tag was to follow me across the Atlantic, the honour of wearing that shirt for Toronto Blizzard in 1982 went to Edmonton-born midfielder Pasquale DeLuca. I wore number twenty.

Because the initial move to Canada had been done in a rush, after our first game both Jimmy and myself flew back home to sort out some personal issues. When I finally arrived in Toronto I was greeted by freezing temperatures. It had been a long winter, I was told, and there was still a lot of snow on the ground. You'd think I'd have been used to the cold coming from England but this was something else. For the teams who travelled to play us from sunnier climes down south, like Tulsa Roughnecks who were our opponents on the night of my home debut, it could be quite a shock to the system. In contrast, when it was hot in Toronto, it was unbelievably hot. During the entirety of my stay there seemed to be no happy medium in terms of the climate.

Saying that, it was a great place to live and the lifestyle out there was one to savour. At first, home for me was a hotel out by the airport. The club was financed by a group that owned it and every new signing was put up there. We each had our own room and it was quite a novelty to begin with. There's only so long you can live out of a suitcase though, and I was soon on the move, renting a room in a house owned by Brian Budd, one of the biggest sporting superstars in Canada. Originally from near Vancouver, Buddy made Toronto his home and became a part of the furniture. Brian had played for the Blizzard and also his country but was perhaps best known for winning World Superstars for three years in succession between 1978 and 1980. It was through his role as the Blizzard's director of public affairs that I got to know him. He was an incredible character, larger than life and someone you couldn't fail to take a shine to. With him and Jimmy 'Nick' as my mates we enjoyed some great fun together and all became great friends.

Being married and having his family there with him, Jimmy rented a house on the outskirts of the city; being single it was decided that I would rent an apartment downtown. I have to admit I didn't fancy that idea; in truth I was nervous about being isolated. Buddy for that matter lived in this huge bungalow, about ten miles outside of Toronto. It seemed the perfect location, so I set about grovelling to see if he could find space for me.

Thankfully he could and, when the time came for me to vacate the hotel, I moved into his place; it was the best decision I made. Also living there, as well as Buddy, was a Can-Am racing car driver and an Irish folk singer. It was very rare for us to all be in the house at the same time so we had our own space and it was just a great place to live.

Buddy was the most athletic man I've ever met. His fitness levels were extraordinary, he could run all day. He also had a degree in physiology so it was interesting to be around him and do some training, even if it was impossible to keep up with him. As you would expect, the football schedule was relentless, but the one weekend when I was left out of the team for a visit down south to Tulsa, Buddy and I went up north to the lakes. It was like something out of the movies, being one of twelve weekend guests at a large wooden country mansion which stood on its own island. It was a retreat owned by Toronto Maple Leaf ice-hockey legend Brian Glennie. I had a fantastic couple of days and football and Tulsa seemed a million miles away. We went out on boats and swam in the lake but Buddy could never just enjoy a gentle dip in the water – he had to swim around the entire island. Another time, he got me involved in a charity run up the famous CN Tower as part of a team with the heavyweight boxer Trevor Berbick – all 147 floors of what was then world's tallest building.

In many ways Buddy became my mentor. It was largely down to him that my time in Canada was so enjoyable and I'll always be grateful to him for that. I wouldn't say I was ever homesick as such but there were certain times when I'd find myself at a low ebb, normally when things weren't going too well on the pitch, and he'd always be there for me as a sounding board or to offer his own wise words of advice. I kept in touch with him for years after and it came as a big shock when I heard the news that he'd passed away, aged just 56, in 2008. Brian Budd was the type of person I thought would live forever and it was an absolute pleasure to have called him a friend.

When I wasn't hanging around with Buddy or my team-mates it was also great to spend some time with a girl named Janet Lamb who I had only recently started dating back in Liverpool. When I told her I was going away to Canada for the summer Jan enquired whereabouts and when I said Toronto she quickly replied that she too was planning a trip there to visit her gran. 'If you want, I can see you out there if you have the time,' she said.

Throughout the early weeks we kept in touch but although she was gorgeous and I fancied her like mad I was still too nervous to openly invite her to Canada. As I was later to find out though Jan was an expert at getting what she wanted and she hatched to come out for the whole of July! I met her at the airport and I think she visited her gran just once in the entire time she was there. It was an amazing month that would change our lives forever.

There was certainly plenty to see and do in Toronto and what was good was the fact that, although it was a sports-mad city, soccer was way down the list in terms of popularity. So much so that the Blizzard players could walk around virtually unnoticed. There were a few bars and restaurants that made a fuss so we didn't have total anonymity and I remember one occasion when I was away with the team, Buddy got a visit from the police who had picked up two lads claiming to be myself and Jimmy Nicholl. We never did quite find out what they'd been up to but apparently they were having a fine time with a couple of girls until running into some trouble. We were flattered if not baffled as to why they would have wanted to be us, and they must have been die-hard Blizzard fans just to have known us because at the 50,000-capacity Exhibition Stadium where we played our games the average attendance would only be between four and five thousand.

Elsewhere in the NASL, particularly the likes of New York, Chicago, Montreal and Vancouver, soccer was more popular and attendances much better, but even in those places it still played second fiddle to other sports. There were no purpose-built stadiums and it was not unusual for us to play games on a baseball field, where the makeshift pitch had grass one side and shale on the other. At the Exhibition Stadium, which we shared with Toronto's baseball and Canadian football (a variant of American football) teams, there would be no supporters behind the goals when we played, just on either side; in terms of atmosphere, it wasn't too different to being back in the Central League.

The press attention we received was also just a drop in the ocean compared to the amount of column inches and TV airtime dedicated to American football, baseball, basketball and ice hockey. In Toronto the main focus of attention centred on the Maple Leafs in the National Hockey League and Major League Baseball's Blue Jays. They were absolute megastars out there.

Although soccer might have been looked upon as the poor relation in a sporting sense, facilities were top class and we wanted for nothing in terms of training and rehabilitation. It was a real eye-opener to see how players were trained over there. The US and Canada were way ahead of their time in this field. In comparison Anfield and Melwood were archaic. I was 25 and thought myself to be pretty fit and strong when I first arrived, but half an hour in the gym on these state-of-the-art Cybex machines made me think again. Still, they were great for building up my fitness.

What my knees weren't prepared for was the rigors of having to play on Astroturf. It might have been a new concept in the Football League, with Queens Park Rangers being the first English club to trial it in 1981, but it was commonplace in the NASL. Two-thirds of the pitches used were artificial and they'd been the cause of controversy a year before when Johan Cruyff returned to Europe early, citing that he could no longer play on them.

Unfortunately for me, the turf at Toronto's Exhibition Stadium was by far the worst. It was as hard as concrete. If I'd have known beforehand just how bad it was then I'd have seriously considered joining a team who played their home games on grass. I remember one of our players falling over and banging his head in training. That was on the Friday and he didn't wake up until the Monday. It could be so dangerous and certainly wasn't made with football in mind. Twisting and turning on it was particularly precarious, especially for someone like me with a recent history of knee trouble.

I didn't get to play on grass until the fourth game in. It was away to Tampa and making it even better was the fact that it had rained for a couple of days before. To me, the conditions were perfect. It was just like being back home and it made such a difference. Later in the season, during a spell playing for the reserves, nearly all games were played on grass and it was no coincidence that I then enjoyed my most fruitful spell in front of goal.

The win over Tampa was our fourth on the bounce. It was the club's best ever start to an NASL season but our 100 per cent record couldn't be maintained. We lost for the first time at home to Fort Lauderdale Strikers. I was yet to open my scoring account and was taken off at half-time without any explanation from the coach. I wasn't very pleased but it gave me the chance to do something I'd always wanted to do – sit up in the stands watching a game while enjoying a Coke and a hot dog. And taking me off didn't make a positive difference – they still slumped to a 4–3 shoot-out defeat.

I found myself in a familiar role for a few games – back on the bench – though at that time out there I had company as they had five substitutes available. I was struggling to adapt to playing on plastic pitches but my form in general wasn't too bad. I felt Bobby Houghton was punishing me because I was yet to score, certainly that's what his interviews implied. Whereas in England I'd been used to getting the ball out wide and dribbling towards goal, here too many balls were being played into me at waist height and, with a defender immediately on my back, it was difficult trying to turn them, especially on those artificial surfaces.

Houghton was also asking me to become more aware of my defensive duties. It was a role that was totally alien to me. He liked his teams to play on the counter-attack and I was not adapting as quickly to the system as he was trying to implement it. Constantly tracking back was not my game. The way he was setting the team up didn't play to my strengths and for this reason we just didn't see eye to eye.

It was a difficult time but I never once thought about cutting short my stay in Toronto. I just got my head down and continued to work hard. On reflection, maybe I was wrong in not attempting to embrace Houghton's ideas but after I rediscovered my touch in front of goal for the reserves, he was persuaded to deploy me in the position I knew best. Cutting in from the left and attacking defenders was a much more familiar role for me and the one in which I produced my best form for the Blizzard. I formed a good understanding with left-back Bruce Wilson. We knew our positions, he'd never run ahead of me and I'd never drop back behind him, it worked a treat.

At home to Montreal Manic in May, on the same day Liverpool clinched the 1981/82 First Division title at home to Tottenham, I finally broke my scoring duck for the Blizzard. Typically, it was after coming on as a substitute. There was just over four minutes left in overtime and the game looked to be drifting towards a shoot-out when I scored the winner. It came via a right-wing cross from our Argentinean midfielder Juan Carlos Molina. The ball fell perfectly for me and I made no mistake in heading it home. It was a great moment to score in this sudden-death situation. I was mobbed by all my team-mates and it was celebrated like we'd won a cup.

I wouldn't say I had been feeling under pressure to score but Bobby Houghton had been making noises in the press that I needed to start firing so it was nice to finally get off the mark. I was always confident that the goals would come but the longer the barren spell continued I was naturally starting to worry. I was becoming frustrated that the Toronto crowd had yet to see the best of me so it was really satisfying to see the feel-good factor that this win created. It ended a two-game losing streak and kept us in contention for the play-offs.

That game was one of nine we played during May. The schedule was relentless. At times we were playing almost every other day. The last thing we needed was another game added to the roster but, in what was a welcome break from the league fixtures, Juventus, the recently crowned champions of Italy, came over to play a showpiece friendly at the end of the month. With such a large Italian population in Toronto this was a game that really captured the imagination. Nearly 36,000 rolled up to the Exhibition Stadium. It was by far the biggest crowd I played in front of during my stay in Canada but unfortunately my participation in this glamour tie was very brief to say the least. I came on as a substitute late in the second half and within ninety seconds had received my marching orders after getting caught up in an incident with the Juve defender Sergio Brio. As I came on and took up a position with my back to goal the ball was played into me, he pushed in and I just used my arms to fend him off. It was a laughable decision but not unusual because the standard of refereeing over there was often questionable.

My memories of this came flooding back after seeing Steven Gerrard sent off in less than a minute after coming on as substitute for Liverpool against Manchester

United in March 2015. The occasions are incomparable but I knew what it was like to be ordered from the field so quickly. Apart from coming to terms with the shock of being sent off in such circumstances I also had to deal with some terrible abuse from the large crowd of Italians who had come to cheer for their fellow countrymen.

I hardly covered myself in glory that night but a few days later I was back on the score-sheet after coming off the bench again in a 4–0 win away to San Diego. As all eyes turned to the World Cup in Spain our season continued. Unfortunately we were about to hit a rocky patch. At the start of July we suffered a fourth straight defeat, so desperate times called for desperate measures.

Ahead of our next game, at home to Vancouver, Houghton called the players in three hours before kick-off. We were baffled. He was a stickler for dissecting what had gone wrong in previous games so we all thought we'd been called in for another re-run of our last defeat. We turned up as requested and were told to get changed before making our way to the video room. We were all dreading it. Another in-depth analysis was the last thing we needed so you can imagine our faces when the film Airplane! appeared on screen. It took us totally by surprise. I'd never seen it before and found it hilarious. We were all roaring with laughter and it really lightened the mood.

I don't know if any other managers had ever done something similar but it was the first, and only, time I'd prepared for a game in this way and it worked to perfection. A few hours later we ran out at the Exhibition Stadium and defeated Vancouver 3–1. I have to say, it was a masterstroke by Bobby and it kick-started a four-game unbeaten streak that fired us to the brink of play-off qualification.

It was during this run that I experienced one of the highlights of my time with the Blizzard. New York Cosmos were still without doubt the biggest scalp in the NASL. It was very rare for them to lose at home and they were just a month away from winning the 1982 Soccer Bowl when we emphatically defeated them at the Giants Stadium in Meadowlands. At one point we were 4–0 up and that would have been their heaviest-ever home loss. I was up against the great Johan Neeskens that day, while up front they had the NASL's all-time leading goalscorer Giorgio Chinaglia.

It eventually finished 4–1, which was still a massive result for us – one of our most memorable – and a great confidence-booster heading into the play-offs. As was an emphatic 9–2 victory over Tampa Bay Rowdies on the final day of the regular season, a match in which I netted my fourth and final goal in a Toronto shirt.

As the joint lowest-ranked team in the play-offs it was always going to be a tall order to progress beyond the first-round stage. Our opponents were Seattle Sounders, who had topped the Western Division. They were considered to be a particularly strong side and had already beaten us twice earlier that season. Leading their attack was former Brighton striker Peter Ward. After helping fire the Seagulls to promotion in 1979, a high-profile move to Nottingham Forest had turned sour but Ward flourished in the NASL and would end the 1982 campaign with the league's Most Valuable Player award.

Situated in the Pacific Northwest region of America, Seattle was one of the furthest away trips for the Blizzard and it was to there that we headed on a five-hour flight for the first in a best-of-three series. The game went to form, ending in a 4–2 victory for the home side, but our hopes of reaching the semifinal were not yet over. Given that the return in Toronto was just two days later, there was no time for the usual post-match reception. With an early flight to catch it was a case of straight back to the hotel, room service and bed. It was far from ideal preparation for such an important game. Our body clocks were all over the place but at the Exhibition Stadium we managed to turn it around and level the tie with a 2–1 win in overtime.

It meant we flew back to Seattle for the decider. Again, it was played at the Kingdome, only this time they closed the roof. It was the first time I'd played indoors. It was great to experience but unfortunately our season was brought to an end with a 4–2 defeat. We were all desperately disappointed but the best team won and there could be no complaints.

My Stateside adventure was over. It had been an amazing six months, an experience I'd never swap. I'd sampled another way of life, visited places I might otherwise never have and met some great people.

It was the first time I'd spent a substantial amount of time away from home and it opened my eyes to what life outside of Liverpool had to offer. For the first time in my life I'd had to really fend for myself and it helped me grow up as a person. Football-wise it wasn't the most glorious of times but it had been a more than worthwhile exercise. I'd overcome the fear of injuring my knee again and was feeling good about myself once more.

It was now time to head home. That was my plan. Unbeknown to me, a spanner had been thrown into the works and moves were afoot to scupper the return I was now longing for. Throughout the entirety of my stay in Canada I'd had no contact with Liverpool whatsoever. Then, as I prepared to leave Canada, I took a call from a journalist at the *Liverpool Echo* who informed me that my name was being linked with a transfer to West German club Hannover.

I knew absolutely nothing about this so immediately got on the phone to Bob Paisley. He confirmed that an agent on behalf of Hannover had expressed an interest in signing me and asked if I wanted to talk to them. I was totally shocked. I was expecting him to play it down as paper talk. He then explained that if I did want to speak with them, I had his blessing and that Toronto would negotiate the fee.

It was the last line that had me confused: Toronto would negotiate the fee. To the best of my knowledge I was still a registered Liverpool player who was due to return from a loan spell. So what exactly was going on here? It required some digging but I finally got to the bottom of it. When I put pen to paper on the deal with Toronto back in April I hadn't read the small print. It had been sold to me as a loan move and that's what I assumed it was. In reality, Toronto had paid Liverpool a fee of £150,000 for my services and there was a buy-back clause in the deal if either Liverpool wanted to recall me or I decided to return. None of this was ever explained to me and the thought that I had been sold was very odd because I was unaware of anyone negotiating this on my behalf. It was certainly the most unusual of arrangements and it seemed as though the press were more clued up about it than me.

I didn't even know if Toronto wanted to keep me. I had done well towards the end of the season but I was never going to stay another year in the NASL. That fact had always been clear in my mind. I went over there on the understanding that I'd be back to resume my Liverpool career six months later. It was as simple as that. To then discover that Liverpool were actually prepared to sell me was a major jolt. The prospect of playing in Germany was half-tempting but I was not yet prepared to throw the towel in.

I had often heard ex-Liverpool players say that only after leaving Anfield did they realise how lucky they'd been to be part of such a great club. With respect to Toronto Blizzard, I now knew what they meant. I dialled Paisley's number again. 'Boss, I've got no intention of leaving,' I said. 'I'm coming back.' And that was that. Not another word spoken. I packed my bags and flew back to Liverpool.

I was 25 and wanted to pick up on the twelve months I had remaining on my contract. My time at Toronto had given me a new lease of life. I felt fitter and sharper than at any time since the injury. I was returning with a better attitude and was determined to give it one last go. I didn't need telling that I was now seriously fighting for my Liverpool future.

15

THE LEAVING OF LIVERPOOL

IT DIDN'T TAKE LONG BEFORE I WAS BACK IN THE OLD ROUTINE.
Morning training at Melwood, a laugh with the lads on the bus as we returned to
Anfield, then a warm shower or bath, followed by lunch in the canteen. It was as if
I'd never been away. And I mean that quite literally. On the day I reported back to
the club I was greeted as though I'd been there every day since the start of July. Not
an eyebrow raised or question asked. Typical Liverpool.

It was late September 1982 and although I'd missed pre-season I was in great
shape having played right through the summer in the NASL. It was the best I'd
ever felt at this time of the year. And it wasn't long before I was pulling on the red
shirt again. It was for the reserves up at Newcastle. We lost 2–1 but I marked my
comeback by netting our consolation goal. It was good to be home.

Two days later, with Bob Paisley facing a striker crisis ahead of the first-team fixture away to Ipswich, I was named on the bench for the long trip to Portman Road.
On the first Saturday of October 1982 I made my first senior appearance in twenty
months, sent on as a late replacement for Sammy Lee. Mich d'Avray had broken
the deadlock for the home side two minutes earlier and my late entrance couldn't
change anything. I only played for nine minutes and the defeat was Liverpool's first
of the season. Still, it was a big moment for me. It seemed like a lifetime since my
last first-team outing and during my time out there'd been occasions when I never
thought I'd experience this again.

I waited two months before my next appearance. This time it was at Anfield, so
even more special. Norwich City were the visitors for a League Cup fourth-round

tie. It was a period of mass unemployment on Merseyside and times were hard. Liverpool supporters never lost their passion for the game but they now had to pick and choose their matches carefully. With Christmas just around the corner the attendance was a poor one. Only 13,235 bothered turning out on a bitterly cold evening and I doubt the game will be remembered by many.

The big-match atmosphere was certainly lacking but that didn't bother me. I came on as substitute midway through the second half in the place of the injured Mark Lawrenson, who had earlier given us a 1–0 lead. I must admit, it was with a touch of trepidation that I raced on that night. Having been out for so long I didn't know what type of reception I'd get. The crowd could have been forgiven for forgetting about me. The majority hadn't seen me in a red shirt for almost two years. I needn't have worried. The welcome I received was tremendous and gave me an instant lift.

Within six minutes of being back on the hallowed turf in a senior game I cut in from the Kemlyn Road side, opened my body up and fired home a shot into the bottom far corner. It was an unbelievable feeling. To come back from Canada, get into the Liverpool first team again and score a good goal proved that I hadn't lost my touch.

After being out for so long I really had been starting to doubt myself. To know I could still produce at this level was a big boost to my flagging confidence, especially given the nature of the goal. One swallow doesn't make a summer, as the saying goes, but I felt I had proved that Bob Paisley was wrong in being prepared to let me leave permanently in the summer. I knew that I was still capable of playing a part in his system.

I think that brief spell away from the club in Canada had actually helped me become a better player. Whereas in the past I'd receive the ball and just set off on a run until I saw sight of goal, now I was thinking more about the positional play of others and how I could link up with them. Of course, there can be no pleasing some people. In the past, one criticism aimed at me was that I didn't stop and think. Now I was being accused of not running with the ball enough. I couldn't win!

The manager described my return as 'a bonus' but it still wasn't enough to guarantee me an extended run in the team. Ever since my injury I sensed that he'd lost confidence in me and, despite my inclusion in the two aforementioned games, I'd seen nothing to change my mind. Come December I'd made only three substitute appearances.

Against my best wishes, it was looking more and more likely that this was going to be my last season at Anfield. Although I was enjoying being back at the club, the situation hadn't really changed and I was approaching that now all too familiar crossroads once again.

On a trip to Sudan for a lucrative mid-season exhibition game in Khartoum Craig Johnston, who carried his camera everywhere with him, even took a photograph of me casually posing next to an exit sign at the team hotel. It was a picture that said a thousand words. You know when something is not right and as the season wore on there were one or two more tell-tale signs that the end was near.

*

FRIDAY WAS ALWAYS A GOOD DAY AROUND THE CLUB; A SHORT team meeting prior to training followed by a light-hearted session. Nothing serious. Just a gentle warm-up and game of five-a-side. This was always the case 24 hours before a match, nothing overly physical and definitely no tough tackling.

On one particular Friday, in December 1982, we were preparing for a game away to the previous season's European champions Aston Villa. It was a big match. Liverpool had been top since early in the season but Villa were just six points off the pace and looking to get back in the title race.

With Craig Johnston rated doubtful, I was hopeful of being handed my first start of the season. I'd recently scored that goal against Norwich and then played the last half-hour of the previous week's win over Watford. Competition for the shirt came in the shape of David Hodgson, a fellow forward signed from Middlesbrough while I was away in Toronto during the summer. Hodgson had enjoyed an extended run in the team during the opening months but hadn't netted since September.

At the meeting Bob Paisley informed us: 'I'm going to wait until we get to the ground tomorrow and have a little look at the pitch before I name the side, I've still got one or two things to work out.' It was nothing I hadn't heard before so I took it at face value and thought nothing else of it.

Later in the afternoon a group of us went for a wander around the city centre, as was often the tradition of a Friday back then. We'd just go to relax and while away a few hours, with the fashion shops and record stores our usual ports of call. While walking through Church Street on this day I picked up a *Liverpool Echo*.

As always I turned straight to the back page, where to my surprise the team to play Villa was splashed across it. Staring back at me in bold type was the news that David Hodgson was to play and I'd be substitute. Paisley wasn't quoted but the story read as if he'd written it himself, with all his thoughts disguised in the words of the writer. This was often the case in the *Echo*, their reporters had always been very close to the manager, ever since the days of Michael Charters, and it was no different now. They'd even travel on the team coach with us at times, that's how cosy the relationship was. There was obviously a huge element of trust and when they wrote a story it was always exactly how Paisley had dictated it.

It was typical of the way he went about things when it came to letting someone down. He would go missing then allow the news to break, so to avoid any face-to-face confrontation. Those who were there knew how he operated but it only affected a certain few of us. There were never any complaints from the likes of Kenny and Souey, for example. Their place in the team was assured week in, week out. Results ultimately proved that Paisley's methods worked and it may sound like sour grapes on my part, but this style of man-management was in no way beneficial to me. If I wasn't going to be in the team I'd have rather been told to my face.

I was furious. 'I'm going back to Anfield on my way home to see if I can find him,' I told the lads as I raced off in the direction of the ground. I'd never done anything like this before, even though I'd probably had plenty of cause to. I pulled into the Main Stand car park, jumped out of the car and headed straight through the main entrance doors. As I arrived the boss was just coming through doorway that linked the reception to the dressing room corridor.

Without hesitation I confronted him. 'I thought you were naming the team tomorrow?' He seemed taken aback. 'What do you mean?' was his reply. 'It says in the *Echo* you're playing Hodgson and I'm sub!' Pointing through the staircase rails he simply said, 'Sometimes you have to do what they say upstairs, they signed him and that's it.'

I was staggered. I thought those days were over when the manager at Liverpool was told what team to pick. That's if he was telling me the truth. I was disgusted with what I had been told and left, returning later as planned for the early-evening journey to Birmingham.

I decided to treat the next day as normal and see if he would elaborate at some point on what he had said. Surprise, surprise – he didn't! No one on the coaching staff said a word. No explanation was given. It never was. That's just how things were at Liverpool back then. To make matters worse, who goes and scores our opening goal? Only David Hodgson! I didn't even get off the bench, but we won 4–2 so could have no complaints, other than the way I found out I wouldn't be playing.

It was like a case of déjà-vu. I'd been in this situation so many times before and my patience was seriously starting to wear thin. After talking it over with Jan (we were now very much an item since my return from Canada) and some of my mates I decided to play it out quietly. I had no idea where I'd be playing my football next season. My name was still being linked with a number of other clubs, including two that constantly seemed to crop up: Brighton, now under the charge of ex-Liverpool star Jimmy Melia, and Manchester City, who had seemingly been monitoring my situation for years. At this point though, there were no offers on the table.

Even if there had been I wasn't sure who I wanted to play for after Liverpool. For some reason, Manchester City always held a certain appeal, even though I'm not quite sure why. They hadn't won a trophy since 1976 so it definitely wasn't for the glory. Maybe it was because Maine Road had always been one of my favourite away grounds. The pitch was an expansive one and it just seemed to suit my style of play. I also got the impression that their flair players were always encouraged to play to their strengths rather than be asked to adapt to a more rigid system. I cite the example of Peter Barnes, who was a good mate of mine.

We were the same age and similar in style yet he gained 22 England caps on the back of his club form. He was a talented player, but didn't score as often as I did. I wouldn't say he had that much more talent than me but his manager indulged him and played him every week. In that type of environment I feel I too could have flourished. I might not have won the medals I did but I'd have been more appreciated in terms of what I had to offer.

Ironically, it was at home to City over Christmas that I next figured in the first team, coming on for the final fourteen minutes of a 5–2 win. After that, I found myself out in the cold once again. Since returning from Toronto, first-team opportunities had been extremely limited, more so than I had imagined. True, I had figured more this season than the one before, but those appearances were still way too few and far between for my liking.

It was clear to see that I was surplus to requirements, gradually being phased out and shunned by the management more than ever before. Like the kid who was being kept out of the gang, I was only ever finding things out second-hand. This was the club I loved and I was disappointed in the way the manager was doing things. I just wanted to be treated honestly and with a little respect, certainly after the service I'd given.

Behind Phil Thompson and Phil Neal, I was now the third-longest serving player at the club but that seemingly counted for nothing. I remember hearing stories from the older players and how they were treated in a similar way when the time had come for them to be moved on. It may well have been the case at other clubs too, I don't know. Liverpool was all I knew and I wanted to believe that they would show a bit more compassion than that.

I didn't want to admit it but I could sense what was happening. My contract was due to expire that summer and although Paisley had announced that he'd be retiring then too I don't think it would have mattered. My time at Liverpool was almost up and, deep down, if I was being honest with myself, I knew it would be for the best.

It was time to face the stark reality of the situation. I'd been here before but never did the end seem so real. Of course, it was difficult to accept. As a local lad and boyhood fan of the club it was never about money. I was on good wages and it would have been easy to just sit on the bench or play in the reserves each week. But as a professional footballer I had to think about my career and at this point I really did want to leave. I had just turned 26 and needed to be playing regular first-team football. No one at the club was telling me I had no future at Liverpool but the signs were there. I could spot them a mile off.

I had learned from being around Ray Kennedy and Jimmy Case. They used to pride themselves on being aware of everything that was going on around the club. Razor, in particular, used to say he was the 'top susser', that he was able to suss everybody out; he knew the character of people and what they were up to. This had been part of my education at the club and like them, as I got older, I often used to just sit back, watch, listen and take everything in. As a result I started to notice an awful lot more than people would have given me credit for.

Knowing that, barring a miracle, I was on borrowed time at Anfield I was determined to make the most of what remained. As the so-called business end of the season approached some big games loomed and I was hoping I could bow out on a high.

In the European Cup, Liverpool faced a quarterfinal against the champions of Poland, Widzew Lodz. I was an unused sub in the away leg but I remember it being a classic example of how a tie can be lost in the blink of an eye. The lads had played quite well over there and didn't do anything drastically wrong apart from one costly goalkeeping error by Bruce. A single-goal deficit would not have been the worst result to take back to Anfield but deep into the closing stages the home side scored another and the task Liverpool faced was suddenly a lot more daunting.

It meant that the situation going into the return game a fortnight later was even more desperate than the one we had faced at the same stage of the competition six years earlier against St Etienne. Lodz were definitely not in the same class as St Etienne though, and there was a genuine belief among everyone that a three-goal margin of victory could be achieved.

The near-capacity crowd certainly thought so, especially when Phil Neal gave us an early lead from the penalty spot. Unfortunately, by the time I was sent on in the 65th minute, the Poles had all but secured their place in the last four with goals either side of half-time. My entrance was seen as the last throw of the dice. It was a scenario I'd faced countless times before but at 2–1 down on the night and 4–1 on aggregate, it was always asking a bit much. I came on and played right wing. Never had I seen so much of the ball in such a short space of time. I'd been told to stay out on the right, get past the full-back and just whip in crosses, hoping that someone would get on the end of them – it was almost like a training ground session. Eventually, Ian Rush did level matters on the night and David Hodgson added a last-minute winner but it was too little too late and we went out on aggregate.

It was my last ever European game for Liverpool and although it ultimately ended in disappointment I was pleased with how I had played. Despite having not figured in the first team for almost three months I'd made an impact and it must have planted a seed with Paisley because ten days later, with Hodgson ruled out of the League Cup final with tonsillitis, I was the chosen substitute for the trip to Wembley.

Our opponents were Manchester United, which obviously stirred some painful memories. I'd not forgotten the desolation of 1977 but it was marvellous to be involved in an occasion such as this again. Having been a frustrated spectator at the last two League Cup finals I was absolutely delighted to be part of this now, even though I was only twelfth man. What a swansong it could have been.

I warmed up for nearly the whole of the second half; I didn't sit down once. I kept glancing back to the bench, hoping for the signal that would mean I was going on, but it never came until the 83rd minute when I replaced Craig Johnston. Alan Kennedy's goal had cancelled out a Norman Whiteside opener and we were heading into extra-time.

It was frustrating that it had taken so long to get on but I was desperate to make an impression on what was, more than likely, going to be my last appearance for Liverpool at Wembley. 'Make the most of the occasion.' That was what I constantly kept telling myself as I ran on. It certainly didn't pass me by, that's for sure, and in the 37 minutes I was on, I was involved in three key incidents.

I managed to test Gary Bailey in the United goal a few times and with one effort he was forced to make a great save to deny me. I had another chance that was not too wide of the mark, while the third is one I'd rather forget. Just minutes remained and we now led 2–1 thanks to Ronnie Whelan's spectacular curler. I ran in on goal, one-on-one with Bailey. It was a gilt-edged chance to wrap things up, win the cup for Liverpool and finish on a high. In situations such as this I was normally so composed, but my boot didn't connect cleanly with the ball and I sliced it well wide. I hold my hands up. I should have scored.

I've seen a lot worse efforts but for me it was a horror moment. I wanted to score at Wembley so much that, with it being so late in the game, I went for glory and tried to burst the back of the net. It was a big disappointment that in four appearances at Wembley I never scored and that miss has haunted me ever since. Even when I see it on television now it makes me wince.

Nevertheless, that whole weekend was a wonderful experience and I finally got my hands on a League Cup winners' medal, meaning, like Bob Paisley, only the FA Cup eluded me. With Liverpool having recently been eliminated by Brighton that was now never going to change, so heading into spring we had only the league to occupy us.

On Easter Saturday, an injury to Ian Rush meant I started my first senior game for Liverpool in 24 months and, despite failing to score in a 1–0 win at home to Sunderland, I kept my place for the Bank Holiday visit to Manchester City. As I explained earlier, it was a venue that always seemed to bring the best out in me and this occasion was no different as we coasted to a 4–0 victory. I managed to net twice, the goals coming towards the end of each half, and it took my tally at Maine Road to five. It also meant I had scored more goals in a Liverpool shirt on that ground than any other, apart from Anfield.

Some things never change though, and with Rushie back fit I had to make do with a seat on the bench when Liverpool hosted Swansea on Grand National day the following weekend. The Swans were still managed by one of my boyhood heroes, John Toshack, and now captained by my biggest friend in football at the time, Colin Irwin. They weren't enjoying the best of seasons and were destined for relegation.

On what was a beautiful sunny day, I came on fifteen minutes from full-time and temporarily had to cast friendships to one side as I proceeded to compound their misery. The ball was played out to me on the right. I took it in my stride and raced towards the Anfield Road goal. I'd missed from a similar position at Wembley a few weeks earlier and was still suffering sleepless nights because of it but I made no mistake this time, firing my shot into the bottom corner. How I wished I'd done the same against United. The game finished 3–0 and it was the last ever senior goal I'd score in a Liverpool shirt. As with my first one, I'm thankful it came at Anfield.

The next week we were away at Southampton. I was handed another starting role but I didn't feel I did myself justice. I felt slightly off the pace and though I have no real outstanding memories of the action, I can clearly remember not feeling as sharp as I'd have liked; it came as no surprise when I was substituted. In all the games I'd started for Liverpool there had been very few times when I was replaced. Plenty had felt the pain when I'd come on to replace them but this time it was me who felt the agony and embarrassment.

We lost 3–2 when a victory would have seen us wrap up another league title. With five games still remaining it didn't seem that big a deal. Liverpool had been way out in front for almost the entire season and the destiny of the trophy was a foregone conclusion. There was no danger of us slipping up now and even though we took just one point from the last fifteen available after the Saints game it was still won with plenty to spare.

I didn't know it at the time but I'd made my last senior appearance in a Liverpool shirt. From Ayresome Park to the Dell. Eight years, 154 games and 55 goals. It had been a rollercoaster of a journey. I just wish it could have ended better. Although I was selected as substitute for the home game with Norwich the following week I didn't come on and I played no part whatsoever in any of the remaining games that season. As was the norm, there was no explanation from Bob Paisley or the backroom staff.

As the season's end approached more rumours about my future began to appear in the press. The papers knew I was about to be released but still there was no official word from the club. For some reason I remained cowardly quiet about going to see the manager. Perhaps I just didn't want to hear confirmation of what everybody already knew.

My final campaign as a Liverpool player petered out in a very anti-climactic sort of way. It had been announced that the championship trophy would be presented ahead of the game with Aston Villa at Anfield on the penultimate Saturday of the league season.

Even though I wasn't selected in the match-day squad I fully expected to be there for the presentation. It was our last home game and there'd be the usual carnival atmosphere. All the focus would be on Bob Paisley, who was taking charge of a game at Anfield for the final time, but I too was looking forward to saying my own goodbyes. After training on the Friday I waited to be told what time I needed to arrive at the ground and hear details of whatever else had been arranged. Nothing was said.

The next day, as the players embarked on the customary lap of honour with the trophy following a 1–1 draw with Villa, I was sat at home listening to it all unfold on the radio.

*

MY CONTRACT WAS OFFICIALLY DUE TO RUN OUT ON THE LAST day of June but on the Friday morning following the Villa game the Daily Mail fell through my letterbox with a thud. In the right-hand corner of the back page was a small headline that simply read, 'Fairclough released by Liverpool'. My heart sank. I knew it was coming and had made my mind up to leave a few months earlier but still, to see it in black and white made it all so real.

I made my way to Anfield and finally broached the subject with the boss. 'It's about this story in the paper,' I said. 'Well, we haven't made up our minds yet,' came the reply, before he added, 'but if you do want to sign a contract we'll offer you a reduced wage and you can go on the end-of-season trip to Hong Kong.'

I wasn't wanted. That was as clear as the sky is blue. But why didn't the club just show some class? Or at least respect my feelings? That's what hurt me most. I'd been a Liverpool fan all my life and a player here since I was thirteen. I'd have rather just been told, however bluntly, that my career at Anfield was over – why all the messing around and playing games?

Seeing as the lads were playing away at Watford the next day and flying straight out to the Far East for the end-of-season tour on the Sunday morning, I was left wondering when they were planning on telling me this if I hadn't asked. 'No thanks,' was my immediate response. No weeks of negotiation were needed here.

His parting shot was, 'I'll still be helping Joe [Fagan] through the year so if you do sign I'll do my best to get you in as much as I can.' For me that didn't change a thing. If he wasn't picking me when he'd been in sole charge I just couldn't see how the situation would change for the better with him in this bit-part role.

The fact the offer from Liverpool was on lesser terms than I was already on meant I was now eligible for a free transfer. At least I definitely now knew that. I told him that was what I intended doing and left to get changed for training.

The final reserve game of the season was away to Huddersfield the following Tuesday night. With Roy set for a well-deserved promotion as part of the managerial shake-up, he was away with the first team in Hong Kong, so John Bennison was in charge of the reserves that night. He couldn't do much to lift my spirits but did say, 'If you are leaving, go out with your head held high and do yourself bloody justice here tonight.'

I tried my best but despite having scored five goals in the last three reserve games – including a hat-trick at Blackpool – I failed to sign off in a blaze of glory. There were a lot of scouts in attendance and it was no secret that a number of us were being closely watched. On what was a frustrating night at the old Leeds Road ground, I struggled to get going and the curtain came down on a disappointing Central

League season with a 2–1 defeat. I just hoped that someone had seen enough in me because I'd soon be a free agent and, as yet, there were no offers to consider.

I PLANNED A QUICK HOLIDAY WITH JAN TO SOUTHERN SPAIN. MY intention was to forget about everything for a few days before coming back to sort my future out as quickly as I could. The night before we were leaving I took a telephone call from Manchester City manager Tony Book. He said he was very interested in signing me and, given that I'd always had a soft spot for City, I agreed that I'd chat with him on my return from Spain.

The break was great. Just what I needed. A change of scenery and the chance to chill out ahead of planned talks with City. My recent troubles were behind me and I felt suitably relaxed. In the days before mobile phones, once in Spain I didn't really expect to be disturbed. Only our parents knew where we were staying so any contact would only be in case of an emergency.

About a week into the holiday though, I was sitting by the pool when I received a message from the hotel reception to say there was a phone call for me. To receive a phone call in these circumstances back then was extremely unusual, mysterious and worrying, because it often meant bad news.

I stood in a little wooden booth at the side of the reception desk and picked up the plastic white telephone. 'Is that David Fairclough of Liverpool?' a foreign voice asked. 'My name is Helmut Epp, I am a football agent and I have traced you via the British Consul.' I was intrigued. Anyone who had gone to that amount of trouble obviously had something serious to say. He continued: 'You are a free transfer, that's right, yes? I have a Swiss club that wants to sign you, do you know FC Basel?'

I explained that I was on holiday and would be for another week. It didn't put him off. 'I will come and see you in Spain tomorrow,' was his immediate reply. He sounded very serious and extremely keen. 'Well, if you want to travel here you know where I am,' I replied.

I returned to tell Jan about the strange call and how this mysterious guy that I'd never met was now coming out to Benalmadena to speak with me the following day. He arrived the next morning but was nothing like the super slick agent I expected him to be. He was probably in his mid-fifties and, like myself, very fair-skinned. Amid the sweltering heat of southern Spain he turned up in a big rain coat, looking all hot and bothered. Upon walking into the hotel reception he announced that he'd left his brief case, containing the details of my proposed new contract, in the back

187

of a taxi. Panic ensued until it was eventually retrieved and that was just the start of a comical 24 hours. He then informed us that he had nowhere to stay and with all the local hotels fully booked I had no option but to let him sleep over at our apartment. That night we went out for a meal, drank too much brandy and ended up rotten drunk. Then the next morning we all overslept and I had to wake him up, by which time he'd missed his flight and in the rush to get to the airport left with a bag containing Jan's toiletries instead of his own! Apart from all that I'd been impressed with what he had to say. My life at Liverpool was over but an exciting new chapter was about to begin.

16

SWISS ROLE

PLAYING IN EUROPE HAD LONG BEEN AN AMBITION OF MINE AND moving to Switzerland was too good an opportunity to turn down. Although the Swiss Nationalliga might not have possessed the glamour and prestige of those nearby leagues in West Germany and Italy, it provided me with the fresh challenge that I was desperately in need of.

After spending the best part of the previous two years in the shadows at Liverpool it was time to move out of my comfort zone and attempt to resurrect my career. Such were my ties to Liverpool that I would have found it hard to pick up the pieces at another English club so soon after leaving Anfield.

Having sampled life abroad with Toronto Blizzard I needed to get away again, albeit somewhere a bit closer than across the Atlantic. English clubs might have been dominating European competition but foreign football had always held a certain fascination for me.

Of course, there was no widespread television coverage of the Bundesliga, Serie A or La Liga back then. Information about the fortunes of teams abroad could only be gleaned from the odd snippets in football magazines. It added to the attraction and there was a certain mystique about it. It's why I used to love playing in European competition with Liverpool so much.

During the 1970s it was rare for British footballers to gravitate towards the continent. Kevin Keegan had moved to Hamburg in 1977 but that was an exception to the norm at the time. By the early 80s it was becoming a lot more common. Tony Woodcock had followed KK to Germany, while Laurie Cunningham had joined

Real Madrid.

Come 1983, there was no doubt that Italy's Serie A was the number one destination of choice for any ambitious footballer. It was where such greats as Platini, Zico and Boniek were plying their trade, helping it become the best league in the world. My old Anfield team-mates Graeme Souness and Ian Rush would soon follow suit and I'd be lying if I said I wouldn't have liked to join them there at some point.

It was virtually unheard of for anyone to move to Switzerland, although I wasn't the first Brit to try his luck there. Former Tottenham striker Martin Chivers had spent two years with Servette between 1976 and 1978, while Republic of Ireland international Don Givens had moved from Sheffield United to Neuchatel Xamax in 1981 and had not yet returned home.

In footballing terms, Switzerland might have seemed an odd choice for me but having played only a bit-part role in Liverpool's success of the past few seasons my stock on the continent had dipped somewhat since the late 1970s; the big clubs were hardly queuing up for my signature. I was aware that I needed to re-establish my reputation and while the land of the lira might have brought untold riches the chance to join the Swiss jet-set was a suitably attractive alternative.

*

I TRAVELLED TO SWITZERLAND IN THE BELIEF THAT I'D BE JOINING FC Basel. Helmut Epp met us at Zurich airport but it wasn't until we arrived at his smart city-centre apartment and were sitting out on his balcony with a cup of tea that he informed us they had pulled out of the deal. My immediate thoughts were, 'Just what am I doing here then?' But before I'd even had time to look at Jan, he announced that there was another club wanting to sign me: FC Luzern. I'd never heard of them. They were by no means the biggest team in Switzerland and traditionally lived in the shadow of those clubs from Zurich, Geneva, Berne and Basel.

With just a solitary Swiss Cup win to their name, success was not a term usually associated with Luzern. Despite this, they were a well-supported club, one of the best in the country. During my time there, we'd regularly attract crowds of between eight and ten thousand and a great atmosphere could be generated at the old Stadion Allmend.

As I was to discover, Luzern (or Lucerne as the English normally call it) was also a beautiful city, an important one in terms of the newspaper trade, and very affluent. Once Epp had delivered his news, and I came to grips with the idea, we set off on the hour-long journey for a meeting at the apartment of the club president,

Mr Simioni. Once there, we sat on the edge of a conversation conducted totally in German. The whole experience felt strange and we were entirely clueless as to what was being decided. I was then told to accompany a smart-looking gentleman for a medical. My immediate reaction was one of panic because I still had no idea what was happening. Thankfully, once Jan and I were in the car, Dr Urs Saner attempted to speak some English and informed us where we were going. In no time we arrived at his private clinic. It put England's medical facilities to shame, but I was still very nervous as he wired me up to all kinds of apparatus. I had an oxygen mask put over my face and was put through a series of fitness tests.

I still didn't really know what was happening and everything was moving too quickly. I was becoming more worried and remember saying to Dr Saner that I wasn't signing anything yet, although that will have been of little concern to him. His job was to make sure the tests were done and thankfully they all went well; this was a relief given that I feared my career could have been over just a year or so before. We returned to see Mr Simioni who personally took us on a private tour of the city before we said our farewells and set off with Epp and his wife back to Zurich. On the way I was told that Luzern had made an offer but I was still reluctant to agree anything at this stage. We spent the night in a hotel and it was nice just to have some time to ourselves so we could digest what had happened. Wandering around Zurich the next morning it began to sink in that joining Luzern would be a good move for us.

We returned to England later that day and the plan was for Luzern officials to come and visit me in Liverpool the following week. During this time there was contact from quite a few other clubs. I was up front with them all and revealed what Luzern had offered. Each time, the answer that came back was the same – 'take it'. One offer that did come close to matching that of Luzern's came from Bayer Leverkusen. The only problem was that their manager, the legendary Dettmar Cramer, was unavailable to sanction the potential transfer until the following Monday. I'd promised Luzern an answer by Friday and was reluctant to mess them around. Though the Bundesliga was highly appealing I now had to be fair both to Luzern and myself. My salary in Switzerland would be four times more than I'd been earning at Anfield and I couldn't run the risk of letting such a lucrative deal slip through my fingers.

It was the first time that I'd really paid any attention to finances in football. Salary negotiations had always been so straightforward at Liverpool and I happily signed whatever had been placed in front of me. At this stage of my career I had to make sure I was getting the best deal and for that I have my great friend, and lawyer,

Jim Davies to thank for negotiating the contact on my behalf.

Although the move had been orchestrated by Helmut Epp, I'd only known him for little more than a couple of weeks, so I was never entirely comfortable about entrusting my future to him. This is where having Jim by my side proved invaluable. Helmut proved to be quite a tricky person to deal with and Jim was more than worth his company's fees when he picked up on the fact that our Austrian agent was planning to take money from both myself and Luzern for helping to push this transfer through. When the Swiss officials came over, we met at Jim's Castle Street office and, in alerting us to Helmut's motives, he saved both parties over £30,000.

I was available on a free transfer but needed my release forms from Liverpool. So that afternoon, while talks between Jim and Luzern officials continued, I drove up to Anfield. It was mid-summer so there was hardly anyone around as I parked in the Main Stand car park and went straight in to see Peter Robinson. While waiting for him to get the forms he said he had something for me, and from the safe he went and got my League Championship medal. While I waited chairman John Smith also came by. He asked how I was doing and I explained that I was about to sign for Luzern. He wished me luck and said, 'Don't worry, you'll be back one day.' What he actually meant by that I didn't really know and never found out.

Without seeing anyone else I walked out of Anfield with the parting gift of a championship medal in my hand. My Liverpool career was over. It should have been a sad occasion but I'd known for a few months that this moment was coming and now I was just relieved. All I could think about now was my new life in Switzerland. By coincidence it was 4 July, Independence Day, and I was now stepping out into the big wide world on my own for the first time.

The following week I jumped on a flight from Manchester. I'd spent a summer in Toronto the previous year but that was on the understanding that I'd be back at Liverpool after a few months. This was for real. Liverpool, my boyhood club, was now a thing of the past. Although I'd forever remain a fan, it was going to be strange not being associated with them as a player any more . . . but there was no turning back.

Switzerland, while only a couple of hours away on a plane, suddenly seemed a million miles from home. It was all a bit nerve-racking but I was quickly made to feel at ease as the red carpet was rolled out for me on arrival in Luzern. As the club's marquee signing I received lots of attention. The president himself came and picked me up at the airport and on the way back to Luzern took me straight to the Adidas factory headquarters where they kitted me out in all the latest gear, before I was then put up in one of the best city-centre hotels.

Initially, I was a novelty and sensed perhaps that there was a hint of scepticism towards me from one or two of the other players. Because of the language barrier it was difficult to really settle in at first. I'd expressed this concern during negotiations, only to be told that it wouldn't be a problem. However, the Yugoslavian coach, Milan Nikolic, spoke no English at all and only three players in the entire squad were able to communicate with me. When you don't know what is being said among your team-mates it's easy to become paranoid but it was still all very exciting and I wasn't going to be put off that easily. I eventually got on brilliantly with Nikolic and he used to invite me round for dinner with his family quite regularly to help me integrate and understand his football philosophy.

As two strangers in a foreign country we shared a common bond. In those days, foreigners were not readily accepted, especially in central Switzerland. With good organisation seen as an essential part of Swiss life, the locals were very protective of the system that existed and wouldn't allow it to be compromised by anyone for fear of it breaking down. There were so many rules and regulations, relating to all manner of things. From parking cars to disposing your refuse, a lot of them seemed fairly minor, but everyone accepted them and they were never flouted. 'Every Swiss is a policeman' was a saying that I soon became aware of, and it was true.

It's also not by chance that everything in this beautiful country seemed to run like clockwork. It's all down to their world-renowned timekeeping. Back home in Liverpool punctuality could be a bit casual. In Switzerland it was a way of life. I quickly realised that being late for training or any other club appointment was not tolerated and fines were readily handed out.

While the locals were very reserved, they were also very polite. It was expected that you said hello (grüezi) to almost every person you walked past in the street, while another ritual that was completely new to me was shaking the hand of every player before and after each training session. I suppose it helped eliminate any bad feeling that might be festering between certain individuals and it was typical of the Swiss nature.

Although all these little nuances took some getting used to, I just couldn't help but be impressed with how they lived their lives and, even if it did test my patience at times, I tried my best to adapt.

Until Jan came over I had too much free time on my hands and, with no English television channels available in the hotel, my solitary life outside of training would see me exploring every narrow Luzern street. I could quite easily have become a tour guide in my spare time. Once I received my car I explored further afield. I also started to knock around with some of the single lads in the team, but the culture among footballers in Switzerland was completely different to back home. Even though it wasn't my style, there were certainly no all-day benders or heavy drinking sessions. One of my new team-mates, Markus Tanner, a big powerful midfielder, had a bit of a reputation for liking a beer or two but compared to British standards it was nothing. Instead, learning to play backgammon on the terrace of a lakeside restaurant, or people-watching while sitting outside a city café bar seemed to be much more what Luzern was all about.

After a week of getting to know the place we went away for an eight-day training camp in the Swiss mountains. It was a rude awakening. We stayed at a monastery and the rooms were very basic. It was like living in a cell. We were woken at 6 a.m. every morning in readiness for a 6.30 a.m. start and would then train three times a day. Breakfast would follow our early-morning hill runs. Then we'd sit down for an hour of theory, which was all conducted in German and was therefore impossible for me to understand as I'd not yet started to learn the language. For two hours before noon we'd be out on the pitch with a ball, then we'd sleep for a bit in the afternoon and train again at 4 p.m. It was a lot different to the tried and trusted training methods I had been used to at Liverpool but come the end of the week I felt in great shape.

As the most high-profile of Luzern's three summer signings, when the real action began I found myself under intense scrutiny from day one. Our first game was in the Intertoto Cup, a competition that was then unheard of in England. It later became the route into Europe for teams that had failed to finish high enough in the league or win one of the cups, but in the early 1980s it was nothing more than a series of friendly matches, played to satisfy the demands of the European football pools business. Against Israel's Maccabi Natanya in our opening game I scored my first goal for Luzern.

When it came to expectations for the season ahead not much was expected of us, especially in terms of competing for the title. Grasshoppers and Servette were the teams to beat. They were the big powerhouses in Swiss football at that time, while St Gallen, Basel, FC Zurich and Neuchatel Xamax were the others considered worthy of challenging for honours. Even qualifying for Europe was thought to be beyond our capabilities.

The Luzern squad was not a particularly strong one and the most well-known player to me was fellow forward Peter Risi. A tough, well-built and hard-working player, I remembered Risi from his time as a player with FC Zurich. A former Switzerland international, he had finished top scorer in the Nationalliga A on three occasions and we'd played against each other in the 1977 European Cup semifinal, when he scored in the first leg.

The standard of football in Switzerland might not have rivalled that of the major European leagues but it was a lot tougher than I imagined and far from the genteel experience that many believed it would be. The fact that Switzerland bordered three of the continent's most powerful footballing nations greatly impacted on the different playing styles in the Nationalliga A. Teams seemed to play in the character of the region they were from; those influenced by the Italians were tactically astute, the French were flamboyant and the Germans, strong and powerful. Luzern fell into the latter bracket.

I enjoyed the pre-season programme and was very optimistic for a good first season. Although I'd scored my share of goals in the warm-up games, once the league campaign started I was slow off the mark and the critics were quickly on my back. Given my status as a former European Cup winner with Liverpool, they expected me to be an instant superstar.

I thought that was harsh and unfair. I was still finding my feet in a new country and trying to adapt to a different style of football. As Luzern's main attacking threat I found myself man-marked every week. Our season opened with a home game against Vevey, who assigned an overly keen defender, Karl Kung, to do everything within his powers to stop me. Luckily, I managed to walk off the pitch in one piece as we celebrated a 1–0 win, while he somehow escaped with just a yellow card.

Our next game was away to FC Basel and I was determined to show them what they had missed out on. However, the pitch at the St Jakob Stadium was in a terrible state after it had hosted a summer pop concert. It was a real mud-heap and we could only manage a draw – I was just glad that we didn't have to play on it every week. I was gradually getting to grips with my new environment and finally, in our third league game against Chaux-de-Fonds, I scored my first goal in a 3–2 win. I was relieved to get off the mark and I think my new employers were too.

In September I was reunited with Sam, my pet Doberman. He was flown over from Merseyside and personally collected at the airport, again by Luzern's president, who then brought him to training as we prepared for a cup tie against our local rivals SC Zug, managed by future double Champions League winner Ottmar Hitzfeld. The following day I scored both goals in a 2–1 win and Sam was deemed my lucky charm.

It was around this time that we also moved out of the hotel. The club had found us a town house, coincidentally right next door to where Hitzfeld lived. The now-famous German had just started out in management, having only retired as a centre-forward with Luzern the previous season. I was signed as his replacement and was a touch apprehensive as to whether my new neighbour would resent me for taking his place but I needn't have worried. Ottmar was a quiet man. He spoke very little English but certainly more than I spoke German. I didn't see too much of him but when I did we got on well.

Jan made very good friends with his wife Beatrice, who spoke excellent English – that was massive help, especially during those times when I was away with the team. Jan's happiness was vitally important because I can't overstate how important a role she had to play in making our transition to Swiss life a success.

Once we settled into our new surroundings our eyes were opened to a wider world that, while testing at times, was so exciting. We lived in a quaint little village overlooking one of Europe's most beautiful cities and were able to enjoy long walks in the nearby forests and mountains. Jan also enjoyed the fabulous shopping and, all in all, it was a great education in appreciating the finer things in life, eating in great restaurants and learning about good food and wines.

On and off the pitch, after a difficult start, life was treating us well. Then, one day in October, Jan and I were summoned to the immigration office. The officer who dealt with us seemed a really nice fella at first. He talked a lot about football and was a big Luzern fan. Although the team were struggling in terms of results he also seemed to be very happy with how I was performing. But suddenly the conversation turned serious and from friendly football fan he switched to hard-nosed immigration official.

It began when he asked Jan when she would be leaving Switzerland. We initially laughed it off. 'She's with me and we're staying for duration of my contract with Luzern,' I said. It then transpired that this was no laughing matter. Jan didn't have a visa to stay in the country on a permanent basis. This was something which had obviously been overlooked by all of us in the negotiations. 'The only way to stay is if you are married,' he explained. Although our relationship was a strong one and it seemed inevitable that one day we would tie the knot, marriage was not something we had ever discussed. But without hesitation, before I had given the situation any further thought, I just came out with it: 'Well, we are getting married.' There was a momentary pause and, realising what I'd just said, I nervously turned towards Jan. She glanced sideways at me. There was a slightly bemused look on her face but thankfully she smiled and nodded in agreement. 'Yes, we are.'

At that point, the visa issue ceased to be a problem, which was just as well because the thought of being there without her was a complete non-starter. We really were getting wed now. It had always been my intention to propose at some point, I just regret that it couldn't have been done in a more romantic way because

Jan deserved better. Fortunately, she fully understood. We left the office and called our families to tell them the news. I think the initial reaction was one of shock but only because it had been announced so suddenly. From the moment I met Jan I knew we would end up together and I think those closest to us thought the same.

While Jan returned home to arrange the wedding, I got back to the business of playing football. Unfortunately, results weren't too good and before the first half of the season came to a close Nikolic was sacked. I felt sorry for him. He hadn't been helped by some unbalanced and over-the-top press coverage but deep down I always got the feeling that he wasn't a big enough character for the club. There'd been an agenda building up against him for some time and so it didn't come completely out of the blue.

His replacement was the player-manager of Young Boys, Bruno Rahmen. As a former Luzern captain who had not long retired, he was a familiar figure with most of the lads in the dressing room but his appointment didn't go down too well and, as a result, the internal politics at the club changed completely. It was clear that he wanted to get rid of the big names in the team and surround himself with 'yes' men. Not surprisingly, this upset a lot of the key players.

It also quickly became apparent that I too was not his cup of tea. I sensed that the writing was on the wall for me when I scored a hat-trick away to Basel in the next round of the cup. I broke the deadlock six minutes after the interval then added another two in as many minutes midway through the half. It was a great result for us and the undoubted highlight of my time in Switzerland up to this point. Hopefully, it made Basel think twice about why they had pulled out of the deal to sign me in the summer. The newspapers were unanimous in their view that I had been man of the match but the coach refused to go overboard with his praise, hinting to the press it was just a lucky day.

Nevertheless, I was enjoying my football. As Christmas approached I was ranked the third-best performing foreign player in the Nationalliga A – a player from FC Sion, Ben Brahim, was top – and I'd played every minute of every game. It was great for my confidence, knowing that my place in the team was virtually assured week in, week out. We played our last game before the break on the first Sunday of December, just as the biggest snowfall of the winter arrived, transforming Switzerland into a scene from a picture postcard. I wasn't hanging around to enjoy it though; I was heading back to Liverpool, where I married Jan a week before Christmas.

While home I also popped into Anfield to say hello and catch up with the latest gossip at the club. A few of the lads were keen to hear about my new adventure in Switzerland so I started telling them about how different it was over there in terms of things like diet, training methods and how we prepared for games. As he went about his business, Ronnie Moran overheard us talking so listened in for a minute. 'Load of bollocks, that,' he barked before quickly moving on. We all laughed but it made me think about just how blinkered we were in England back then. I remember having a conversation with Milan Nikolic once and he said, 'The problem with England is it's an island and it thinks like an island.' On reflection he was right. English clubs had a great record of winning in Europe so it was easy to think our way was the best way. Maybe we were all guilty of this. Not until the influx of foreign managers in later years did this mindset change, although I do remember Souey being criticised for 'thinking like a foreigner' when he took over at Liverpool in 1991. In reality, he was just way ahead of his time.

I enjoyed my first experience of a mid-season break and after a few days back in snowy Switzerland it was off for a two-week training camp in Gran Canaria. With a new coach at the helm and some disappointing pre-Christmas form to turn around it was serious stuff. The training was tough, with lots of running in the sand dunes. We had two sessions a day and I definitely felt the benefit. Rahmen complimented me on my fitness levels and how well I had applied myself to his methods during the camp. We played a few games and I featured in each of them. Everything seemed to be going fine. So I thought. I then heard that Rahmen was not happy because I didn't speak enough German. It suddenly developed into a much bigger issue than it should have been and he ordered me to take daily lessons. From that point onwards our relationship became even more strained and would not recover.

On 26 February the season restarted at home to FC Zurich. Almost three months had passed since our last match and we got off to a winning start. Rahmen had experimented with some new ideas while we had been away and I had now been moved into an attacking midfield position. Despite that victory we knew our next fixture, against a strong Servette side that would go on to win the Swiss Cup, would be a much tougher test. We started well but after falling behind, our organisation disappeared and in a 3–0 loss I scored my only ever own-goal. I was devastated. Even though there was nothing I could have done about it. We got caught on the counter-attack and I was the one left chasing the striker has he raced through on goal. Our 'keeper saved the initial shot but the ball rebounded off me and back over him into an empty net.

I managed to pick myself up and bounced back to score twice in the next three games before we were back in cup action against Vevey. I scored again, the first in a 2–1 win, taking my tally in the competition to six. Luzern hadn't reached the cup final since 1960 and hopes were starting to rise until we were disappointingly beaten

3–0 at home by FC Aarau in the quarterfinal.

Between the cup games I got a measure as to how important I still was to the club. In a rare midweek fixture away to Neuchatel Xamax, which we lost 1–0, I broke my hand. If I'd have suffered a similar injury while a Liverpool player I'd have been ruled out of the first-team picture for weeks, but a few days later we were due to play St Gallen away and there was never any talk of me not being involved. After discussions with the referee it was agreed I could play with a full plaster cast on my arm. Although it came in handy for a bit of protection, which was always useful in the Swiss League, it wasn't very comfortable and was so heavy that if affected my balance.

With nothing but a respectable league finish to play for, Luzern arranged a friendly that packed out the Stadion Allmend. Udinese were the opposition and the majority of supporters had come to see one man only, Brazilian superstar and reigning World Player of the Year, Zico. It was a great thrill to share the same pitch as him and he didn't disappoint, scoring one of his trademark free kicks by bending the ball around a wall I was part of. We lost 3–2 but I at least had the consolation of joining him on the score-sheet.

After that, the season drew to a low-key close and I watched on television, with a mixture of envy and delight, as my former Liverpool team-mates won a fourth European Cup in Rome. The following day, as I prepared for our penultimate league fixture, I thought I was seeing things when I looked out of the window and saw my uncle and cousins walking down the road towards our house. They were on their way home from the final and had casually decided to call in and say hello. It was great to see them and they regaled me with tales of what had been another wonderful night in Liverpool's history.

A week later the curtain came down on my first season in Swiss football. I'd scored a more than satisfactory sixteen league goals but the final table showed that Luzern had finished just one place above the relegation zone, even though we were never in real danger of the drop, collecting ten points more than the team below us.

During the summer there was a mass clear-out of players. It had been on the cards since Rahmen took charge and once the season was over he wasted no time in getting rid of those he saw as a threat to his command. Among others, out went the likes of Peter Risi and a talented German forward called Detlev Lauscher. I was one of only six players to survive the cull and the only one over 25 years of age. I've no doubt that Rahmen would have dispensed with my services too if he could but I was on too big a contract to be easily offloaded.

As a result the team had been severely weakened and we went into the 1984/85 season with a much younger and inexperienced squad. It was a tricky summer for all concerned. A few new faces were added but it came as no surprise that we struggled. Although we defeated Borussia Dortmund to win a local pre-season tournament, the signs were ominous when we won just one of our six games in the Intertoto Cup.

Surprisingly, our league form during the first half of the season was an improvement on the previous campaign and we actually got ourselves up into fourth place for a short while. Unfortunately, we struggled to maintain that early momentum and also exited the Swiss Cup at just the second-round stage.

My place in the team was now no longer automatically assured either. I missed four weeks through suspension after being sent off in the last minute of a win over Wettingen and to fill the void Rahmen brought Walter Hemmeter, a young German striker back, to the club. He started to alternate us, which was a far from ideal situation. I made my feelings known and we had a frank conversation, in which he outlined his plans for the future. Rahmen wanted Luzern to play a more defensive style and that didn't suit my strengths. We had an obvious problem on our hands and I was concerned about my position at the club.

The press back home must have been keeping tabs on the situation because around this time I took a few calls from English journalists asking if I had any intention of coming back. Up to that moment I hadn't really thought about the possibility of leaving but I was soon being linked with a return home. A couple of agents started sniffing around and I spoke with Southampton and Stoke. There was also some mention of a possible move to Germany that quite interested me. Although nothing materialised it was all a bit unsettling and would remain that way as we headed into the winter break.

To maintain my fitness during this time Howard Kendall kindly arranged for me to train with Everton at their old Bellefield training ground, near to where I used to live in West Derby. It was great of Howard, I'd always got on really well with him and come the New Year he declared an interest in signing me. I can remember it well. It was a Friday morning and Everton were due to play Leeds in a televised FA Cup third-round tie that night. As the team coach prepared to leave for Yorkshire, Howard said he'd speak to the chairman over the weekend and get back to me on Monday.

I must admit, it took me by surprise but until there was a firm offer on the table it wasn't even worth thinking about. I'd been here before, of course, when Gordon Lee had apparently wanted to sign me, and my feelings hadn't really changed. It would have been difficult to pull on that blue shirt after so many years wearing the red but as I waited to hear back from Howard I kept an open mind.

As it was, the late Philip Carter, Everton's then chairman, vetoed any potential move. He did not want to risk the wrath of the Goodison faithful by signing another player with Liverpool connections, following on from the recent acquisitions of David Johnson, Kevin Sheedy and Alan Harper. I could see his point and it wasn't a problem. Everton were flying at the time. Howard had totally transformed their fortunes and there was no guarantee I'd have got in the team anyway.

Still, it was flattering to know that he thought I could have done a job for him because this was one of the greatest periods in Everton's history. There were no hard feelings and I continued to train with them until I was due back in Switzerland. Before then though, my relationship with Luzern took a major turn for the worse.

Completely out of the blue I received a telegram from the club, informing me that they wanted to cut my contract and were willing to let me leave. Apparently, I had purposely 'attacked the coach in training' and he felt I was against him. I might not have seen eye to eye with Rahmen but to say I'd attacked him was totally untrue. I remember losing my rag on one occasion in training and smashing him in a challenge but I'd hardly class it as an attack. After all, I was only eleven stone wet through, whereas Rahmen was supposedly a tough centre-half in his day.

For reasons only known to him he decided to pick a fight with me and tried to get me out the door on a technicality. He also tried to claim that I had returned to England during the winter break without the club's permission, which was another fallacy because it was written into my contract. After seeking some advice it was clear that I was well within my rights to appeal this and I employed a lawyer in Switzerland to fight my case.

After the initial excitement of setting up home in a foreign country, life in Switzerland had suddenly fallen a bit flat. My disenchantment had begun to set in long before this latest episode and the homesick blues, which happen to most people who have ever moved abroad sooner or later, were kicking in.

Because I was in dispute with the club I was unable to play and this situation rumbled on for a few weeks before I was eventually offered a financial settlement and handed a free transfer. Given how I felt, when the time came to return home it wasn't too difficult to say my goodbyes.

The way it ended for me in Switzerland was a disappointment and I came home feeling a bit of a failure. My intention had been to really make a go of it out there and hopefully stay abroad, eventually moving on to a bigger club in a better league.

When I look back, I enjoyed my time with Luzern immensely but in hindsight I'd say it probably wasn't the right club for me. They just didn't share my ambition. I sensed that from day one but somehow hoped my arrival might have sparked a change in their thinking. Instead, they were just happy to plod along and therefore saw no reason to invest in the team. With respect to my team-mates there, I was used to being (and needed to be) surrounded by better players.

There's no doubt that my deteriorating relationship with Rahmen was the cause of my career in Switzerland being curtailed. Before the end of February I was home. Back to square one and looking for another new club. Come the end of the season, Rahmen was sacked. In my eyes, some justice had been served.

17

THE NOT SO GREEN GRASS OF HOME

WHILE JAN STAYED BEHIND TO TIE UP THE LOOSE ENDS OF OUR LIFE in Switzerland, I returned to England in the hope of picking up my career as quickly as I could. It was February 1985, I'd just turned 28 and was now in footballing limbo.

I was approached by a few agents who offered to take me all over the place. The first club to express any real interest was Wolves, managed at the time by Tommy Docherty, whom I met for lunch. It was always great to talk with the 'Doc'. He possessed a Shanks-like enthusiasm for the game and I was instantly lifted by his energy. We came to a kind of semi-agreement that I'd sign. It was a deal that appealed to me but by the time I'd got back to Merseyside the Professional Footballers' Association had heard about our meeting and warned me off. They explained that the Molineux club was experiencing severe financial difficulties and I was advised not to join them.

Instead, they asked if I'd meet with Walsall. Out of courtesy I went and spoke to manager Alan Buckley but the prospect of dropping down into Division Three was not an enticing one.

I then took a call from Manchester City boss Billy McNeill. Although they were in the Second Division at the time this was a move that really captured my imagination, not least because it meant I could commute from Liverpool. Also, as I've already explained in a previous chapter, I'd always had a soft spot for City and might have joined them two years earlier had it not been for the offer from Switzerland.

I met McNeill and immediately felt comfortable in his company. He was a legend in the game, captain of the Celtic team that had become the first British club to win the European Cup in 1967 and a manager I could see myself playing for. Before discussing the possibility of a contract the plan was to give me a run-out in a couple of reserve games. The first was away to Huddersfield, ironically, the ground at which I'd played my last game for Liverpool reserves.

I lined up in a City side packed with highly promising youngsters. The likes of Paul Simpson, David White, Paul Moulden, Paul Lake and Andy Hinchcliffe were known as the 'Golden Generation' and big things were expected of them. The Huddersfield game went well even though it ended goalless and I played again the following week, this time at my favourite ground other than Anfield, Maine Road. It was against Sheffield Wednesday reserves and I scored two in a 4–0 win.

I really enjoyed playing with such an exciting group of attack-minded young-sters. I chatted with McNeill afterwards. He said he liked what he had seen and offered to sign me on loan until the end of the season. It wasn't ideal from my point of view but I could see the sense in it from their perspective and was fully prepared to sign until Norwich City manager Ken Brown rang me.

I kept McNeill fully informed and, although I'd signed nothing yet, out of re-spect, I asked for his permission to speak with Norwich. He didn't stand in my way but I could sense he was a bit put out.

I travelled down to Norfolk to play for Norwich reserves against Tottenham at Carrow Road and stayed the night at the home of Canaries skipper and fellow Scouser Dave Watson, who I had played alongside for Liverpool reserves. The fol-lowing day I met with Ken Brown to discuss the way forward.

'What have Man City offered you?' asked Ken. I explained the situation and he replied: 'You don't want that, we can offer you the same deal, with a view to offering you something more permanent at the end of the season.' In terms of security it was a slightly more attractive proposition and, with Norwich already in the First Division, I was really torn as to what was best for me.

At this point I was still thinking that Manchester City was the better option for me. The Maine Road club was closing in on promotion and I wouldn't have to move house. I rang McNeill back but he wasn't around so I left a message with his assistant Jimmy Frizzell. If they could match what Norwich had offered I'd have signed. McNeill never did return my call and I often wonder whether it was because I'd not agreed to sign initially. Or had he simply not received my message?

I was left waiting in a hotel room with a decision to make. During this time I was also contacted by Willie Maddren, manager of Middlesbrough. Willie was another great ex-player and a good friend of Souey's from their time together at Ayresome Park in the 1970s. But, like Wolves, they were going through a period of financial strife so it wouldn't have been an ideal time to go there either. Instead, Maddren went out and bought a then unknown striker called Bernie Slaven, so Boro fans owe me one because he went on to become a legend up on Teesside!

With no word back from McNeill I accepted the offer from Norwich. Ken Brown had got a good team together at Carrow Road, one that had potential but also plenty of experience. With the likes of John Deehan, Mick Channon, Asa Hartford, Steve Bruce, Chris Woods and Dave Watson at the club it seemed a good mix. Just a few weeks after I'd joined they beat Sunderland to win the League Cup and were sitting comfortably around the mid-table mark in Division One.

Back in the early days of my Anfield career I was often referred to as the team's lucky charm for the fact that we always seemed to win when I played. At Norwich it was the complete opposite. From the moment I signed we won only three more league games and suddenly became embroiled in an ultimately unsuccessful battle to avoid the drop.

Not that Norwich's alarming dip in form can be entirely attributed to me. I only made two appearances. After playing a few times for the reserves I was eventually handed my debut away to Arsenal on Easter Saturday. My reintroduction to top-flight English football though was soured by a 2–0 defeat. The following week, at Watford, I started on the bench again but entered the fray much earlier after Mark Barham was forced off through injury in the first half. However, it was another afternoon to forget. We lost by the same scoreline and, despite having been sent on to play out wide on the right I found myself operating as an extra right-back for much of the game due to the threat posed by Watford's future Liverpool winger John Barnes. After that I didn't get back in the team but that wasn't my only problem.

After staying in a hotel for the first few weeks of my time at Norwich Jan naturally started to get a bit fed up so I asked the club if they could find us some suitable accommodation elsewhere. When told that they'd got us a flat we were delighted. On the Saturday night after we'd played Arsenal I got the keys and we drove to the address I had been given. During the day Jan had been out to buy some nice food and we planned on enjoying our first home-cooked meal in weeks. In high spirits we headed to a place called Caister-on-Sea near Great Yarmouth.

As we got nearer to the destination I suddenly realised it was where I had been on a caravan holiday as a ten-year-old. We carried on driving and the directions took us to that exact same site, California Cliffs. Surely this must be a mistake, I thought. Or a wind-up. Much to our dismay, it wasn't. The flat Norwich had arranged for us to rent was a holiday apartment above an amusement arcade. We couldn't believe it.

It had been vacant since the previous summer and was freezing cold. It was that cold we had to cuddle up under a duvet on the floor right under a solitary wall heater which we had to leave on all night, constantly feeding it with fifty-pence coins. The walls were paper-thin and the noise of the fruit machines throughout the night almost drove us insane. It was totally demoralising. From the jet-set lifestyle of Switzerland to this. 'You take me to some places,' said Jan, 'but how did we end up here?'

We eventually laughed about it but there was no way we were staying. First thing the next morning we packed our bags and returned to Norwich. That night we stayed with John Devine and his wife Michelle, while the club hastily found us somewhere else to live.

Keith Bertschin had recently left to join Stoke so it was arranged that we could move into his old place. It was in a lovely little village called Bawburgh. The contrast couldn't have been greater. Situated in an idyllic countryside setting, with the River Yare running through it, it was so quiet and homely that you could leave your back door open and the only thing that would wander into the kitchen were the local ducks.

It certainly made our stay in Norfolk a much more pleasant one, even though I was struggling with an excruciating pain in my right foot. It was partly because of this that I had no further involvement in the first team and this underlying problem was now starting to worry me. I first encountered it when training with Everton over Christmas but had tried to play through it. I had no idea what was causing it and was sent to a specialist. A condition called Morton's Neuroma, which affects the nerve that runs between the metatarsal, was mentioned but the doctors quickly tried to discount that by saying it would have been impossible to play football for any length of time if suffering with that.

Before the season was over I managed a few more games for the reserves, with the final two squeezed into as many days down on the south coast, first at Portsmouth and then Southampton. As the match with the Saints entered the last few minutes I was thankful that the season was almost over but there was to be one last nasty surprise lying in wait. With barely seconds left on the clock I went in for a header. It was going to be my last act of the campaign and it ended with a size-nine boot in my face. Apart from a broken nose, my face was a mess. It was cut to pieces and for the next few days I resembled a panda. Some years later I met up with Andy Townsend, who informed me that he'd been the owner of the boot that caused the damage and I sarcastically thanked him for the agony he'd caused.

To compound the misery of a season that I'd rather forget, Norwich were relegated. Because of this they had to readjust their budget and were therefore unable to extend my contract. Although it hadn't worked out as well as I would have hoped at Carrow Road, it was an amicable parting of the ways. I wished them luck for the future and was delighted to see them bounce straight back up to the top flight the following season.

While the imprint of Townsend's size nine on my battered and bruised face eventually disappeared, the mystery surrounding my injured foot rumbled on. I headed back to Merseyside and, in a bid to get to the bottom of what was causing me so much pain, immediately booked myself in to see the Liverpool-based specialist Dick Calver. It was starting to handicap me more and more, and I can only liken it to walking with a big stone in your shoe. Calver gave me an injection then waited a week before confirming what I suspected while at Norwich. Morton's Neuroma was diagnosed and the only cure was to have the nerve completely cut out. It wasn't the most straightforward of medical procedures and, for a while, I was unable to put any weight on my foot all. I virtually had to learn to walk all over again, it was that bad, and I underwent physio at Walton hospital every morning for almost a month.

I concluded that I'd handled the last six months really badly and made some terrible decisions. My Liverpool upbringing had made me plod on with an injury when I should have looked into getting treatment earlier and I was now paying the price. Conscious that the new season was drawing ever closer and that I was still without a club, I sought advice from the PFA and sent out handwritten letters to every club in the Second Division and a few selected teams in the first. I received only three replies. Graham Taylor was one of the managers to get back to me; he couldn't offer me anything but wished me luck, which I thought was a nice touch and I appreciated his reply. I've still got the letters somewhere at home.

Around that time Carlisle United manager Bob Stokoe also contacted me and asked if I would play for them in a friendly against Newcastle. The prospect of moving up there on a permanent basis was not one that particularly appealed but I was in need of a run-out to help build up my match fitness so I set off on the two-hour drive northwards. There was a cracking turnout at Brunton Park. Peter Beardsley and Chris Waddle were in the Newcastle team and the match ended 1–1. Afterwards I was offered a deal but it was never going to happen. Jan didn't fancy it and there was no way I would have been able to commute on a daily basis.

Not long after that game I bumped into the Oldham striker Mick Quinn, who I knew from the days when we both lived in Cantril Farm. I told him about my situation and a few days later his boss at Boundary Park, Joe Royle, got in touch with an invite to go along and train with them. It wasn't long before I was offered a contract and, although Oldham might have been the windiest place on earth, it was a move that suited me fine.

I was grateful to Joe for handing me this chance. I'd always got on quite well with him when our paths crossed during his playing days and I was looking forward to my first experience of playing in English football's second tier. I made my debut on the opening day of the 1985/86 season, ironically away to Norwich. We lost 2–0 and not long after I came on my old mate Dave Watson went over the top on me to prove that there are no such things as friends in football once you cross that white line.

There were some really good players at Oldham, including the likes of Andy Goram, Willie Donachie, Nick Henry, Roger Palmer, Ron Futcher and, of course, Quinny. When I signed, Joe explained that he expected one of his regular front two to be sold and that's where I would then step in as their replacement. Unfortunately for me, that never transpired and I found myself spending a lot of time on the bench or in the reserves. Although I believed I was worthy of a starting place, Quinn and Futcher formed such a good strike partnership that I didn't have much of a case to argue.

What perked me up was the news that Oldham had been drawn to play Liverpool in the second round of the League Cup. I was out on the training ground when it came through and the prospect of going back to the ground I still called home immediately put an extra spring in my step.

We made the short trip to Merseyside for the first leg in late September. Some things never change and, as substitute, I reacquainted myself with the Anfield dugout, albeit the away one. It was quite a low-key affair, there was a crowd of only around 16,000 inside the ground that night and I don't recall there being much fuss made about my return. It seemed strange going into the opposition dressing room, a throwback to my days as a Liverpool apprentice, but I enjoyed the occasion and it was great to be back. Although I hadn't left on bad terms I was still a bit unsure about what type of reception I'd receive when I eventually came on for the last fifteen minutes. We were already 3–0 down at the time but I couldn't get on quick enough. I remember we were defending a corner down at the Kop End and as I ran on it seemed as though everyone was applauding. It was a humbling experience, one that helped ease the pain of defeat.

As a contest the tie might have been over but I for one couldn't wait for the return leg. Especially when I was told that I'd be in starting eleven. It was a massive thrill. I'd started only one previous game for the Latics and this was the big one for me. Any faint hopes of causing an upset on the night were quickly extinguished as Ronnie Whelan and John Wark put Liverpool two ahead inside the first 25 minutes.

Whelan then added a third just after half-time before I seized the opportunity to grab a couple of memorable goals. The first was the result of a defensive mix-up between Mark Lawrenson and Bruce Grobbelaar and I nipped in between the pair of them to score. For the second, I simply controlled the ball and slammed it home from the edge of the six-yard box.

It's not often you can enjoy a 5–2 home defeat but I was proud as punch to have scored two against Kenny's double-winning Liverpool team that night. I never thought we'd win so this was the next best thing and on the way home I remember stopping off at a pub on the East Lancashire Road for a celebratory drink.

Those two goals were enough to see me retain my place for the next game away to Crystal Palace. I netted again, my only league goal in an Oldham shirt, and started a couple more matches before returning to the bench as Oldham battled to consolidate their position in the division. Just after the New Year I played on the right wing in a hugely disappointing home loss to Leyton Orient in the FA Cup third round. It was a terrible team performance and, not surprisingly, Joe was furious. The following day he announced 'this team has no spine, and up to seven of you could be moving on'.

There had been a lot of discussion between the lads that the manager's recent experiment to play a sweeper system wasn't working. He overheard the whispers and asked who didn't agree. Thinking we were all in agreement that it was a bad idea, I put up my hand. As the room fell silent I looked around and noticed I was the only one. So much for solidarity, I thought, and my face went so red that it could have lit up the room. My honesty backfired and, after that, I felt Joe's attitude towards me totally changed.

Frankly, he acted immaturely. Despite our differences of opinion over whether I should have been playing or not, he'd always been pleasant enough towards me but an obvious frostiness quickly set in. He'd been a player himself until just a few years before and I found it remarkable that he was now behaving in such a way.

I soon found myself completely cut out of his first-team plans and forced to train with the reserves under the charge of Billy Urmston. According to Billy, I was still in the manager's thoughts and he kept telling me that I'd soon be back in the first team but I'd been made the scapegoat and no matter how well I did, there was never any sign of a recall.

One night after playing for the reserves I was informed that Doncaster Rovers manager Dave Cusack and his assistant, my old Liverpool team-mate Phil Boersma, wanted to speak to me. We met and they expressed an interest in taking me on loan for the remainder of the season. They were pushing for promotion from the Third

Division and needed some extra firepower in attack. I was their number one choice, they told me, with their back-up option being a young lad from Millwall called Teddy Sheringham. Boey did his best to persuade me and said I could stay with him, but on the strength of the good vibes I'd been getting from Billy Urmston I politely declined their offer. I'm not sure who Doncaster did eventually sign but it wasn't Sheringham. I brought it up when I bumped into him at an event many years later and it was something he knew nothing about.

In hindsight I probably acted too hastily in not accepting the Doncaster offer but I wasn't to know then that I'd never play for Oldham again. I went on to captain the reserves to the title and finished top scorer, but Royle's mind had been made up where I was concerned. I'd only signed a one-year contract and as the season's end approached I didn't need a genius to tell me that it wasn't going to be extended.

Come the final few weeks of the campaign I couldn't wait to get away. I had realised much earlier in the year that leaving Switzerland had been a mistake. I missed England while I'd been over there but little had changed and I was left wondering why I had been so keen to return. It was like when you get to the end of a foreign holiday – you can't wait to get back in the house for a cup of tea and some toast but after a few hours you're pining to be back on the beach with a cocktail.

That's how I felt. The green grass of home was not as lush as I remembered it. My passport was ready and the bags were waiting to be packed again. I had unfinished business on the continent and would soon be back on foreign soil.

18

BELGIUM
BOUND

I HAD NO IDEA WHERE MY NEXT MOVE WAS GOING TO TAKE ME. For the second successive year I faced a summer of uncertainty and it required the intervention of a psychic palm reader to direct me down the right path.

During a three-week holiday in Florida and California I did a lot of thinking and it only confirmed what I already knew: that I was desperate to try my luck abroad one more time. Apart from our families there was nothing else to keep us in England. We were still young and yet to have kids. It hadn't worked out for me at Norwich or Oldham and I didn't fancy dropping any further down the Football League ladder.

I still harboured regrets over my premature departure from Switzerland and felt that my playing style was more suited to the continental game. It was World Cup year and watching the action unfold in Mexico only whetted my appetite to broaden my footballing horizons once more.

There had been a number of tentative enquiries, mainly from Scandinavia, but nothing serious. There was also interest from Cyprus and a guy hounded me to go out and see what they had to offer. We'd just found out that Jan was expecting so we quickly ruled it out, but he wouldn't give up. In the end I agreed to go over and speak with them, partly just to get him off my back. The club in question was EPA Larnaca. They were so friendly and welcoming that I was talked into playing a friendly game for them while over there. It was so hot though, and with my fair skin it was definitely not the climate for me to be playing football in on a permanent basis.

Apart from that match, we treated the rest of our stay like a holiday and while walking along the beach one night I was shocked when a group of Cypriot lads recognised me. We got chatting and it emerged that they owned the famous Blue Star chippie back in Liverpool. They enquired as to what I was doing there and when I told them they were unanimous with their advice. 'Do yourself a favour and get back home,' they said. To be fair, I had no intention of signing, but the chairman still wouldn't take no for an answer. He treated Jan and I like royalty. He couldn't have been nicer and the deal he put before me was fantastic. The money just kept going up and up. It was amazing. I felt bad rejecting his advances and in the end I had to say I was returning home to think about it. I gave it a few days then called him to say I couldn't accept.

There was still a bit of interest from one or two other clubs but nothing seemed to be happening so I started pre-season training in the familiar surrounds of Melwood. It would have been nice to say that I had secured a dream move back to Liverpool. Unfortunately, the reality was that the club was just allowing me to use their facilities until I fixed myself up with a new team.

I would have loved nothing better than to be offered a chance to rejoin the Reds. That goes without saying and I'd be lying if I said I hadn't let that possibility cross my mind. What if there was an injury crisis and the manager had no one to turn to but me? What if I impressed enough in training to warrant the offer of a contract? Of course, it was nigh-on impossible that this was going to happen so I just tried my best to enjoy it for what it was, a chance to build up my fitness alongside some old friends.

Plenty had changed at the club since I'd left. Not least the man in charge, my former strike partner Kenny Dalglish. In his first season as player-manager he'd just guided Liverpool to a historic League and FA Cup double so there was a good atmosphere about the place that summer and it was an enjoyable experience, even if I did find it a bit embarrassing to be temporarily back at the club as an unattached player. Everyone made me feel welcome but I still felt like an outsider.

As the days passed by with no new developments on the transfer front my frustrations grew. Although I was confident that the situation would eventually resolve itself, I must admit I was starting to get slightly concerned. My livelihood was at stake if I couldn't find a club soon.

Then I was contacted by a gentleman named Andre Delrue. He said he was acting on behalf of Belgian club KSK Beveren and I thought he was an agent. I came off the phone excited about what he'd said but slightly spooked because of something that had happened a few weeks earlier. Jan had gone to have her palm read and I tagged along. When we arrived the palmist insisted that she read mine too. Not being a believer in this type of thing, I politely explained that I wasn't interested. She kept on at me, however, and, although reluctant, I eventually gave in. I was then informed by her that my next career move would be to Belgium. It was a nice thought, but I treated it as just a bit of fun and had totally forgotten about it until I took this call.

My preconceived ideas about mediums changed in an instant. Jan had overheard the telephone conversation and when I put the receiver down we looked at each other in complete shock. 'It's meant to be,' we both thought. I quickly did some research to make sure it wasn't a wind-up and then arranged for us to go and see what they had to offer.

Before I travelled out to Belgium, Rochdale manager Vic Halom got in touch to express an interest in signing me. I politely told him of my plans to go abroad but he asked if I could do him a favour by playing in a game that coming weekend away to Blackburn in the pre-season Manx Cup. There's some confusion over whether I did actually sign for Rochdale, so let me clear this up. It was a few days before I was due to meet officials from Beveren and I didn't want to run the risk of getting injured. At the same time I quite fancied a run-out and therefore agreed to play.

I was reluctant to sign any forms but on the morning of the match I was informed by Halom that unless I did, the rules of the competition wouldn't permit me to play. I'm not even sure what it was that I signed. As far as I was concerned it was just an agreement to play in this game only. It was not an official contract and I was never registered as a Rochdale player. For the record, I did play and scored our only goal in a 1–1 draw. Halom was keen to make it a permanent deal but I was off to Belgium.

Two days later Jan and I travelled to Ostend to meet Andre and later he took us to Beveren, a small village located on the outskirts of Antwerp and just 45 minutes from the capital Brussels. It was arranged that I would play in a friendly game on Wednesday night. It was part of a summer tournament called the Flanders Cup and the semifinal was against Kortrijk. It went well and I scored the winner in a 1–0 win.

Afterwards I spoke to the manager Ladislav Novak, a former full-back who had captained Czechoslovakia in the 1962 World Cup final. He appeared quite deadpan and didn't give much away but he was keen for me to stay on for the final a few days later. Jan had been really impressed with the place and tried to put words into Novak's mouth, saying how well I'd done. He remained tight-lipped and I began to think that maybe I hadn't done as well as I thought. As I later discovered, that was just a trait of his personality. He was always very slow to commit and show any real feeling. The next day I unfortunately fell ill with a stomach bug and it was decided

I should return home. We parted amicably before I came back to sign the following week.

I couldn't wait to get started. These were halcyon days for Belgian football and I was more than delighted to be a part of it. The national team had just reached the last four of the World Cup in Mexico, where only a Maradona-inspired Argentina had halted their gallant march. At club level Belgium always seemed to be well represented in the latter rounds of European competition and, unlike other countries of similar size, its domestic league had managed to hold on to the majority of its many home-grown stars. The prospect of rubbing shoulders with players such of Jan Ceulemans, Francois Van Der Elst, Rene Vandereycken, Franky Vercauteren and Enzo Scifo was an exciting one.

Like Luzern, Beveren were not a household name on the continent, nor one of the top clubs in their own country. That mantle belonged to the likes of Anderlecht, Bruges and Standard Liege. But in what was a highly competitive league, they were more than capable challengers and clearly a much better fit for me than Luzern had been. Beveren were regular competitors in Europe and had won the domestic championship as recently as 1984. The club certainly didn't lack ambition and the team was a good one. Their other big signing during the summer of 1986 was Eugene Ekéké, a Cameroon international who is probably best remembered for scoring against England in the 1990 World Cup quarterfinal, while other characters included Marek Kusto, a veteran of three World Cups with Poland, and Filip de Wilde, a goalkeeper likened to the legendary Jean-Marie Pfaff.

My latest move abroad might have slipped slightly under the radar of the British press but it was headline news on the back pages in Belgium, so all eyes were on me when the season opened. Luckily, we got off to a good start and were unbeaten up until Christmas, alternating between third and fourth in the league for much of this time. What prevented us getting closer to the top was the fact that we drew too many games. I opened my goalscoring account in mid-September. It was against Charleroi, for whom a young Philippe Albert, later of Newcastle United, made his debut, and I netted twice in a 4–0 win.

It was always a relief to get off the mark for a new club and on this occasion it felt even better because I'd just returned from suspension after foolishly getting sent off at home to RWDM Brussels. It was a far from ideal way for me to start life in the Belgian league and I only had myself to blame. As I went up to challenge for the ball the opposition player had his hands all over me. I lashed out with my elbow and caught him right in the stomach. It was so blatant and right in front of the referee. It was a straight red and I had no case to argue. When I watched it back on TV later that night it was embarrassing. I feared a lengthy suspension and as I nervously awaited the outcome I was quick to hold my hands up and admit that I had been in the wrong. Coupled with what was almost a personal begging letter to the Belgian FA, a potential four-game ban was thankfully halved. Still, it had been a shameful incident and one that wouldn't have done me any favours in the eyes of my new bosses, so I was grateful when quickly restored to the team.

After the handsome win at Charleroi we started our run in the UEFA Cup. It was exciting to be back playing in European competition and I was delighted to find my true form. It began when I scored the only goal of our first-round tie against Norway's Valerenga. In the next round we were drawn to play Athletic Bilbao and not many people fancied our chances. The Basques had been double-winners in Spain in 1984 and with a team that featured the likes of goalkeeper Andoni Zubizarreta and the infamous 'Butcher of Bilbao', Andoni Goikoetxea, they came armed with a tough reputation. There was a lot of interest in the tie and our tidy little Freethiel Stadium was packed to the rafters. We relished the chance to upset the odds and I netted again, our third in an impressive 3–1 win at home.

The atmosphere in the San Mamés for the return leg was one of the best I ever experienced until we silenced the vociferous Basque crowd with a highly disciplined first-half performance. It was goalless at half-time and when I broke the deadlock in the 57th minute our passage into round three was secured, even though Bilbao hit back with two late goals to win on the night.

It was a great result and my UEFA Cup scoring streak continued at the next stage against Torino. In the first leg at the Stadio Comunale we conceded twice just after the break but six minutes from the end I snatched what we all hoped was a vital away goal, drilling a left-footed shot into the bottom corner from a tight angle.

It left the tie evenly poised going into the return leg in Belgium and we threw everything at Torino, only for them to hit us on the counter-attack with a 75th-minute goal by Giuseppe Dossena. It was a massive disappointment because after beating Bilbao we really believed that we could have gone far in the competition. Still, we'd given a more than decent account of ourselves, one that boded well for the future. Personally, it had been great to be back on the big Euro stage. It reminded me of my early days with Liverpool and made me even more determined to experience it again.

The first half of the season with Beveren had been fantastic and I was really enjoying it. There was such a fun atmosphere around the club. On the last Monday of every month a local restaurant would be booked and we all went out en masse. It helped forge a great team spirit, which in turn made us a very hard team to beat, as proved when we played away at league leaders and eventual champions Anderlecht. We trailed 1–0 but refused to buckle, really dug in and eventually got ourselves back on level terms before coming away with a well-earned point.

On the field, whenever fit, or not suspended, I was an automatic starter and my importance to the side hit home ahead of a game away to Racing Jet of Brussels, who played in a small ground next to the Heysel Stadium. After being struck down with a form of enteritis, I was confined to my bed and seemingly had no chance of playing. Not wanting to rule anything out, Novak decided to see how I felt the following day. I was no better but was persuaded to join up with the team for the trip to the capital. I was still desperately ill and couldn't believe it when I was named in the team. God knows how I got through the ninety minutes. All I remember is the warm-up. Like with the broken hand incident in Switzerland, moments like this really made me feel wanted. It was something that I thrived on in football. Man-management at its best, and a feeling I very rarely experienced in England. In contrast, Novak appeared to appreciate what I brought to the team and didn't like to make changes unless really necessary.

Our performances tailed off slightly after Christmas – maybe the winter break affected our momentum – yet we still ended the season with only five league defeats and comfortably finished in the top four to secure European qualification. We also won an award for the longest unbeaten run in the league, a sequence that we stretched to March before losing for the first time against Bruges. In the Belgian Cup we were unlucky to be eliminated by eventual winners KV Mechelen at the quarterfinal stage. From what I'd seen there wasn't that big a gulf between us and the leading teams in Belgium.

On a personal note I was more than happy with how my first season in Belgium had gone. Off the pitch we had settled in smoothly to the local way of life and, in February, we became forever connected to the small town of Beveren when Jan gave birth to our son, Tom.

As I headed into the summer there was even talk that Ajax were considering a move for me before they eventually signed Frank Stapleton. Although it was flattering to be linked with the Dutch giants, for the first time in a long while I was content with how my career was going and it felt great to be free of any uncertainty about my future.

I was optimistic that Beveren could again challenge for honours in 1987/88 but during that close season we lost a couple of our experienced key players. Strangely, our captain Paul Theunis, a real leader in the Graeme Souness mould, and someone who all the lads looked up to, was released. Defensive midfielder Patrick Gorez also left. With them gone we lost an edge. Ekéké also moved back to France and de Wilde would soon join Anderlecht. Given that the team had picked itself towards the end of the previous campaign it came as no surprise that we struggled without them.

Our style of play – a defensive 3-1-5-1 with me up top – remained the same. We signed a new midfielder, while a couple of younger fringe players were promoted to help fill the voids. Unfortunately, it didn't work. We lost the solidity that had previously been our strength. There was a quite noticeable weakness in our game and performances suffered as a result. We lost three times as many league games as the season before and eventually finished fourteenth, just two points clear of the relegation places.

One of the rare highlights was a terrific game against a Bruges side that included a young Ronnie Rosenthal and the great Jan Ceulemans. I scored twice and we won 5–2. Bruges went on to win the league and this was the heaviest defeat they suffered. Unfortunately our inconsistent form was causing concern in the boardroom and, sadly, even a couple of great results could not save Ladislav Novak's job. As so often happens in these situations, it's the coach that pays the price and I really felt for Novak when he was dismissed. He was a lovely guy and immensely popular. When he came into the dressing room to say his goodbyes it was the first time I'd seen genuine tears among footballers. It was very emotional and I started to well up myself. Granted, we were going through a tough time in the league, but we all believed it was just a minor hiccup and that we could eventually turn the poor run of form around. His sacking was a harsh one in my opinion and I think subsequent results proved that because there was no improvement.

In that season's UEFA Cup the first round saw us paired with Bohemians Prague and I scored both goals in a straightforward 2–0 victory at home. Next up was Vitoria Guimaraes of Portugal. We lost 1–0 away from home in the first leg, which we didn't think was too bad a result, but after only winning by the same score in Belgium the tie went to penalties and we lost. What sticks in my mind about that night was how the Guimaraes players all stood with their arms around one another as the shoot-out took place. It's common practice nowadays but was unusual back then.

Another first for me early that season came in a Belgian Cup game when I netted four times in a 6–1 victory over the minnows of FC Liedekerke. It was the most goals I'd scored in a competitive league or cup game during the course of my professional career and it took me back to my days as a schoolboy when I would regularly help myself to a hatful of goals. Sadly, I was unable to replicate this prolific scoring form in the league.

I'm not using it as an excuse but the period of change that followed Novak's departure certainly didn't help. Initially, it was the assistant coach and masseur who took joint charge of team affairs, which was a bit odd, before Belgium legend Wilfried Van Moer was brought in as manager. Born and bred in Beveren and a former player of the club, big things were expected under Van Moer. He had a great reputation but his arrival failed to have the desired impact.

There could be no doubting his determination and will to win. But while it was only natural that he'd experiment with different line-ups and formations, the way he chopped and changed the team was unsettling for everyone concerned. As he searched for a system that might change our fortunes my place in the side suddenly was no longer assured. I was tried on the left side of midfield but the new boss was a lot more critical of all our performances and nowhere near as patient as Novak. As a result I found myself being substituted more often.

It came to a head in a game where he brought me off. In a fit of pique I reacted angrily. I thought I had played well and didn't shake the hand of the player coming on to replace me. Then, as I made my way straight towards the tunnel, I publicly questioned the manager's decision. It all happened in the heat of the moment. I regretted my actions afterwards and knew there'd be repercussions.

As expected, that night I got a phone call from one of the directors and was summoned to a meeting the next day. It was all quite cordial and we had lunch but it was made clear that the club wasn't happy with my behaviour, which, on reflection, I could understand. I was given a telling-off and told, in no uncertain terms, that such a show of dissent towards the manager could not be tolerated. As an example to the rest of the team it would be announced that I'd been fined, although it was agreed privately that I wouldn't have to pay it.

I wouldn't say I had a great problem with Van Moer. In fact I had quite a lot of respect for him and used to enjoy his training sessions. He always seemed to speak well of me in the press but I often sensed that he was a bit harder on me in training than some of the other players. Because of my reputation as a player with Liverpool maybe he expected more from me, I don't know. Our relationship certainly didn't get off to the best of starts and towards the end of the season his no-nonsense style showed through when I broke my nose just before half-time away to Cercle Brugge. During the interval I was sat there feeling sorry for myself when he turned to me and asked, 'Are you going to stop worrying about your face and get going in this half, worry about that tomorrow.' He would have fitted in perfectly at Anfield. In the days before masks I played the following week against Kortrijk.

Compared to the season before, it had been much tougher and it was somewhat of a relief when the campaign came to a close. I still had a year left on my contract so the thought of leaving didn't enter my head as I headed back to England for the summer. As I did, it was announced that Van Moer was packing in.

However, in shades of the episode with Luzern three years before, as I packed my suitcase ready to go on holiday, a telegram arrived from Beveren telling me they'd agreed to sell me to Bastia, a French club based on the island of Corsica. It was a total shock. In truth, I wasn't sure exactly where Corsica was. All I knew was it was home to the Foreign Legion. I'd had no inkling whatsoever that they were thinking of letting me go and, with a sixteen-month-old baby, there was no way I was prepared to uproot the family again. I contacted Beveren but it was made clear that I at least had to go and meet the agent who was negotiating the deal.

That meant I had to cancel our planned holiday and, with young Tom in tow, Jan and I flew to Corsica. We were met at the airport by Bastia's assistant coach who, as it transpired, was the only English speaker we would come across during our stay there. He took us to collect a hire car and lent us a car seat for Tom. As we drove across the island towards our hotel we couldn't fail to be taken in by the beauty of the place, it really was stunning.

There was no sign of the agent though, and the following day, before any talks had taken place, I trained with the Bastia team. That was on a Tuesday and the agent didn't arrive until Thursday. In the meantime Bastia had a friendly. I played and scored in a 3–2 win, and even featured on the pre-match team photo. Despite the searing heat, I was in decent shape fitness-wise because the Belgian season hadn't long finished, so I enjoyed the run-out. Still, I was adamant that I wouldn't be joining them. It was nothing personal against the club. The likes of Johnny Rep and Roger Milla had played here in the past and I could see the potential. The supporters were passionate and Bastia had a decent team.

From a footballing point of view I possibly could have been persuaded but there were other factors to consider and I knew Jan was dead set against it from the start. The prospect of trying to learn yet another language held no appeal for her whatsoever, especially with an overactive young Tom to look after. Corsica was a great place to spend some time on holiday but in terms of culture it was the exact opposite to what we were used to and also not the environment for us to raise a family. As with Cyprus, nor would my red hair and fair complexion have enjoyed the intensity of the Mediterranean sun.

When the agent finally arrived a meeting was arranged with the Bastia president and the terms of the proposed deal were laid out. A fee of £52,000 had been agreed and, to be fair, the contract was an attractive one. The club president had an intimidating presence about him. I sensed he was used to getting his own way and he was certainly putting pressure on me to sign. After his first offer, I returned to see Jan and outlined the impressive terms he'd offered. 'I don't care, no way am I staying here,' was her immediate response. When I delivered the news that I wouldn't be joining it was like a scene from the Godfather films, with him playing the role of the mafia don. He was not amused, throwing his pen across the room, slamming his fists on the desk and declaring Bastia would not be covering the cost of our stay in Corsica if I hadn't changed my mind by the time he returned a couple of days later. The agent wasn't best pleased either as he was in danger of losing face and missing out on his commission.

I wasn't going to be bullied into signing though, and because I didn't want to be stung with a hotel bill that the club had promised to pay, we hatched a plan to escape without him knowing. We went into town and booked the only two available stand-by flights back to Manchester for the following day. Under cover of darkness that night I loaded the hire car with our suitcases and parked it just down the road away from the hotel. The next morning we got up early and casually left, aware that we needed to be as discreet as possible. The last thing we needed was for someone to get wind of our departure and alert the president. We quietly left the car seat on the porch of the coach's house before he'd woken up, then sped across the island in the direction of the airport, carefully negotiating the hairpin bends of the hilly terrain with Jan holding Tom in the back. It was a pretty hazardous journey and along the way Tom was sick all over her, forcing us to briefly pull over while she changed.

At the airport I returned the car, which had been hired in the president's name, and rushed inside to the check-in desk before any questions could be asked. Two passengers had not shown up so it was looking good for us with the stand-by tickets, but the flight was then delayed so we had to wait anxiously for a further two hours until it was confirmed we were on. Every time a police officer walked by, our hearts skipped a beat in case the hotel had realised we'd done a bunk.

After what seemed like an eternity our names were finally called to board the flight. There was nothing for us to feel guilty about but we felt like fugitives. Nevertheless, our escape plan had succeeded and I never did hear back from the Bastia president or the agent. It's comical when I think back to this entire episode but I can assure you that we didn't see the funny side at the time. When the plane finally took off the relief was palpable. Almost three decades have now passed but I'm yet to return to Corsica for fear of possible retribution!

Beveren were totally surprised when I turned up back in Belgium ready to resume pre-season training. Just like Bastia, they were also furious that the deal had collapsed as they'd missed out on a decent payday. Initially there was a bit of a stand-off but I reasoned with the club secretary, who I had always got on well with, and the matter was eventually resolved.

A few weeks later I took a call from *Liverpool Echo* football writer Ric George. As well as covering the fortunes of the Reds, Ric was also the font of all knowledge when it came to the European scene, particularly France; sensing he was on to a scoop, he got in touch to enquire why I was on the official Bastia team photograph for the new season.

Of course, he wasn't the only one who thought I'd be starting the season as a Bastia player. Having sent me to Corsica, Beveren wasted no time in drafting in my replacement. They brought in two young players from PSV Eindhoven. One of them – Eric Viscaal – was considered something of a whizz kid and he was lined up to play the lone striker role that I'd occupied for the past two seasons.

A bit of competition couldn't do me any harm, I thought, and any ill feeling over the proposed moved to Bastia was quickly cast aside as I set about trying to impress new boss René Desaeyere, a former Antwerp player who had recently managed Standard Liege. He took us to a pre-season camp on the beaches of Dunkirk. It was very intense, facilities were basic but it had the desired effect. We trained and ate well. By the time it came to start playing games I felt really good and was looking forward to the campaign starting for real.

Before then, he arranged for us to play two friendly games in 24 hours. I took part in the first one but suffered a knock. Although it was nothing too serious I mentioned to him that it might be best if I sat out the next game as a precaution. It was the worst thing I could have done. I watched from the stands as Beveren strolled to a double-figures victory – I can't remember if we scored ten or eleven. I would have been able to have got through the game on one leg. In my absence Viscaal played, scored a hatful and became the first-choice striker. I had really shot myself in the foot and was jettisoned to the back of the queue for a starting place. It meant I had to patiently bide my time for another chance but I never got much of a look-in and it was to be a dismal season from my point of view.

To be fair, Viscaal was a very good young goalscorer and he was to finish the season as the country's joint-fifth top marksman with seventeeen goals. There were ten years between us in age and he represented the future. It was clear that I was now fighting a losing battle so I started to think about moving on from Beveren.

It was bad enough being out of the team when I was living in my home city. Having to suffer the same frustration in a foreign country just exacerbated the situation. I did get a short run before we broke up for the Christmas break but upon my return I was informed that Dutch side Willem II had enquired about the possibility of taking me until the end of the season. They were based in Tilburg, which was commutable from Beveren, so it seemed a reasonable option. I joined them on a week-long break in the south of France, where we trained and played a couple of games. It was here that I was first introduced to pilates and yoga, which Willem II were convinced was their secret to limiting muscle injuries. It was a hugely beneficial few days but on my return the clubs couldn't reach a financial arrangement so I stayed with Beveren.

KV Oostende then expressed an interest in taking me on loan. They were owned by James Storme, a former Standard Liege player who had scored at Anfield in a European Cup Winners' Cup tie back in 1965. He had big plans for the club and it was a move that would have tided me over until the end of the season. Unfortunately, Beveren refused to play ball unless it was a permanent deal. Two French clubs also made an approach, Guingamp and Gueugnon. I'd always fancied the idea of playing in France, even after my brief experience with the Bastia president, but they could only afford to sign me on a free transfer and, again, Beveren were not prepared to compromise.

I was stuck between a rock and a hard place. Tom was still young and Jan was now expecting our second baby. With this in mind, it was only to be expected that she was wanted to move back closer to our families. I spoke to Mick McGuire at the PFA and it emerged that because I had left England on a free transfer I was entitled to return there on a free transfer. Although I could have stayed on at Beveren our minds were made up and my release negotiated. We were going home and, this time, it would be for good.

19

APPROACHING
FULL-TIME

ONE OF THE MAJOR SOURCES OF FRUSTRATION WHEN I LOOK BACK ON MY football career is the times when, for one reason or another, I was unable to hold down a regular first-team place at the various clubs I played for. Yet one of my happiest and most enjoyable years as a professional came during a season when I made just a fleeting contribution to a club's cause.

It was in 1989/90 and I made only thirteen league appearances for Tranmere Rovers in the old Division Three. Yes, I'd have loved to play more. That goes without saying. But rather than complain to the manager or sulk in silence, like I had done many times in the past, I did nothing because off the pitch I had never felt more settled.

After three years in Belgium I was living back home on Merseyside and with a club that was on the up. Tranmere liked to play good football and the team spirit was second to none. It was a squad full of nutcases, but in a good way. They were the funniest bunch of lads I'd ever shared a dressing room with. The likes of Dave Higgins, Eddie Bishop and Eric Nixon would constantly have us in fits of laughter. So much so that I used to look forward to training with them every day.

The atmosphere was like what you'd experience in a Sunday League team; a group of mates all in it together and playing football for the fun of it. Don't get me wrong, when they had to be serious they were and there was no messing around when it came to the job of getting results, but they went about it in a fun and light-hearted manner.

What made it even more remarkable for me was that the players came from a wide variety of backgrounds. Some were rough diamonds, plucked from the local non-league scene. Others were seasoned professionals who had been around the block a few times but still maintained that all-important desire to give it their all. They all just clicked and it was no surprise that Tranmere did so well that season.

After years of languishing in the lower reaches of the Football League, manager Johnny King had transformed their fortunes. From the ashes of administration in 1987, and almost dropping out of the Football League, came the most glorious era in the club's history. No longer were Merseyside's poor relations having to apply for re-election or seen as cannon-fodder when drawn against bigger teams in the cup. They were now pushing for a place in the previously uncharted land of English football's second tier and making their presence felt in the knockout competitions.

While the club's owner Peter Johnson financed this incredible turnaround, most of the credit has to go to King. There's a statue of him outside Prenton Park now and he's fully deserving of it. The team he assembled became rightly regarded as one of the best in Tranmere history and although I played only a bit-part in what they achieved in 1989/90 I'm proud to have been involved.

He was a very wise manager; a former Everton player in his day, but a self-confessed student of Shankly-ism. Like the players, he too was a bit barmy and I mean that in the nicest possible way. His team talks were legendary. He'd come out with stuff like, 'The ship's all painted and the mast is repaired, we're ready to set sail,' or talked about 'rockets bound for the moon'. His style of management was in keeping with the whole atmosphere surrounding the club. The players would constantly take the mickey out of him. At the same time he was so highly respected and this was reflected in the performances of the team. It was his second stint in the Prenton Park hot seat and the previous season he'd guided them to promotion from Division Four. No one was expecting anything more though.

I was signed during the summer of 1989. The squad was a settled one and I'd been brought in to provide extra attacking cover. Big Jim Steel and the vastly under-rated Ian Muir were the established front pair and together they formed a fearsome strike-force. I was also used on the right wing, although that position was predominantly filled by Johnny Morrissey and, sometimes, Chris Malkin.

Even though I probably played more than I wanted to for the reserves under War-wick Rimmer, at 33 I was just happy to be there. My career was winding down and because I was enjoying my time at the club so much it wasn't a problem.

I made just thirteen league appearances that season and scored only one goal. It came at home to Rotherham in September; a diving header, late in the game that earned us a 2–1 win. It capped a great month, one which also saw the arrival of our second child, Sophie.

We also enjoyed a decent run in the League Cup, beating Preston, Ipswich and

Millwall before being drawn at home to Tottenham in round four. A 2–2 draw earned us a replay at White Hart Lane, before which we stayed in a really nice hotel on the outskirts of London. For me, it was a rare taste of being back in the big time. It was a novelty for a lot of the other lads and they were like big kids on holiday, jumping in and out of the pool on the morning of the match when normally we'd be told to relax and conserve our energy.

That night Tranmere lost 4–0, which was no disgrace as Spurs, under Terry Venables, had a very good team that would go on to win the following year's FA Cup. Their undoubted star was Paul Gascoigne and I got talking to him as we walked off at the end. Given all the publicity that used to surround him I was intrigued to see what he was really like but he was more interested in asking me about my Liverpool career.

With our cup adventure over we pushed on in the league. Our form was good and, against the odds, we established ourselves as genuine contenders for promotion. I managed to string a few games together around Christmas but broke my collarbone away to fellow challengers Bristol Rovers. It happened in a collision with Geoff Twentyman, Rovers' big centre-half, whose dad had scouted me for Liverpool all those years before. He really clattered into me and I knew straight away that it was serious. I couldn't move and had to be carried off. It was agony. How Gerry Byrne played in the 1965 FA Cup final with the same injury I don't know.

With my right arm strapped up and totally immobilised I was unable to drive so Johnny King went completely out of his way to take me home that night. It's a measure perhaps of just how much he cared for his players. I was impressed and certainly couldn't have imagined some of my previous managers doing that for me. It was an injury that ultimately ruled me out for about six weeks and that was really frustrating because I'd just got myself into the team. Now I couldn't do much other than try and do exercises at home or run along Formby beach.

In my absence the team continued to do well, maintaining their chase for at least a place in the end of season play-offs and securing a ticket to Wembley for the final of the Leyland DAF trophy. I had played in the competition earlier in the season but was an unused substitute beneath the twin towers as Tranmere came from behind to beat Bristol Rovers 2–1.

Reaching Wembley and winning a trophy was an unexpected bonus and we were back there the following week to contest the Third Division play-off final. It was such an exciting time for everyone at the club. We might have missed out on automatic promotion by eleven points but we qualified comfortably for the play-offs, finishing fourth in the table.

After defeating Bury in the semifinal, Notts County stood in our way at Wembley.

I again started on the bench but, seven years after I'd last played there in the red of Liverpool, I came on. Sadly there was to be no repeat of the joyous scenes of a week before. County had finished seven points clear of us in the league and it was they who deservedly won the right to go up alongside the two Bristol clubs, beating us 2–0 with a goal in each half.

To miss out on promotion this way was hard to take and there were a few tears shed in the dressing room afterwards. Having not been at the club for as long as the other lads I was perhaps not as gutted as most. Still, it was a painful end to a season that I thoroughly enjoyed.

Our efforts were recognised with a civic reception at Birkenhead Town Hall and I was already looking forward to the following season. I was fully expecting my services to be retained so to then be told that I was being released came as a massive disappointment. Money was tight at Tranmere, I knew that, but I wasn't on a big contract and I'd never given the manager any trouble. I was content to play wherever and whenever he saw fit. When King called me into his office to deliver the news I was totally shocked. Not getting promoted had impacted on the manager's future plans and I was now surplus to requirements. Twelve months later Tranmere returned to Wembley and clinched promotion. I was delighted for them but wished I'd have still been part of it.

Because we had now settled back in Merseyside I was keen to find a club I could commute to and thankfully it wasn't long before I was contacted by Wigan Athletic manager Bryan Hamilton. We met at a hotel in Standish and discussed terms in a sauna, of all places. Bryan was a bit of a charmer who could talk the birds out of the trees and he convinced me to sign. In hindsight, it was a decision I rushed into. Although Wigan were also in Division Three, they were nowhere near as strong as Tranmere. They had a young team, featuring the likes of Nigel Adkins in goal, Peter Atherton and Joe Parkinson, but the make-up of the squad was not right. I was by far the oldest player at the club and felt that I didn't fit in. Within days of being there I feared that I had made a mistake.

In terms of size, Wigan and Tranmere were quite similar but this was a totally different world to what I'd known. Ahead of the first pre-season game one of the coaching staff was handing out tie-ups for our socks and as he did, he reminded everyone to take care of them because they would be the only two we'd get all season. Everything was done on a shoestring budget. They were still playing at Springfield Park back then, the pitch was terrible and facilities not much better. We had no training ground and wouldn't know where we'd be training from one day to the next. Sometimes it would be at a nearby school, other times on a local field. We'd be informed in the morning and then told to run there. Wigan was to be the graveyard of my career and I quickly came to hate it.

There was also a general feeling of apathy around the place. I sensed that from day one and it didn't get any better. I picked up an injury early on, which didn't help matters, and when I did play I struggled to really make an impact. It was a tough season and highlights were few and far between. The stand-out memory for me was an FA Cup third-round tie away to First Division Coventry City. On my 34th birthday we drew 1–1 at Highfield Road. In the replay, four nights later, we should have beaten them. I had a goal disallowed and we lost 1–0. The following weekend I did manage to score. It came in a 2–0 win over Grimsby, but it was to be my one and only goal for the club.

By this point, my relationship with the manager had become pretty strained. It began over a newspaper column I used to write. I'd started journalism training the year before, while at Tranmere, and was approached by the *Wigan Evening Post* to submit a weekly article. It was something I enjoyed and, with an eye on what I might do when I did eventually hang up my boots, I looked upon it as good experience. I would generally work on my writing after training, in the afternoons or evenings, but Bryan could be one of the most difficult managers over what time we left and many a time he'd say that he wanted to see everybody after lunch, meaning we had to hang around. What he'd do then was go around the dressing room and select players to stay behind and do more training. Those who weren't picked were free to go home, although by that time, once I'd driven back along the M58, much of the afternoon had been wasted.

After about six weeks of writing the column, Hamilton suddenly decided that any money I earned from it had to be put in the players' pool. I argued that I was doing it with a view to building a future career for myself and that because I did it in my own time I deserved the money. He wouldn't back down so I packed it in.

It was an incident that completely changed my view of him. Hamilton was a control freak and the most awkward manager I worked under. Like with Joe Royle at Oldham, he hadn't long finished playing himself so surely he should have been able to still see things from the players' perspective.

Football-wise I believe he could also have made more of my experience. I was the senior professional at the club but that meant nothing to him and he treated me like he would one of the kids. After my time in Europe this was a world away from what I'd been used to. His attitude irritated me and it was the same on the pitch; I grew to loathe the whole experience. We just didn't play in a way that was ever going to fully utilise my strengths. He'd tell me to hang on to the ball longer because my thought process was sometimes quicker than those I was playing with. The problem was, in that division, if you hung on to the ball for any length of time a defender would come clattering through the back of you. I wasn't a target man. Never had been. He must have known that before signing me so, unless he was going to change the way Wigan played, it was a move that was doomed from the start.

Wigan's style was to lump the ball forward from the back and if it didn't reach me direct I was expected to chase it into the channels. I specifically remember one game, against Bradford reserves, where the ball was continuously being played over the top and they kept urging me to run after it. Former Wales international winger Leighton James was a player-coach with Bradford at the time and during a break in play I was stood by him and he said, 'Even if we combined our old pace together you still wouldn't be catching these balls.' And he was right. It was soul-destroying and I was getting to the stage where I couldn't take any more.

Away to Mansfield later in the season it was the same. I was constantly being kicked up in the air by George Foster. It was not my idea of fun. Five or ten minutes into the second half Hamilton substituted me and it was a relief. As I trudged off I thought to myself, 'What am I doing here?' I knew then that it was time to pack in once the season ended. Playing this way was killing my enjoyment of the game and I'd lost my appetite for it. Little did I know, however, that this match at Mansfield on Saturday, 19 January 1991, was to be my last as a professional footballer.

*

After seventeen years, many goals, a box full of medals and countless memories I'd reached the end of a remarkable life-changing journey. It was one that had taken me all over the world, to places I'd have never visited. Along the way I was fortunate enough to meet so many wonderful and interesting people.

If someone had told me as a young boy on the streets of Everton about the career that lay ahead of me I'd have snatched their hands off. Yet still there are regrets. Of course there are. Anyone who looks back on their career in football and says they wouldn't change a thing is not telling the truth.

Before turning my back on professional football for the final time I went to see Bryan Hamilton in his office at Springfield Park. After signing a few forms I said my goodbyes and turned to leave with no hard feelings, I have to say. As I walked towards the door he said one last thing, and it's a sentence that has lived with me ever since. It was that I never fulfilled my potential. And it's true. Part of me still feels I didn't achieve as much as I should or could have. There are a number of contributory factors as to why that is and I know I could have also helped myself a lot more. That is why I'll forever have some regrets about my football career.

EPILOGUE

THROUGHOUT MY CAREER AS A PROFESSIONAL FOOTBALLER I'VE been placed in many testing situations, faced numerous challenges and had to overcome countless obstacles. From start to finish it was a roller-coaster ride of emotions. I experienced the highest of highs and lowest of lows. Nothing though, could have prepared me for what life was about to throw at me twenty years into retirement.

The cards I'd been dealt up until this point had been pretty good. Aside from losing my dad at an early age I couldn't complain about how everything had turned out. I count myself very lucky to have achieved my boyhood ambition of playing for the club I love. I fulfilled nearly all my dreams and, in return, left a few nice memories behind.

I married the most engaging and vivacious wife in Jan. We had two great children, Tom and Sophie, and enjoyed so many fantastic times together as a family. Yet it's only when bad things happen in life do you fully appreciate just how precious it really is.

*

DESPITE ALWAYS CONSIDERING MYSELF TO BE RELATIVELY FIT AND healthy, I was floored by a massive shock in the autumn of 2010 and it was nothing to do with Liverpool's poor form at that time. It was a Friday morning and I was training in the gym, like I normally did, when I experienced some very unusual pains in my chest. They were bad enough to curtail my workout so I headed home.

On the way I stopped at the shop for a newspaper and, with the discomfort easing slightly, I even found time to discuss what had been a dreadful start to the season for Roy Hodgson's team. Once I arrived home the pain came again and this time it was severe enough to floor me. I was lying on my back in the bedroom when my phone rang. Fortunately it was Jan and on hearing that I was in trouble she quickly raced home. I refused an ambulance but accepted that I needed to see a doctor.

Jan rushed me round to the surgery where we were told to get to a hospital as quickly as possible. I didn't like what I was hearing and just wanted to get to the LFC TV studio for my usual Friday evening stint in front of the cameras. But in no uncertain terms I was told to forget about that. I was going nowhere. After undergoing a series of tests I was informed that I'd suffered a heart attack and that it was a good job Jan had reacted like she did.

I couldn't believe it. I was only 53. Three years older than my dad when he'd passed away because of the same problem, but it had never crossed my mind that I might one day suffer a similar fate. To hear those words was, at the time, the biggest shock of my life.

News of my plight travelled far and wide. I was totally blown away by the interest and get-well wishes that came in from all over the world. It was an emotional time and it took me a while to come to terms with why it had happened to me.

Against my best wishes I was told to try and forget football for the time being and it was just as well, because the following day Liverpool suffered a home defeat to Blackpool that left them languishing in the bottom three of the Premier League. It was almost as unthinkable as me being confined to a hospital bed with a worrying heart condition.

I was kept in for a while then once home Jan made sure I took things easy. It was typical Jan and I don't know what I'd have done without her at that time. The heart attack was an almighty scare and the recuperation process meant I had plenty of spare time on my hands. It allowed me to take stock of all that was good in my life and spend more time with those closest to me. The kids were growing up fast but as a family there was plenty for us to look forward to.

I gradually got back on my feet and everything seemed to be returning to normal. Then one day, without warning, our lives were tragically turned upside down and changed irrevocably.

When I set out to write this autobiography, I knew at some point I would have to relive the everlasting anguish of this moment. Retracing my career as a professional footballer has been a thoroughly enjoyable experience, despite having to ponder some of the disappointments along the way, but this is the one part of the book that

I dreaded confronting. Thinking how I could explain it in the best possible way was the cause of many sleepless nights.

Just where do you start trying to put into words the pain of losing your soulmate and life partner so suddenly and prematurely? It was the most harrowing of periods and it puts everything I have previously written about firmly into perspective.

It was a normal spring morning in 2011, around a quarter past nine, and I was enjoying myself out on the local golf course in Formby. My game couldn't have been going that well because I was fourth to tee off on the seventh fairway. While I waited my turn I noticed the club greenkeeper frantically racing towards me. 'Dave, you need to call your son,' he was shouting. My initial thought was that Tom must have locked himself out of the house. If only.

I quickly turned my mobile on and was amazed to see I had 32 missed calls. Either my phone was playing up or there was something seriously wrong. We somehow managed to contact Tom and my instructions were clear: 'Get to the hospital as quick as you can!'

Jan had collapsed at work and my mind was now racing as to just how serious this was. How I made it to the hospital I don't know as I couldn't think straight, let alone drive. But somehow I managed it and I screeched to a halt outside the doors of the emergency unit.

Jan's sister was with the kids and the look on her face told me this was as serious as it gets. Tom's first words were, 'It doesn't look good,' and within moments of me arriving at the hospital I was whisked in to see my stricken wife. She looked ill and there was little sign of life in her eyes.

I was stunned, speechless, and thought this had to be a nightmare that I'd soon wake up from. I took her hand but there was no sign of acknowledgement. Jan was whisked away and we were taken to a side room. In that time I telephoned her best friends, who were holidaying in Spain.

It was only minutes before a doctor arrived and delivered the most devastating news: 'Jan has suffered a massive, massive, brain haemorrhage and she won't survive.' We looked at each other in disbelief and hugged tightly as the room filled with the sound of crying.

I've often heard it said that in situations like this, despite being surrounded by close family and friends, you can still feel so lonely. I was never sure how that could be possible. But now I knew. It's something you can only appreciate if you've been through it yourself.

I was panicking and could feel myself struggling for breath. It felt like I was going to have another heart attack. In the moments that followed we questioned the prognosis. Had the best people available delivered this decision? I was lucky to have a friend, Paul May, who was a leading consultant in neurosurgery, and after receiving our call he was at our side at the hospital within minutes. Paul gave us an outside chance of hope and Jan was transferred to the Walton Centre, a centre of excellence for neuroscience.

For the next three days we kept vigil at her bedside before I had the most painful decision of my life to make – to give up our fight and admit defeat by agreeing to turn off Jan's life-support machine.

For Tom, Sophie and me, the world instantly became a different place. Adjusting to life without Jan has been the biggest challenge I have ever faced. If it wasn't for the hope of a bright future for the children I wouldn't have known what to do. Jan left behind a marvellous legacy in how she moulded two outstanding young people and the strength she instilled in them has shone through in the crucial situations they have faced since we all lost our best friend.

Each of us relied on Jan for so many different things and my ability to cope was severely tested in the immediate weeks and months that followed. Jan and I had been almost inseparable ever since we'd first met. A life without her just didn't seem plausible. The feeling of loneliness was an unbelievable one and, at first, I would do anything to avoid being in the house. I spent a lot of my time walking the dog in the countryside where, in the expanse of solitude, I was able to shout about my inner torment.

As anyone who has been through a similar bereavement will tell you, there are times when it seems like there's no end to the suffering. When it comes to coping with grief there is no timescale. There comes a point, however, when – for everyone's sake – you have to try and move on and it was only thanks to the love and support of my family, plus some very close and caring friends, that I was eventually able to do that.

Another important part of this process is getting back to some sort of normality. I had to slowly reintegrate myself into the routine of daily life and that meant returning to work. LFC TV quickly welcomed me back into the fold and, even though I might have appeared pretty vacant at times when first back on screen, it's perhaps fitting that football was the light at the end of my darkest tunnel. Ever since I was a young boy it's been such a constant part of my life and it was to offer me an escape route from the depression I was sinking into.

*

EVEN AFTER HANGING UP MY BOOTS I COULDN'T TEAR MYSELF away from the game I love. As any ex-footballer will tell you, the best days of your life are your playing days. Nothing can ever beat that and in hindsight maybe I was too hasty in calling it a day when I did.

I've often heard my former colleagues say that it's not the playing they miss but the dressing room atmosphere every morning, the banter. I'd agree that at times it was good fun, but I definitely missed playing most of all. I retired on impulse and secretly regretted it. I should have tried to play on for at least one more year.

During the summer of 1991, not long after I'd left Wigan, there was interest from a club in Sweden but I took it no further because it would have meant uprooting the family again. I was keen to remain involved in football though, and soon started working for the Professional Footballers' Association, helping players plan for retirement both financially and practically.

I often get asked why I didn't go down the coaching route and the truth is I might have done, had my old Liverpool team-mate Steve Heighway contacted me before the PFA. It was not long after I'd started my new role that Steve got in touch to see if I'd be interested in getting involved with coaching the kids at Liverpool. After years in America, he had recently returned to the club as director of youth development. It was something I would have previously jumped at but I was now on a different career path and reluctantly passed up the chance.

At the same time I also pursued another of my boyhood ambitions and looked for an opening in sports journalism. After speaking with my old journalist friend Martin Leach, then of the News of the World, he mentioned my name to his sports editor Bill Bateson and before I knew it I'd been offered an opportunity. I was thrown in at the deep end, sent to Bramall Lane to cover Sheffield United versus Southampton. I remember Alan Shearer was playing for the Saints and the experience was both fascinating and enlightening. I instantly loved the buzz of being in such a pressurised position.

One day, while reporting on a game between Blackburn and Bournemouth, the final whistle was approaching and we all had our stories written, ready to file in time to meet the deadlines. To our horror the visitors then grabbed a dramatic late equaliser. At which point, veteran reporter Alan Thompson turned and, to howls of laughter, shouted in my direction across a packed press box, 'Now you know why we used to hate you so much.' I knew exactly what he meant and had to hastily rewrite my report.

I really enjoyed my Saturday afternoons in the press box and couldn't get to the paper shop quick enough the next morning to read my copy. That was until Piers

Morgan arrived at the News of the World in 1994 and I became a casualty of his mass cull.

The majority of my media work these days is on TV, while I also do some co-commentary for the local radio stations on Merseyside. It will come as no surprise that football is never far from my thoughts. Scousers live and breathe the game and there's just no getting away from it. I'd want it no other way.

I'm still a massive fan of Liverpool Football Club, probably more so now than when I was a player, and whenever I get together with my friends it's the fortunes of the Reds that more often than not dominate our conversation. It was during one of these regular footy talks not so long ago that I unearthed one of the little mysteries surrounding my career – why Bob Paisley completely ignored me during the final weeks of the 1982/83 season.

It came about when I was spending some time with Colin Bridge, who was perhaps my closest friend. Colin was battling cancer at the time so I would often go round to see him. During my playing days he was a regular visitor to Bob Rawcliffe's garage and therefore often came across Paisley. The football gossip was rife within the four walls of this place and it's where many secrets were exposed down the years.

Colin was the funniest person you could ever meet. He loved life and would always have me in fits of laughter, even throughout his illness. Sadly, he passed away early in 2015, but I'll never forget the friendship we had, even if I wished he'd have told me the following tale years earlier.

I can't recall what we were actually talking about on this particular day in question but, as always, it was something to do with Liverpool and while sitting at his kitchen table he casually dropped the following line into our conversation: 'Well, we all know why Bob Paisley fell out with you, don't we?'

'Do we?' I asked, with a rather puzzled expression on my face.

'It was because you wrote that piece in the paper and got thousands for it.' I was lost for words. I'd known Colin for almost 35 years and only now did he decide to pass on this information.

I often wondered why I was shunned by the boss after what proved to be my last game for the club away to Southampton in April 1983. Now it all started to fall into place, because around that time I remember doing an interview for the Sunday People. It was just the basic type of interview many players did, talking about how the season had been going and my plans for the following season and so on.

When I saw the headline I wasn't happy – 'I owe Liverpool nothing,' it roared. I'd been stitched up and was annoyed at how my words had been reported. What they chose to omit was the bit, 'but they owe me nothing too.' Paisley took offence and immediately decided to bomb me out, telling anyone within earshot at the garage, 'We give him his chance and that's how he pays us back, selling his story to the papers for thousands.'

Apart from the fact that I didn't receive a penny for the interview, it came as a real shock to discover the reason why my Liverpool career ended so abruptly, and I couldn't believe the boss never confronted me over it. Years later, he was misquoted by the press himself, regarding a remark he made about John Aldridge, so it can easily happen and I just wish I'd had the chance to explain myself.

Thankfully my association with Liverpool didn't completely end after that incident and three decades on I'm proud to say that I'm still heavily involved at the club, whether that be as a pundit for its in-house television channel, as a match-day host in one of the lounges or through my association with the former players.

When I set out to become a footballer all those years back I didn't expect to still be involved with LFC at this stage of my life. I may be biased but Liverpool really is a truly unique football club. I'm convinced of that and it will always have a special place in my heart. The relationship between the supporters and the players, old or new, is like no other. I can vouch for that from both sides.

It's over three decades now since I last pulled on the red shirt. And while there have been players who have since played more, scored more and won more than me at Liverpool, I've still not been forgotten. Above all, I'm best known for my exploits when coming off the bench. Being so synonymous with the Liverpool number twelve shirt, being the original and perhaps ultimate Supersub is something I've grown to live with. When I play a round of golf someone will comment that they were only expecting me to turn up for the final couple of holes. Or if I attend a meeting I'll get, 'we didn't think you'd be here until ten minutes from the end'. It's just a bit of banter. I'll smile and play along. It's nothing new and I'll never hear the end of it. If I'm honest, I don't want to hear the end of it. If that's what people remember me for that's great. Just to still be remembered by so many people is, for me, a huge honour.

ACKNOWLEDGEMENTS

Tom and Sophie for being strong and loving.

Susan, Rob, Mathew and Sarah Blackwell, always there through the best and the worst times.

My Mum and sister, Lesley, for all that we've shared.

Jim Davies, who has always been there for me.

Sharron and Alan Stockton and their boys, Luis, Jordan and Lloyd without whom we could never have got through the last few years.

Colin Bridge for all the fun and laughter.

Sadly this summer Colin and Alan both passed away, I'll miss them so much.

John Curtis for taking me under your wing.

Mark Platt for our friendship and all the hard work and commitment you put into this project.

James Corbett and everyone at deCoubertin Books for publishing my story

And Liverpool fans all over the world for your love and support through the ups and the downs.

For their statistical assistance, a special mention must also go to Ged Rea, Tim Johnson, Jonny Stokkeland, Arnie Baldurrson, Steve Hunter, the Swiss Football League and Patrick Van Wesemael.

S T A T S

DAVID FAIRCLOUGH

Date of birth: 5 January 1957
Birthplace: Mill Road hospital, Liverpool
Schools attended: Major Lester Primary & Evered Avenue Grammar

CAREER

Club	Years	Games	Goals
Liverpool	(1975-83)	154	55
Toronto Blizzard	(1982)	23	5
FC Luzern	(1983-85)	44	15
Norwich City	(1985)	2	0
Oldham Athletic	(1985-86)	20	3
SK Beveren	(1986-89)	90	27
Tranmere Rovers	(1989-90)	18	1
Wigan Athletic	(1990-91)	10	1
Total		361	107

HONOURS

League Championship: 1975/76, 1976/77, 1979/80 & 1982/83^

European Cup: 1977*, 1978

UEFA Cup: 1976

League Cup: 1983

European Super Cup: 1977

Charity Shield: 1976*, 1977, 1979*, 1980*

International caps: England under-21 (1), England B (1)

Central League: 1974/75, 1975/76, 1976/77, 1978/79, 1979/80, 1980/81, 1981/82

Central League Division Two: 1985/86

Leyland Daf Trophy: 1990*

^*made just 8 appearances but was awarded a medal*
unused sub

*

It's for his role as Liverpool's Supersub that David Fairclough is best remembered, hence the title of this book. These are his vital statistics as the Reds number 12…

Of his 154 Liverpool appearances 62 were as a substitute and 18 of his 55 goals were scored when coming off the bench. He was an unused substitute on a further 75 occasions.

SEASON BY SEASON BREAKDOWN AS A LIVERPOOL SUBSTITUTE

Season	Unused	Apps	Mins on pitch	Goals	Mins per goal
1975-76	6	12	257	5	51.4
1976-77	14	13	319	2	159.5
1977-78	11	8	166	3	55.3
1978-79	8	3	55	0	-
1979-80	20	14	357	6	59.5
1980-81	3	4	83	0	-
1981-82	-	-	-	-	-
1982-83	13	8	154	2	77.0
Total	75	62	1,391	18	77.3

INDEX